Teacher Education and the Challenge of Development
A global analysis
Edited by Bob Moon

Education Quality and Social Justice in the Global South
Challenges for policy, practice and research
Edited by Leon Tikly and Angeline Barrett

Learner-centred Education in International Perspective
Whose pedagogy for whose development?
Michele Schweisfurth

Forthcoming titles

Professional Education, Capabilities and Contributions to the Public Good
The role of universities in promoting human development
Melanie Walker and Monica McLean

Nomads, Development and the Challenges of Education
Caroline Dyer

Gender, Education and Poverty
The politics of policy implementation
Edited by Elaine Unterhalter, Jenni Karlsson and Amy North

Professional Education, Capabilities and the Public Good

The role of universities in promoting human development

Melanie Walker and Monica McLean

LONDON AND NEW YORK

First published 2013
by Routledge
2 Park Square, Milton Park, Abingdon, Oxon OX14 4RN

and by Routledge
711 Third Avenue, New York, NY 10017

Routledge is an imprint of the Taylor & Francis Group, an informa business

British Library Cataloguing in Publication Data
A catalogue record for this book is available from the British Library

Library of Congress Cataloging in Publication Data
A catalog record for this book has been requested

ISBN: 978-0-415-60471-0 (hbk)
ISBN: 978-0-203-08389-5 (ebk)

Typeset in Galliard
by RefineCatch Limited, Bungay, Suffolk

Printed and bound in Great Britain by
TJ International Ltd, Padstow, Cornwall

Contents

Illustrations

Acknowledgements

Bringing a book to fruition is always as much a social as an academic project, depending on collaborative work and a network of peers who contribute generously in different ways to the unfolding ideas and a critique of the ideas. We both led the research and were ably supported by research assistants, Arona Dison in South Africa and Rosie Vaughan in the UK, and by Martina Daykin who provided splendid administrative support. Pippa Segall in South Africa also assisted with some fieldwork and organisational support. We are especially grateful to those people in the three universities who agreed to work with us and to be interviewed. Similarly, we are grateful to alumni, members of professional bodies and NGOs who also gave their time to speak to us. We gratefully acknowledge our funders, ESRC/Dfid (Award No. RES- 167-25-0302) who made the project possible.

During the life of the project, our colleagues at the School of Education at the University of Nottingham, where we both worked while conducting the research, were always supportive and interested in the work, providing a rich and challenging environment in which to undertake research. We thank Carol Hall who was head of school at the time the bid was prepared and was unwavering in her support, as was her successor Chris Hall. We were able to try out some of the ideas with our students on the MA in Higher Education at the University of Nottingham, some of whom did not agree with our approach, encouraging us to think about what would make the ideas more accessible to students in a developed country. Linda East and Rebecca Stokes took up our ideas and applied them in a UK context; we appreciate their interest and learned from their thinking about the Index in relation to the UK. A number of our Ph.D. students were exposed to the theoretical ideas and their taking up or criticising them again contributed to our own learning; we would like to thank Melis Cin, Earl Kehoe, Aurora Fogues, Tham Nguyen, Lesley Powell and our students on the part-time Ph.D. in Higher Education. Ideas from the project have been presented at conferences and seminars in Australia, Europe and South Africa over several years; we are grateful to participants in all these events for engaging productively with us. The Human Development and Capability Association community, and especially the education thematic group, have offered productive and challenging space to think well about capabilities ideas. In particular, Sandra Boni, Vivienne Bozalek, Enrica

Chiapperi-Martinetti, Louisa Deprez, Severine Deneulin, Caroline Hart, and Elaine Unterhalter have responded to our evolving ideas. The EU-funded Marie Curie EDUWEL initial training network has provided a tremendously rich environment to think through ideas about capabilities with all the early stage and senior researchers, especially Hans Uwe-Otto, the project leader, Anasofia Ribiero, Petya Illeva and colleagues in Working Group Three. Other colleagues have contributed substantially to our ideas at seminars, conferences and in conversation, especially Marie Brennan, Joan De Jaeghere, Carolin Kreber, Brenda Leibowitz, Tristan McCowan, Martha Nussbaum, Leon Tikly and Lew Zipin, and at the University of the Free State, Jonathan Jansen, Andre Keet, Lis Lange, Sonja Loots and Merridy Wilson-Strydom. The series editors, Madeleine Arnot and Christopher Colclough, read and commented in detail on draft manuscripts; their wise observations and meticulous comments assisted greatly in improving the final version of the book.

We would also like to acknowledge our respective families. For Melanie, Milo, Lexie and Tessa knew nothing about this book but were wonderful companions and a welcome distraction! As always, she owes her greatest debt of love and unwavering support both to her sister Vicki Gilham and her partner Ian Phimister. Monica is lucky to have an extended and extending family that revives and sustains her – special thanks to Iraj Hoshi, her husband; her children and their partners, Darren and Stella, Gavin and Rosa, Bijan and Julie; and her grand-children, Gus, Vince and Zahra. Special gratitude to Shân and Garry, wonderful friends on Salt Spring Island.

Introduction

This book makes a case for how university-based professional education in South Africa might contribute to the public good, in particular to poverty-reduction. Our arguments are located within the domain of human development which recognizes that while economic well-being is necessary to human well-being, it is insufficient. In this conception of human development the focus is on improving lives and expanding choices and opportunities in a range of dimensions of life (Haq, 1999). Specifically, we raise the questions: How might professional education orient professionals towards social justice and to be aware of the potential of their profession to reduce the poverty that exists in their local contexts? Can universities educate and train individuals in the professions to possess knowledge and values that help them address inequalities and poverty in their countries, and to be effective leaders in poverty alleviation in their own fields?

The concept of public good is not one that is normally researched empirically in developing countries. The goal of this book is to show how we have combined theoretical resources with an analysis of the views of university educators, trainees, and practitioners to identify indicators of public good professionalism that can focus professional training and education. In so doing we demonstrate how the research was democratically engaged to develop a normative conceptualization of the public good.

In an innovative manner, we have used the yardstick of an orientation to the public good in professional education to explore and understand in more depth the values and potential which higher education – universities in particular – have in societal development. We hope that readers will be encouraged to consider the arguments and claims and be moved to actions for change within the context of democratically inspired work within universities. To this end we offer a theoretically informed, empirically grounded study of professional education which might open the door to more such studies.

Using a theoretical framework drawn from the human development and capabilities approach of Amartya Sen (1999, 2009) and Martha Nussbaum (2000, 2011), we propose the term 'public-good professionals' to convey the concept of professionals with the values, knowledge and skills to provide services to the public which expand the opportunities to lead better lives (capabilities) and the achievements (functionings) that their clients have reason to value. In particular, graduate professionals who work with people living vulnerable and precarious lives in conditions of poverty would aim for more justice and less inequality.

At the centre of the book is a normative 'Public-Good Professional Capabilities Index' (for brevity's sake also referred to as 'the Index') generated by combining insights from the capabilities approach and 'ideal-type' professionalism literature with interviews and discussions with students, lecturers, managers, alumni and non-governmental organizations (NGOs) in five professional fields (engineering, law, public health, theology and social work) in three universities in South Africa. In the Index, the capabilities are the educational goals, and the educational arrangements and university dimensions which we develop in Chapters 4 and 5 support those goals. The Index (see Chapter 5, p. 74) comprises:

- Four 'meta-functionings' of public-good professionals: to recognize the full dignity of every human being; to act for social transformation and reduce injustice; to make sound, knowledgeable, thoughtful and imaginative professional judgements; and to work/act with others to expand the full range of human capabilities of clients.
- Eight public-good professional capabilities conceptualized as the normative goals of professional education: knowledge and skills; informed vision; affiliation; resilience; social and collective struggle; emotional reflexivity; integrity; and assurance and confidence.
- A set of educational arrangements likely to produce public-good professionals at university departmental level (transformative curriculum; appropriate pedagogies; and inclusive departmental culture) and, at university level (having a transformative culture and environment; being critical, deliberative and responsible; and being socially engaged).
- An element for identifying in any specific national context the social, economic, political, cultural and historical constraining and enabling factors for public-good professionalism.

Some readers may prefer first to go straight to the detailed Index in Chapter 5 and then to work back and forward from there; even though earlier chapters refer forward to the Index.

The Index is intended to provide an evaluative space for thinking about public-good professional education and practice. While the inequalities in the case-study country of South Africa are especially stark, in our view the case we make for educating public-good professionals holds for all countries struggling to reduce inequality. Wealthier countries can be included – as a recent OECD (2012) report reminds us, inequality continues to rise in both rich and in poor countries.

Formal education systems comprise political, cultural and social action, bound up in the interplay between state and civil society. Systems of education comprise networks of workers, practices and policies for nurturing learning capacity for the benefit of individuals, the economy and society. Education has then been discussed both as a potential force for social change and as the vehicle for reproducing existing social hierarchies. This book focuses on university-based professional education as a potential force for change.

Delanty's (2001) history of universities charts how modernization, nation states and capital accumulation is inextricably linked with the rise and growth of universities: beginning in the eighteenth century, universities have provided states with professional elites, technological and economic services, and scientific advances. Yet, Jurgen Habermas (1989) has commented that the social role of universities has been ambiguous. On the one hand, knowledge-generation within universities has mainly depended on a 'defensive' relation to society and an 'affirmative' one to the state (ibid.: 109); on the other hand, during the late twentieth century universities become spaces for the expression of democratic citizenship and the encouragement of 'radical imagination' (Delanty, 2001: 19). We should not be romantic: Delanty's (2001) history clarifies that the role of universities in liberal and organized modernity has been, on the whole, to place knowledge at the service of nation-state building in the post-Enlightenment era. For the most part of their history, far from being progressive, universities have legitimized the dominant social and political values. Nevertheless, for our purposes we can draw on other ideas of the university (a phrase coined by Cardinal John Henry Newman in a series of lectures and published as *The idea of a university* [1852]): the critical and emancipatory power of knowledge and reason; the usefulness of knowledge for society; and, equality, citizenship and democracy.

Potentially, universities can contribute to reducing poverty by how they prepare professionals for their work. Universities do not stand apart from urgent problems in society, whether scientific or ethical, and it is important, as recipients of public funding and spaces for generating critical knowledge, how universities understand their purposes and how their graduates situate themselves in relation to urgent problems in society. Poverty and inequality are among the greatest of what Habermas (1990: 211) calls the 'moral-political liabilities' of the age. In our view, it is reasonable and right to educate so that professional graduates are in a position to choose to contribute to the public-good and human development in society.

Future professionals will arrive at university with already formed social justice commitments grounded in a wide variety of personal experiences and biographies of (in)justice (for example, of race in South Africa, or social class in the UK; of gender unjust or abusive families; conversely, of being entitled or of being of service). The curriculum and pedagogies that students encounter can enable them to frame the problems of justice and injustice in relation to their own professional field; to think about them critically and compassionately; and to acquire specific professional knowledge and skills which might enable them to act to reduce injustices and in their future working lives, increase the well-being of individuals and groups.

We start the book in Chapter 1 by discussing the situation facing higher education globally, arguing that, at present, it appears that an ideology emphasizing human capital and economic growth shapes higher education policy, with the effect of obscuring other discourses and purposes. Simultaneously, we begin to trace an alternative more expansive image of higher education, one in which, in policy and practice, the public good enjoys equal status with university contributions to prosperity and the economy. In Chapter 2 we outline in some detail the conceptual approach we took in our ESRC/DfID funded research project in 2008–2009 which resulted in the Public-Good Professional Capabilities Index. Here, as an alternative and challenge to a narrow economic growth perspective on development, we sketch the relevant concepts and ideas from human development and capabilities, complementing them with those from theories of public-good professionalism. Chapter 3 describes the situation in our case study country of South Africa, and its historical, political, social and higher education context.

Next, in Chapters 4 and 5, we aim to establish the legitimacy of the Index by explaining in detail the methods of data collection and the methodological and analytical processes that resulted in its production. Crucially these chapters demonstrate the iterative and collaborative way in which we tested our theoretical ideas empirically to ascertain the robustness of capabilities as a useful approach to professional education for social justice in higher education. Chapters 6, 7, 8 drill down to the five professional field case studies located in three historically different South African universities. The qualitative data derive from interviews with 120 diverse stakeholders in professional education and participatory discussions with people at the South African universities. It is interpreted in the light of social theory and debate within the broader scholarly and policy community.

While the views conveyed in this book are ours alone, by developing the Index we hope to contribute to debates on the role and responsibilities of universities in different international contexts to educate professionals for the public good. Such dialogue would include attention to how university graduates might make societies go better, and to graduates' obligations to make contributions to social and democratic change in those societies. In this way universities' professional education departments and schools might enhance the cognitive, skill and ethical bases of their professional fields by shaping professional and personal identities oriented to public good.

We aim also to contribute to human development and capabilities knowledge. In the last 10 years, the capabilities approach has been taken up in a wide range of education studies, including gender equality, disability and higher education (see Walker and Unterhalter, 2007 for a range of examples, and the special issues on education of the *Journal of Human Development and Capabilities*, August 2012 and the *Cambridge Journal of Education*, September 2012). Here, we take it up in relation to the specificity of professional education; this book is the first attempt to apply the ideas in the field of professional education to offer an original contribution to capabilities literature.

Part 1

Higher education, the public good and professionals

1 Higher education in a global context

Working for the public good

Infant dies on grandmother's back

In March 2009 in South Africa, Cape Town newspapers (see West Cape News 30 April 2009) reported the story of a black child living in a poor African township[1] located, because of apartheid geography, some distance from the city and its health services. Seventeen-month-old Unabantu Mali had fallen ill with diarrhoea, so his grandmother, Ntombizodwa Mali, strapped the child to her back and walked to the nearest community health clinic, where she found a long queue. Realizing that Unabantu needed urgent treatment, she walked to the KTC Hospital two hours away but was told that it only treated adults. She then walked to the Gugulethu community health clinic, another kilometre away. She approached a nurse asking for emergency treatment; the nurse told her she would attend to the child, but failed to do so. After an hour, she was told to return the next day. Walking home, she had a feeling that her grandchild was dying; the weight on her back felt 'cold and heavy', as though she was carrying 'stones'. She sensed Unabantu was dead, but because she was exhausted from a six-hour journey she carried on walking home, arriving at about 3.30 p.m. where she put Unabantu on the bed. Realizing he was not moving, she called the baby's mother, Nomantombi Mali, who started trying to stretch Unabantu's stiff fingers.

Nomantombi later told reporters that she wished her dead child was with her so that they could 'sing or dance' together because Unabantu had loved dancing. She said she had hoped that her first-born child would one day become an academic so that he could assist the family. 'Every day to me feels like hell. I don't know the reason why I am here and he is gone,' she said. Nceba Matinyana, who had acted as a spokesperson for the family, blamed a lack of service delivery for Unabantu's death. In the Freedom Park area where the family live, faeces can be seen in the street and shacks have been built next to the workers' hostels, leading to overcrowding. A resident said children used the streets as toilets and played in dirty puddles. 'Children are dying here. The government is failing us. We can't just sit and do nothing,' he said.

Three years later, Ntombizodwa Mali said that she was still too scared to go to the clinics, 'I think I'm still heartbroken at the way Unabantu passed on, but the main problem is that I'm scared because I don't know how the nurses are going to treat me when they see me again.' Nomantombi said that when last at Nyanga Community Health Clinic, the nurses had talked in whispers and pointed fingers at her, making her feel uncomfortable. 'I don't think about him as much as my mother does, but whenever it's his birthday or if I see other children his age, I always think of him. I still get hurt at the way he died. I think if he had died at the nurse's hands or in hospital, the pain would have been better because we would also have closure into his death . . . We would know that the nurses did all they could do to save his life,' she said. 'Nothing has really changed at the clinics though, especially at Nyanga CHC. Patients are still treated badly by staff . . . there's no dignity to patients at all. Just like Unabantu was turned away three years ago, even today people are still turned away,' she said. Earlier that week it had been reported that scores of patients at Nyanga CHC had to deal with a staff tirade as they patiently waited to be helped, while others were turned away after arriving 'too late'.

(*IOL News* 20 March 2012)

Higher education and the challenge of global inequality

This story is not intended to pathologize individual health-care professionals struggling under very difficult circumstances in a seriously underfunded public health system in South Africa. Rather it is recounted here as an instance of how inequalities in infrastructure and public service provision have tragic and shocking effects, both physical and emotional, in the lives of ordinary people. South Africa is one of the most unequal countries in the world, a country in which 10 per cent of the population earns 58 per cent of national income, and the poorest 10 per cent just 0.5 per cent (Keeton, 2012); and, where inequality has recently been described by the World Bank as a 'corrosive reality' (Isa, 2012: 1).[1] Yet Unabantu's story is not specific to South Africa, it can be multiplied across the world, exemplified in Narayan *et al.*'s (2000) *Can Anyone Hear Us?* in which they draw on 40,000 'voices of the poor' across 50 countries, capturing stories of poverty in action in people's lives – too little food, long hours of work, deaths from preventable illnesses, inadequate public services, a lack of dignity, and so on.

Two further examples illustrate the problem of unequal lives and unjust life chances. In 2002 Tanzania with a population of 35 million had a GDP of $10.15 billion (World Bank cited in Basu, 2006: 1361), compared to the net worth of the 10 richest individuals in the USA in the same year of $127 billion (Basu, 2006): 10 people who together were richer than 35 million. Comparing countries, Norway was the richest of the 152 countries surveyed and had a per capita income of $43,400 in 2002 compared to Burundi, one of the three countries ranked at the bottom of the per capita income table, with a per capita income of $90 (World Bank 2005 in Basu, 2006: 1361). Basu (2006: 1361) asks whether in the future people looking back to today 'will wonder how primitive we were that we tolerated this'. And yet, writes Judt (2010: 7), 'the materialistic and selfish quality of contemporary life is not inherent in the human condition'.

So that Judt's implicit challenge can be addressed, the aim of this chapter is to locate our study, which is based in South African higher education, more broadly in literature about the potential role of universities in development, specifically for us, human development (Haq, 1999). The chapter gives an overview of global higher education policy directions and key issues. It situates higher education in the context of globalization and the widespread influence of neo-liberal ideas which result in policies strongly focused on responding to market forces and free trade at a global level. In a variety of ways, such policies can have the effect of exacerbating inequalities and they tend to silence questions related to broad conceptions of human flourishing.

Given the figures above about discrepancies of wealth and arguments about the sustainability of continuing economic growth in conditions of scarce resources, it is reasonable to suggest that university goals might include improving the lives and well-being of the poor and vulnerable in society and to ask: What kind of society do we want, what is important in a democratic society, and hence what kind of higher education is valuable, relevant and desirable? What educational aims and practices might promote *both* economic growth and individual prosperity in regions and countries *and* a broader conception of human flourishing? In particular, what versions of equity and equality underpin what it is that universities are doing when they address professional education?

Globally, nationally and locally, higher education is not disconnected from society and the economy or the myriad challenges of growth and inequalities, nor is there any reason to doubt a general concern about poverty reduction within the sector. Yet, the connections can appear remote. For example, the Global University Network for Innovation (GUNI), whose membership is drawn from universities across Europe and the developing world including Africa, Latin America and the Caribbean, Asia and the Pacific, acknowledges that the problem with higher education thinking about its contribution to the Millennium Development Goals (MDGs)[2] (which we might take as an imperfect proxy for poverty reduction) is that 'the vast majority of academics are not aware of them, and cannot therefore even start thinking about how their institutions can contribute to them' (GUNI, 2008: xxxvii).

In the rest of the chapter, we begin the discussion of universities' contribution to poverty reduction first by focusing on the contexts of globalization and of neo-liberal agenda that impact on universities, then by considering higher education as a means of social reform, and finally by introducing the notion of 'public-good' as a way of thinking about universities' social role.

Globalization, human development and higher education

Scheuerman (2010: 1) argues that globalization 'contains far reaching implications for virtually every facet of human life'. He notes (ibid.) that there is a range of ways in popular discourse to define and describe the concept of globalization: the pursuit of classical liberal ('free market') policies in the world economy ('economic liberalization'); the growing dominance of Western forms of political, economic, and cultural life ('Westernization'); the development of new information technologies ('Internet Revolution'); and the idea of a unified and co-operative global community ('global integration'). What encompasses all definitions is the notion of '*deterritorialization*' by which increasingly social, including educational activities, are not tied to geographical locations. Scheurman identifies the growth of social interconnectedness across geographical and national boundaries; in particular he draws attention to how distant events can have an impact on local and regional endeavours. This phenomenon might include the exchange of ideas in cyberspace or the internationalization (in terms of students, research and other partnerships) of what were previously local or regional universities.

Anthony Giddens' (2001: 245) uses the term 'stretched' to describe the new relationship between 'local involvements' and 'interaction across distance' in which geographical boundaries are blurred, and flows of movements of people, information, capital and goods have become faster. Examples include transnational forms of production, around-the-clock financial markets (and their influence), and supranational organizations such as the European Union. While globalization has the effect of minimizing the state's role in driving national economies, the state, nonetheless, plays a crucial role in providing the conditions, laws and institutions to maximize economic participation and competition in global markets. At a political level, Scheuerman (2010) argues that it is no longer self-evident that democracy and justice are solely pursued in the domestic arena since domestic and foreign affairs are now irrevocably intertwined.

In Giddens' definition, globalization is a neutral phenomenon; the result of 'stretching' is that 'modes of connection between different social contexts or regions become networked across the earth's surface as a whole' (2001: 245). But the effects are contested, seen as leading either to uniformity, standardization and homogeneity (sometimes called 'Macdonaldization') or – paradoxically – as leading to fragmentation and differentiation. Moreover, some see global benefits: Norberg (2001), for example, argues that the diffusion of capitalism has lowered poverty rates and created opportunities for growth and employment all over the world, raising living standards and increasing life expectancy. We are positioned with Amartya Sen (2002) – on whose work we have drawn substantially – who locates himself between proponents and sceptics on the question of the effects of globalization.

To start Sen argues that globalization is not new. Moreover, he claims, the active agents of globalization have historically been located at some distance from the West, citing the high technology of the world in 1000AD and China's reach and influence at that time, and the mathematical influence spreading from India to Arab mathematicians. He argues that 'global civilization is a world heritage' (2002: 2), and that resistance to the globalization of ideas and practices as western is a 'misdiagnosis' (ibid.: 3). He points to evidence that the global economy has spread prosperity in Europe, America, Japan and East Asia. The question he emphasizes concerns how to ensure participation in the 'remarkable benefits' (ibid.) of economic contact and technological progress is fair; that is, how to share the gains of globalization between rich and poor countries, and among different groups within a country.

Such redistribution, he argues, requires reform and attention beyond the mantra that the rich are getting rich and the poor poorer: 'the attempt to base the castigation of economic globalization on this rare thin ice produces a peculiarly fragile critique' (ibid.: 4). Yet, at the same time, he is not sympathetic to claims that the poor are better off because of globalization. He explains:

> When fairness is at stake, the questions are not whether people living in poverty gain something from the global system; or whether they are made poorer by global contacts; or whether they would have been better off had they excluded themselves from globalized interactions. These questions are wrong because '*Again, the real issue is the distribution of globalization's benefits.*'
>
> (Sen, 2002: 5–6; our emphasis)

Similarly, for Sen, dispensing with a market economy is not the solution to reducing poverty and inequalities, rather it is that a market economy can be seriously defective in its operations; furthermore, the globalization of markets on its own is a 'very inadequate approach to world poverty' (ibid.: 7). He notes that the outcomes of dealing in markets (however fair or not they are) are 'massively influenced' by public policies, including those concerning education, so that public action can 'radically alter the outcome of local and global relations' (ibid.: 6). For Sen, then, it is precisely the reach of globalization and the abundant opportunities that 'makes the question of fairness in sharing the benefits of globalization so critically important' (ibid.: 8).

So arguments for reforms to globalization processes and outcomes should follow an evaluation of inequalities in society. It follows that we can ask the same kind of questions of global and national higher education: as UNESCO (2009) notes, higher education cannot opt out of the new global environment. In its ten-year follow-up report to the 1998 UNESCO conference on higher education, UNESCO (ibid.: 7) described globalization as 'the reality shaped by an increasingly integrated world economy, new information and technology, the emergence of international knowledge networks, the role of the English language, and other forces beyond the control of academic institutions' all of which have 'profoundly affected higher education' in contradictory ways.

On the one hand, across the world, the appetite for higher education is sharp and there is a dramatic increase in wider participation in higher education (Altbach, 2009; Schofer and Meyer, 2005; Unterhalter and Carpentier, 2010). The numbers of the age cohort worldwide enrolled in tertiary (which can include further and not only higher education) grew between 2000 and 2007 from 98,303,537 to 150,656,459 students (UNESCO, 2009: 205) although the proportion varies from country to country and the least dramatic gains are in low income countries where participation has only increased from 5 to 7 per cent. Sub-Saharan Africa has the lowest participation in the world, but, even here, absolute numbers increased from 2,342,358 students to 4,139,797 (Unterhalter and Carpentier, 2010.) The impact of ICT on science, scholarship, teaching and learning 'has been particularly profound' (ibid.: 3) Gender equity is also being addressed, with UNESCO (1998) having identified women's participation in higher education as an urgent priority. There have been gender gains globally with the number of female students rising from 10.8 million to 77.4 million (World Bank, 2009). There is now significant global student mobility with 2.5 million students studying outside their home countries (UNESCO, 2009: 7.)

On the other hand, in all countries access to and participation and success in higher education is unfairly distributed. Across the world systematic inclusions and exclusions by social class, gender, race and other categories of people are to be found. So, even as globalized higher education offers 'a myriad of possible futures' (Marginson, 2007: xii) actual achievements are patchy. It is argued that one of the reasons for the patchiness is that as a response to a globalized market for higher education, universities have embraced a neo-liberal ideology whereby profit is pursued at the expense of human transformation and development. It is to this argument that we now turn.

The neo-liberal agenda for higher education

Commenting on the University, Pierre Bourdieu describes the ideology of neo-liberalism as 'a program capable of destroying any collective structure attempting to resist the logic of the "pure market"' (Bourdieu 1998 in Stromquist, 2002: 6). In the field of higher education there is substantial body of work from a critical perspective that draws attention to various distorting effects on the core missions of teaching and research of a minimalist state, free trade, de-regulated open economies, decentralization, privatization, and competition (for example, Aronowitz and Giroux, 2000; Stromquist, 2002; Zipin and Brennan, 2004; Olssen and Peters, 2005; Field, 2006; McLean, 2006; Rizvi and Lingard, 2006; Rizvi, 2007; Badat, 2010). In recent times, the argument goes, higher education has prioritized its role in forming human capital to enhance national economic competitiveness within a global knowledge-driven economy (Singh, 2001; Marginson, 2007; GUNI, 2008; Lebeau, 2008; Boni and Gasper, 2009). From a human capital perspective individuals consciously and rationally invest in themselves to improve their own economic returns through promotion or better earnings, which, in turn has positive effects on the national economy (Keeley, 2007).

From our perspective, though, we want to understand the relationships between universities and socio-economic policies in the light of Sen's (2002) reasoned defense of globalization and his question about who benefits. As we see it, the problem is not so much market principles or practices in themselves, but rather *how* they are extended into non-economic areas of life. For example, commenting specifically on England, Holmwood (2011) writes on the website of 'The Campaign for the Public University' that public anxieties about change are greatest in relation to proposed government reforms to higher education and to the National Health Service. In his view, the anxieties are justified because opening these public institutions to competition in the name of efficiency and profits is inimical to their core values. He claims that an analysis reveals: 'market reforms are promoted in the name of efficiency, but in each case what we are being offered is a more costly, less efficient system designed to secure shareholder value and executive bonuses' (ibid.: 1). Harvey (2005) agrees, arguing that once neo-liberal goals and priorities become embedded in a culture's way of thinking, institutions engage in practices that mime and extend neoliberal principles — privatization, competition, the proliferation of markets at the expense of publicly funded services.

In terms of universities specifically, academic commentators are often with Naidoo (2010) who argues that neo-liberal market mechanisms and 'new managerialism' have led to the growing and relatively unmediated influence of economic pressures and the prioritization of economic capital in the field of university education. Commentators argue that higher education is shaped by market images and leads to such trends as managerialist practices; narrow forms of accountability; an emphasis on science and technology at the expense of the arts and humanities; and the projection of specific kinds (e.g. 'entrepreneurial' Vernon, 2011) of academic and student identities (Stromquist, 2002; Bok, 2003; Olssen and Peters, 2005; Field, 2006; Rizvi, 2007; Nussbaum, 2010; Molesworth *et al.*, 2009, Brown, 2011). Not untypical of this critique in relation to university practices is the report by Grove (2011) reporting on a UK conference titled 'Universities under attack' at which academics called for a fight back against neo-liberal language of employability, value for money and a focus primarily on universities economic value. At the conference, speakers from the UK and the USA decried the 'market trap' for universities, universities having to become businesses, and user-pays agenda focusing students on making money and replacing academic values with business values.

But neo-liberal polices cannot be entirely reproduced in the discursive practices of universities and in the consciousnesses of people who work in them. On the ground in the everyday lives of students and academics the picture is more complex, as we have found in our own research. For example, academics struggle to preserve the 'sacred knowledge' (Bernstein, 2000) of their discipline in the face of official discourses that threaten it (Abbas and McLean, 2010); in the course of their studies, students expand their ambitions for a job to encompass personal transformation and contributing to the improvement of society (McLean *et al.*, 2012); and, the core value of disinterested critical thinking is promoted (Booth *et al.*, 2009; Walker, 2009). While it might be that the social benefits of universities have become as Marginson (2010: 51) describes 'shadowy and diffuse', they are by no means obliterated.

In the same vein, the rise of 'employability' as a goal for higher education has drawn criticism, yet there is merit in human capital formation: the acquisition of skills and knowledge of use in employment is necessary and desirable. McMahon's (2009) detailed study is a careful and persuasive description of the wider benefits of higher education from a human capital perspective. He presents evidence that higher education accrues significant social as well as private benefits and develops a sustained evidence-based argument for the wider non-monetary benefits of higher education, arguing that higher education is important for personal success and well-being as well as economic growth. His empirical research suggests that a university degree brings better job opportunities, higher earnings and even improved health. Higher education, he claims, also improves democracy and sustainable growth, and generates social benefits such as reduced crime. He therefore argues for increased investment in higher education, *both* for its contributions to human capital *and* its wider contributions to society.

Higher education then generates both private and public benefits, but from an equality perspective these benefits need to be in balance (Hall, 2012a). Participation and success in higher education for students from less privileged backgrounds – thanks to the expansion of access which has accompanied globalization and knowledge-economy drivers – represents real and positive changes in their lives and their family circumstances (ibid.). We can also argue that universities have played and will continue to play a significant role in distributing fairer opportunities and attainments, even as they simultaneously focus on brand and status and advance the interests of elites in society (ibid.). Elites may make choices to contribute socially, (see for example Spreafico's [2010] study of elite Barnard College in the US). Possibilities exist in complicated tensions and leave open spaces in which universities might choose contributions to fair societal development.

Developing countries have not been immune to global higher education shifts (Altbach, 2009). The World Bank (2003), in a major policy reversal from its earlier emphasis on primary education as the way to promote economic growth, now promotes the importance of technological development, knowledge and information in economic development and emphasizes the need for highly-skilled knowledge workers with a capacity to learn and adapt to changing contexts, and to contribute to innovation. The emphasis is on 'knowledge as a main driver of growth' because '[k]nowledge accumulation and application have become major factors in economic development and are increasingly at the core of a country's competitive advantage in the global economy' and 'central to the creation of the intellectual capacity on which knowledge production and utilization depend' (ibid.: xvii). Thus higher education has been positioned as a 'powerhouse' for development (Singh, 2010: 66). The idea is to transform poor countries into information/knowledge-rich societies in a global knowledge economy. But the new policy orthodoxy, Singh (2010) argues, is primarily instrumental in its growing demand for a well-educated workforce to drive economic development.

Overall, then, neo-liberal ideology – its characteristic emphasis on markets and its associated practices and policies – influences but does not completely shape what happens in higher education. The question of overriding importance to us here is Sen's question about the extent to which benefits are fairly distributed. UNESCO (2009: 9) notes that 'inequality is part of the global higher education landscape': for example, when universities in richer countries employ talented academic staff and graduates from poorer regions, and when knowledge partnerships are entered into between richer countries, excluding poorer countries, globalization trends might work to increase poverty and wealth gaps. Yet mobilities of higher education staff and students and knowledge partnerships represent both opportunities to alleviate and threats to increase inequalities between countries (Unterhalter and Carpentier, 2010).

Contributions to equity are also strained by the impact of the rapid rise of international comparative university rankings (increasingly taken as the proxy for university quality) in the last 10 years. The two primary international rankings currently are those produced by Shanghai Jai Tong University and the QS/*Times Higher Education*, both of which emphasize research productivity and quality, which correlate with the wealth of universities. Moreover, other indicators (for example, staff–student ratios and student entry qualifications) also relate to university wealth and established status, thereby confirming the reputation of universities as if it is the natural order (Amsler and Bolsmann, 2012). Indeed, Marginson (2010) suggests that the greater enemy of the public good for universities is not the economic market but rather the status hierarchy and competition between universities, and between nations which play strongly to the self-interest of some universities. For example, our personal conversations with a Pro Vice-Chancellor (International) at an elite English university turned on the University wanting to establish North–South links only with those South African universities which featured in the top 500 universities. Internationally, the rankings, suggests UNESCO (2009: 11) are 'taken seriously' by the public, universities and governments. A 'world class' university 'is less likely to stress teaching, public service, providing access to under-served populations, or other important social services' (ibid.). Higher-status universities maintain their status, and newer entrants to the game seek that status by doing and being that which earns them high rankings.

Notwithstanding, in developing countries there are competing views about the value of league tables. In South Africa, for example, four universities are currently in the top 400 of the *THE* League Tables for 2012–2013. On the one hand, Adam Habib (2011), then Deputy Vice-Chancellor of the University of Johannesburg (UJ), has argued that rankings privilege one reality of higher education and impose indicators related to that reality across multiple global systems, overlooking history and contextual specificity. In his view, the most benign effect of rankings is to promote institutional uniformity. The most dangerous, 'would be the derailment of the development agenda and the continued reproduction of poverty, inequality and marginalisation in the developing world' because contributions to human development do not influence rankings (ibid.: 28). Similarly, the Vice-Chancellor of Rhodes University, Saleem Badat (2010), argues that rankings ignore the value of community engagement and are only marginally concerned with high-quality teaching and learning, which he sees as central to advancing development in the South. Further, the vertical hierarchy of universities devalues those which fall outside the top 500 with the 'burden of these characterizations weigh[ing] disproportionately on universities in the South' (ibid.: 130). On the other hand, Cheryl Potgieter (2013), Deputy Vice-Chancellor at the University of Kwa-Zulu Natal (in the top 400 unlike UJ and Rhodes) has recently argued in favour of rankings. In her view, research is vital in South Africa, and can be encouraged by the rankings, and indeed can be 'the engine that pulls the whole university forward' (ibid.: 2).

Opinions about the effects of university rankings vary, nevertheless, the broader point is that global trends, including the use of league tables, play out in specific ways in Africa, the developing region in which our empirical study is located and to which we now turn. Much of the research on higher education in Africa has called for its revitalization (Sawwyer, 2002; Brock-Utne, 2003; Sall *et al.*, 2003; Lebeau, 2008; Singh, 2011). We regard the capabilities-based project which is the subject of this book as a part of such initiatives. 'Revitalization' is, as Singh (2011) explains, a policy imperative (e.g. World Bank, 2002, 2003a, b, 2009; UNESCO, 2009) and the focus for research and debate. Moreover, the term suggests confidence in the potential of knowledge societies: drives for revitalization tend to be framed by possibilities for knowledge-driven development in global times, which is regarded as crucial to development trajectories in Africa (Singh, 2011). Thus employability and individual economic opportunities are critical: professionals without jobs cannot use their knowledge and skills to contribute to society; unemployed graduates will not be socially mobile and are likely to be dissatisfied with their lives: a graduate without job prospects is a wasted national resource in any developing country.

While not gainsaying the importance of economic development, Sen's (2003) question about fairness remains crucial: we should ask what the fruits of growth are for; and how they are distributed and to whom. Economic growth and a productive business environment undoubtedly increase human well-being: insecurity is reduced; health promoted; and opportunities for leisure are presented. Integration into economic life matters if people are to possess a sense of belonging in society by participating in income generation and securing remunerative employment. That said, income alone cannot capture the full range of contributions to a state of well-being in a person's life. A strong economy ought to be a means to good lives, but as Sen (1999) has reminded us, we cannot evaluate resources as an end; rather we need rich and full information about how resources are being realized in actual human lives, activities and achievements. In the next two sections, then, we turn to how higher education might make strong contributions to the full range of human capabilities.

Higher education as social reform

Even though universities round the world, and perhaps especially in developing countries, face equity and growth challenges and contradictions (Unterhalter and Carpentier, 2010), those of us who work in universities know how potentially transformative a university education can be. Universities can be spaces where relations of equality, respect for difference, and concerns for contributing to society are nurtured; and where original, creative and life-enhancing knowledge is produced. Universities' missions and practices have not been entirely captured by neo-liberalism as an ideological force. As Marginson (2006: 47) argues, the problem with 'irresistible force' descriptions about the potency and widespread grip of globalization and neoliberal policies is that they risk reducing the complexity of how things work out in different higher education sites. He writes:

> The transformation is never so complete, nor solely engineered from above by managers and governments, let alone cosmic forces of 'capitalisms' and 'globalization'. It also involved changing identities and desires, and new kinds of reflexivity and self-investment. And there is much more national and local variation.
>
> (ibid.: 46)

The Public-Good Professional Capabilities Index is grounded in discussions with stakeholders, so it is an expression of understanding the local and particular and the scope for agency. Yet, as we have argued above, while the scope for agency is being taken up in universities in similar ways across the world, the dominant, hegemonic discourse of neo-liberalism undermines a focus on issues of social justice. Thus, how residues of 'subjugated' discourses (Williams, 1977) about universities will survive under current policy conditions is tremendously important if we are not to give mere lip service to universities as a public good or, as Martha Nussbaum (2010) states, to 'prune away' all those parts of the higher education project that are crucial to citizenship in any democratic society. The recent financial crisis suggests that it is precisely the moral and ethical dimensions of human life, rather than the quantity and level of education which has let us down so badly.

Yet as Habermas (1989: 118) implies, we should not be unduly worried, the traditional four functions of the university still stand: the generation of technically exploitable knowledge for producing wealth and services; the academic preparation of public service professionals; the transmission, interpretation and development of cultural knowledge, and 'the enlightenment of the political public sphere'. Castells (2001) inflects university functions rather differently. As well as producing knowledge, he suggests that universities play a role as ideological apparatus, expressing ideological struggles present in all societies; and they select and socialize dominant elites, of which the education and training of professionals is a part (Larson, 2013). Castells (2001: 141) also draws attention to how universities must manage 'a complex and contradictory reality' with local pressures to contend with, alongside having also a universal role. Speaking in South Africa, he reflected further on the role of universities in development for both economy and society, arguing that 'the quality, effectiveness and relevance of the university system will be directly related to the ability of people, society and institutions to develop' (2009: 1) by its capacity to train and educate a good quality labour force. By the same token, universities are 'a critical source of equalisation of chances and democratisation of society' (ibid.). At the same time, in echoes of Habermas's (1989: 118) 'enlightenment of the political public sphere', Castells identifies for universities the function of the production and consolidation of values, drawing attention to the importance in a fast changing precarious world of a few 'solid' values (2001: 4).

For statements on the public value and role of universities we can turn to declarations such as the Magna Carta of European Universities (1998),[3] the international Taillores Declaration (2005),[4] and the UNESCO (1998)[5] declaration on higher education for the twenty-first century, reconfirmed in 2003. While we draw here on a theoretically pluralistic literature, it has in common a concern for universities as places both where critical knowledge is created and where contributions to equity in society and democratic life are possible and desirable. Thus, in contemporary times GUNI (2008) proposes that critical discourses can be generated in higher education to enable societies to reflect continually on and to advance positive shifts towards social transformation. Lobera and Escrigas (2009) cite a Delphi study of 214 experts (higher education specialists, vice-chancellors and other university employees, policy makers, and members of civil society involved in development work) from 80 countries of whom the majority agreed that universities should play an active role in human and social development. They note that the key challenges prioritized by these respondents included: poverty reduction (60 per cent); sustainable development (58 per cent); critical thinking and ethical values in the globalization process (50 per cent); and the improvement of governability and participative democracy (44 per cent).

The disparities that can be found between the dominant discourses of human capital and many university practices recall Raymond William's (1977) conceptualization of a complex of dominant, residual and emergent (policy) discourses. While neo-liberal discourses might be dominant, there are continuing beliefs, values and practices about university education as intrinsically valuable which persist and there is an emergent discourse at the margins of higher education around human development and capabilities (Walker, 2006; Boni and Walker, 2013; Leibowitz, 2012), quality as well-being (nef 2008), and the call to imagine other globalizations (Rizvi and Lingard, 2010). Higher education, as UNESCO (2003) affirms, is a vital component of cultural, social, and political development, of endogenous capacity-building, the consolidation of human rights, sustainable development, democracy, and peace, in a context of justice.

The public dimensions of universities in Africa in particular are dealt with by Sall *et al.* (2003). They discuss African universities in civil society, explaining that while they may have reproductive effects, they also have the potential as part of the public sphere to hold the state and business accountable and provide critical discussion and direction on changes in society. Importantly, they note that universities produce most of the people employed at the higher echelons of the public and private sector, including we might add, professions in law, engineering and so forth. The university is then both a participant in changing social processes and affected by processes of change and transformation. Moreover the social significance of university expansion lies in graduate social mobility and integration into the labour market, both critical for the transformation roles and functions of universities (ibid.). Crucially, the choices and experiences of young people in higher education in Africa will themselves be critical to whether it fulfils a reproductive role for privilege and private advantages only, or also encompasses a transformative role for well-being across society.

This depiction of possibilities does not deny that higher education should be expected to deliver structural change in macroeconomic policy, unemployment, health, poverty and so on. We can consider simultaneously how the public-good contributions of universities reduce inequalities in society. As we have indicated, possibilities exist for both reproductive and transformative action in and through higher education, allowing a space for us to re-imagine universities as a public good, to which we now turn.

Re-imagining universities and their public-good contributions

In developing our understanding of the concept of 'the public good' we have drawn eclectically from a range of scholarship, added to it by a consideration of professionalism for the public good (dealt with in Chapter 2), and then made it concrete and operational in our research project. In the first place we considered the knowledge that professionals acquire as a public good. The economist, Paul A. Samuelson (1954: 387), is usually credited as the first to develop a theory of 'public goods', which he defined in opposition to private goods as '[goods] which all enjoy in common in the sense that each individual's consumption of such a good leads to no subtractions from any other individual's consumption of that good'. This is the property that has become known as 'non-rivalrous': for example, a poem or a book can be read by many people without reducing the consumption of that good by others. In addition, public goods possess a second property called 'non-excludability', that is, it is impossible to exclude any individuals from consuming the good. Relevant to an ethical stance on the part of universities, is that knowledge, as Stiglitz (2003) suggests, is a public good because it retains its value. For example, a mathematical theorem can be used over and over again across the globe, or a book read by millions across the world without diminishing in value. But in current times university-produced knowledge can be excludable through intellectual property rights, patents, commercial distribution, the selection of students and so on, and is then not equitably distributed. Further, as Calhoun (2006) points out, while knowledge (when made freely available) is not used up by sharing, it can be collected in the form of credentials based on access to the same knowledge, thereby transforming it into a private good. If credentials are too widely shared they diminish in professional and financial value. The issue then is how or if the credentialed elite use their knowledge to contribute to the wider good, as professionals or as citizens participating in the public sphere. The relevant question concerns how the knowledge produced, reproduced or disseminated in universities is circulated and made more equally accessible. Our answer centres on the production of graduate professionals whose accumulated acquired knowledge is used in society as a public good. As Nixon (2011: 26) suggests, higher education can educate people 'who are not only efficient and effective in their use of acquired knowledge, but who can use that knowledge to make complex choices regarding the right uses and application of that knowledge' – for the public good.

Second, we have considered 'the public good' in the singular as a 'fundamental goal' of higher education'. GUNI (2008: 8) describes the public good as relating 'directly to the roles that academic institutions can play in society [. . .] a public commitment to the general interests of the society of which they form part'. Higher education trains people for positions of responsibility – their decisions can have a positive or negative impact on people, communities and society:

> Higher education can be focused on training professionals or on educating citizens who will interchange value with society through the exercise of their professional responsibilities. This second approach implies the education of citizens knowledgeable about the human and social condition, with ethical awareness and civic commitment.
>
> (GUNI, 2008: 11)

Seeing professional education as educating people to be able to contribute to the common welfare connects the singular public good of higher education to the notion of plural public goods. Nixon (2011) argues that the public good can reside both in individuals working inside and in graduates outside the academy, and in the ethos and democratic mission of the university itself. In higher education, individuals and institutions together produce 'outputs' of wide public benefit such as informed citizens, health professionals, business people, and so on (Calhoun, 2006). 'Public good' then captures, as Leibowitz (2012) suggests, the idea that a university as a whole leans consistently towards the values, practices and policies of social justice and inclusion both within the institution and in its external dealings.

Yet, as UNESCO points out, public-good university education is 'easily neglected in the rush for income and prestige' (2009: 21). Moreover, Deneulin and Townsend (2007: 25) argue that public goods cannot be provided satisfactorily through unfettered market mechanisms, mainly because the market demands tangible outcomes, whereas, 'the good of the community which comes into being in and through' higher education inheres in the quality of relationships that are built internally and externally. For Moellendorf (2009), a public good association would produce goods and powers that are useful to all members of society, nationally and internationally; furthermore, the poor should be included in conversations about global and national issues (including, for our purposes, global higher education inequalities).

What is developed is an idea of universities and the public good based on: consistent values; associational life which is egalitarian and collective; commitments to human well-being for all members of a society; the university community and society more broadly having a voice in decision-making processes, whether direct or indirect. These are some of the conditions for sustainable and shared public goods accruing from university education.

We have drawn on this broad idea to develop our own innovative concept of public-good professionalism in the chapters which follow. To regard professional education as a public-good contribution by universities is to conceptualize professionals educated to provide a good-quality public service for their societies; and to be supported in doing so by public policy and funding. Helpfully, Salais (2010) notes that we need to revisit the idea of what we mean by 'public services', in order to revive the understanding that a service is 'public', not so much because it is publicly funded, but rather because it should be understood to *serve* the public – that is, citizens have legitimate claims on state resources which can improve their lives (legal aid, health care, social welfare, urban infrastructure, clean water, and the like). Yet the burden and challenges of transformation should not fall entirely on professionals in the public sector, leaving those in private work free of obligations for social change. From our perspective, societies need professionals educated with the knowledge, awareness and social values for operationalizing inclusive public services (even if universities cannot be held accountable for graduates' actual public-good choices once they leave university).

Public policy actions must align: to promote a social and collective paradigm requires a public culture that places human dignity and the alleviation of remediable injustices at its core (Escrigas, 2008). It requires universities' engagement with the moral-political urgencies of poverty, human security, environmental sustainability and fair access to technology. University-based professional education and training is a key function of universities and is a pivotal point at which social needs and economic and political imperatives meet advancing knowledge and aspiring talent. While there can be no direct connections between specific curricula and pedagogic processes and the production of professionals with specific attributes and dispositions, desire for social transformation demands questions about public-service professional education and what it means to train professionals in conditions of inequality and unfairness.

In sum, this chapter has set out the global context and global challenges of and opportunities for higher education. On the one hand, what Sen (2002) calls 'globalism' has brought real benefits and gains including in the arena of higher education: expanded student access, more diverse students, more gender equity, more interaction and mobility internationally fuelling graduate capacity building and research collaborations, and economic opportunities and employment. On the other hand, there are also inequalities globally in higher education and a push by economic policy makers to see higher education as contributing primarily to economic development and human capital so that other significant purposes of higher education in relation to society and higher learning become obscured. Yet, such shifts are neither hegemonic nor uniform across higher education and whatever policy intentions are, they do not wholly determine actual practices. Universities continue to operate under competing pressures and also remain spaces for equity and human development. To this end we have outlined how the public good is understood to foreshadow how we take this up, both theoretically and empirically in relation to the formation of public-good professionals in universities.

In the next chapter is an explanation of the conceptual framework that was brought to bear on the problem of universities' role in poverty reduction. We show how we drew on both ideas about public-good professionalism and the 'capabilities approach' to human development; and how we brought them together to provide a framework for thinking about university-based professional education oriented towards the public good.

2 Capabilities-based public-good professionalism

> And, in educating for freedom, how can we create and maintain a common world?
>
> (Maxine Greene, 1998: 117)

The previous chapter noted a dominant economic growth–human capital model driving higher education policy globally, and also began to sketch an alternative image of university professional education that is oriented towards the public good. In this chapter we outline how we arrive at a conceptual framing of public-good professionalism. As we explained, spaces exist for universities to contribute towards defining and working towards addressing social, national and global problems. Higher education does not always legitimize the interests of the powerful in society; it can disrupt hierarchies and instill altruistic values and outcomes. As we also noted, Habermas (1989) points out that one of the important social functions of the university is the academic preparation of professionals.

The chapter draws on two sets of ideas: first, ideas from literature about professionalism (Freidson, 2001; Sullivan, 2005; Larson, 2013), and second, ideas from the capabilities approach (Sen, 1999, 2009; Nussbaum, 2000, 2011). We explain how during the project theorizing professionalism was a resource to illuminate professional education oriented to poverty reduction, to more justice and to less inequality. Throughout the project and for the purposes of this book we are proposing that university-based professional education is thought of as professional education explicitly for the public good, rather than education which takes little or no account of the potential of professionals to reduce poverty and other forms of inequality.

Our version of professionalism seeks to advance human development (Haq, 1999) in society, by which we mean, 'to create an enabling environment for people to live long, healthy and creative lives'; and, 'a process of enlarging people's choices' (UNDP, 1990: 1). A human development perspective gives rise to such questions as: Do people have the opportunities for moving about freely and safely?; do they have decent housing?; are they able to read and think critically?; do they have good friendships?; are they treated by others with dignity?; do they have economic opportunities, and so on? Human development is underpinned by core principles of empowerment, equity, and security and sustainability of people's valued achievements and opportunities; and we are applying these principles to public-good professional practices.

In the next section, following a specific reading of the history of professions (drawing on Magali Sarfatti Larson's seminal work *The rise of professionalism: monopolies of competence and sheltered markets* 2013, first published 1977) we explain how the discourse or ideology of professionalism might be employed as a resource to elaborate and illuminate the task that faces the educators of professionals in a transforming South Africa. The concept of professionalism is deconstructed to show that the aspect that links its social functions and the public good can be mobilized in any democratic society in the contemporary world, and in South Africa in particular.

Public-good professionalism

A large literature in the sociology of the professions concurs that the historical rise of professionalism was a response to the increasingly complex social and economic needs of modern society which called for specialized expertise; and professionals have now become integral to the modern welfare state (for example, Abbott, 1983; Barber, 1963; Brint, 1996; Derber, 1983; Downie, 1990; Larson, 2013; Macdonald; 1995; Witz, 1992). This literature tends to expound an ideal type of professional occupation: autonomy and prestige is granted by the state in return for expertise in areas central to the needs of the social system and in return for devotion to public service. Two main elements of professionalism justify the special status of professions. The first is the cognitive element – that is the body of specialized and theoretical knowledge and techniques which are applied to work, the acquisition of which requires long and substantial training and education; the second is the normative element which resides in the responsibility of care and gives rise to professional ethics. In this literature, professions are characterized by relatively stable and common affiliations, values and interests. They are marked by professional associations; professional university-based schools/departments[1] and a self-administered ethical code (Larson, 2013).

Magali Sarfetti Larson (2013) regards the picture drawn above as over-simplified and over-valorized because it ignores what professional groups have done to negotiate with states and publics to secure a special position for themselves. Her interpretation is the result of a painstaking historical study analysing how professions were established in modern time. In brief, in her view the processes of professionalization have amounted to a 'project' to gain market power and control, they represent 'an attempt to translate one order of scarce resources – special knowledge and skills – into another – social and economic rewards' (2013: xvii). She proposes a 'double movement' that secured for professionals both the market for services and social status: on the one hand, professional groups mobilize the resources of skills and knowledge; on the other, they have generated and shared an ideology which simultaneously satisfies members of the professional group and persuades the public to trust them.

In this view, Larson is 'disturbed' to note that competence and the service ideal play as central a role in the sociological ideal-type as they do in the self-justification of professional privilege' (ibid.: xi). Certainly, professions do not emerge as disinterested. For example, they work to maintain a monopoly of services; professions are inextricably linked to social hierarchies, serving the middle classes and upwardly mobile; and, there are wide discrepancies of status and reward within professions (ibid.: xii). Nonetheless, there are three aspects of this view that have relevance for our argument for public-good professionalism. First, there is nothing fixed or stable about professionals' prestige or autonomy; second, there is a contradiction or tension within the professions that can pull either way; and third, connected to the tension, there is the notion that the ideology of professionalism can be (and often is) used to shape actual policies and practices. We discuss each in turn below.

First, in practice, professional work is complex, and a theory of professionalism cannot hold everywhere for all time (Larson, 2013). Different professional groups have arisen from historical conflicts and political situations; claims to moral and technical superiority are contested; and gains in privilege and autonomy negotiated with the state can always be withdrawn, so must be defended (Fournier, 1999; Larson, 2013). Professionalism has never been neutral and apolitical and can be understood as a discourse, as part of an ongoing politics of knowledge, power and social organization. In other words, the actual needs of societies and the structures of specific professional markets will impact on professional work. As Larson puts it:

> The stage of economic development, the volume and distribution of national income, the class structure and ethnic composition, the average standard of living, the nature of the state and its policies, and ideology – including a variety of cultural traditions – define the potential, the characteristics, and the dynamics of a profession's market.
>
> (Larson, 2013: 50)

In our case, the ideology of 'transformation' in South Africa supports a construction of professionalism that is oriented to poverty reduction. The Finance Minister, Trevor Manuel, then publicly said that public servants, who should be the 'mainstay for transformation', have lost the passion for their work. Manuel continued: 'Our ability to deliver a deep and durable democracy focused on improving living standards will never be attained without the commitment of our public servants in the key social sciences' (Joseph, 2008: 3). As Freidson (2001: 71–72) puts it, if a profession's work 'comes to have little relationship to the knowledge and values of its society, it may have difficulty surviving'.

Second, Larson asks whether professionals can be acquitted of the charge of having a 'capitalist profit motive' (ibid.: xiii), but, in one sense, this charge is not relevant. What we are interested in are the actual uses and social consequences of expert knowledge, even if the individual and collective professions must protect their interests. Larson (ibid.) clarifies that there are two orientations to professionalism – entrepreneurial and vocational, which are analytically distinct, even if they appear together in the actual lives of modern professionals. She notes that certain social conditions might put emphasis on the entrepreneurial to the point that it becomes 'mere economic instrumentalism' (ibid: 62). The vocational orientation relates to what she calls the 'intrinsic' (ibid.) value of professional work: it encompasses self-realization, creativity and an authentic interest in making contributions in the field of work. For Larson, the combination of entrepreneurial and vocational orientations 'generates tensions, both for the individual professional and for the profession as a whole' (ibid.: 61–2) which inevitably harm the intrinsic qualities of the work and which cannot be resolved without solidarity with 'all workers [to] find the means of claiming and realizing the full human potential of all work' (ibid: 244). We do not take as uncompromising a view. We accept that there is a pull 'towards an ethos of individual competition and the reproduction of a hierarchy of social advantage' (Jonathan, 2001: 48) and many commentators diagnose self-interest in the professions and remark a decline of public trust (Brint, 1994; Drydal and Karseth, 2006; Freidson, 2001; O'Neill, 2002; Sullivan, 2005). On the other hand, everyday experiences provide evidence of professional altruism and integrity, and internalized personal professional virtues, motivated, we might assume, by the ideology of public service (Drydal and Karseth, 2006). From our perspective, Larson underestimates the draw of the intrinsic meanings of professional work.

Third, then, and perhaps most importantly for our purposes the ideology of professionalism can be mobilized as a resource to promote public-good professionalism. In Larson's (2013) view the ideology of professionalism has been used to justify high status in society and the tight definition of criteria for gaining access to the professions. Nevertheless, even the sceptical Larson concedes that the common image of ideal-type professions has come from actual practices as well as ideology: while ideology 'unconsciously obscures real social structures and relations [it also] consciously inspires collective or individual efforts' (ibid.: xvii). At this point, we draw on the idea that professions can and should build their moral missions because there is a close relationship between the integrity of professional life and the health of civic cultures (Freidson, 2004; Sullivan, 2005; Strain *et al.*, 2009).

As a starting point for defining public-good professionalism, Sullivan (2005) provides a pragmatic and neutral definition with three interlocking constituent features – human capital, collective enterprise and civic politics, thus revealing the springboard for turning the ideology of ideal-type professionalism into policies and practices:

'(1) professional skills are human capital that (2) is always dependent for its negotiability upon some collective enterprise, which itself (3) is the outcome of civic politics in which the freedom of a group to organize for a specific purpose is balanced by the accountability of that group to other members of the civic community for furtherance of publicly established goals and standards.

(Sullivan, 2005: 184)

What must be added here to make sense of a claim for public-good professionalism is what Larson called the 'intrinsic' value of the work. The potential meaning and value of professional work are strongly evaluated by both R.H. Tawney (for whom the professions serve a civilizing function) and by William Sullivan:

> [T]he successful doctor [may] grow rich, but the meaning of their profession, both for themselves and for the public, is not that they make money but that they make health, or safety, or knowledge, or good government, or good law.

(Tawney, 1948: 94)

> [W]hat makes one free and renders life worth living is finally neither satisfying one's desires nor accomplishing one's purposes, valuable as these are, but instead learning to act with the good of the whole in view, building life act by act, happy if each deed, as far as circumstances allow, contributes to general welfare. Anyone who has been stirred and inspired by a committed teacher, an attentive health care provider, a dedicated pastor or rabbi; anyone who has experienced a well-functioning business firm or public agency, school or cultural institution has glimpsed the enlivening possibilities inherent in communities of professional purpose.

(Sullivan, 2005: 290)

In this section, we have established a rationale for building a notion of public-good professionalism by taking up the dominant ideas of ideal-type professionalism, which should be viewed with some scepticism, to argue that ever evolving professional projects will respond to local circumstances (in this case the need for 'transformation' in South Africa); and that, despite the pull towards self-interest, professionals are attached to work that makes contributions to the improvement of their clients and the societies in which they work.[2] We are now in a position to explain how the capabilities approach provides a framework for developing a multidimensional definition of public-good professionalism that is specifically oriented to poverty reduction.

A capabilities-based professionalism

Education, including higher education is central to development agendas globally, as we noted in Chapter 1. Higher education is seen as driving high-level skills and knowledge for competitive global economic growth and graduate employability. However, higher education is rather less central to debates around development for poverty reduction. Nor does poverty reduction figure explicitly in professionalism discourses, including progressive versions. Therefore we need to bring together professionalism, higher education and human development/ poverty reduction, and the capability approach offers a means of doing so.

A detailed step-by-step explanation of the practical processes by which we drew up a list of public-good professional capabilities is found in Chapters 4 and 5. The rest of this chapter provides an overview of how we drew on the capability/ies approach to human development, first by way of a brief introduction; and then by discussing overarching issues that relate the approach to education and to the concept of a capabilities-based public-good professionalism. The last part of the chapter explains the background thinking involved in defining public-good professional capabilities.

According to Sen, human development consists in 'expanding the real freedoms that people enjoy' (1999: 1) through 'the removal of various types of unfreedoms that leave people with little choice and little opportunity of exercising their reasoned agency' (ibid.: xii). Freedom is, for Sen, fundamental to the quality of human life and well-being. Each person should be free to generate reflective, informed choices about ways of living that they deem important and valuable. He focuses on self-determination and on what people are actually able to be and do, personally and in comparison to others. To evaluate human well-being in these terms, Sen proposed the 'capability approach', also referred to by some as the 'capabilities approach', which is the term we use to capture both the development over time of ideas about what counts as a capability and Nussbaum's assertion that capabilities are 'plural and qualitatively distinct' (2011: 18).

In the capabilities approach, poverty is seen as a multidimensional erosion of human well-being and agency; and poverty reduction as the expansion of a range of human capabilities which are the freedoms or opportunities people have to be and do what they value. Capabilities are the freedoms of each person to choose and exercise a combination of ways of being they have reason to value, and functionings are what a person chooses to do (their 'doings'). The approach was conceptualized first by Sen (1985, 1999) as an alternative to other ways of thinking about welfare economics and human well-being. From a capabilities perspective how well people are doing is evaluated neither by looking at GDP or average income in a country alone, nor by asking how satisfied people are with their lives (because people may resign themselves to bad circumstances). Rather, it aims to assess what people are actually 'capable' of being and doing in terms of living lives they regard as good. Sen argued for five elements in evaluating capability: evidence of real freedoms when comparing a peoples' (dis)advantages; an assessment of individual differences in the ability to convert resources into valuable achievements; attention to the plurality of achievements which contribute to well-being; making a balanced account of materialistic and non-materialistic factors; and a concern for the fair distribution of capabilities in society. So the approach rejects the view that improved lives can follow from economic growth only – there is a complex range of valued human ends which requires a correspondingly expansive understanding of human development. Interpersonal comparisons are made on the basis of a person's capabilities, rather than their economic resources or the satisfaction they may claim with regard to aspects of their life.

Most significantly for public and international development policy, Mahbub ul Haq (see K. Haq, 2008) worked with Sen to apply the capability approach to develop the United Nations Human Development Index which includes what might be considered basic capabilities in health, education, and income, and assesses them across developed and developing countries as a measure of quality of life. The capabilities approach, then, is fundamentally concerned with justice in the context of the complexities of the individual lives of the disadvantaged, thus offering an attractive normative orientation to professionalism that is focused on well-being and human development (Robeyns, 2011).

Our thinking about education is informed by Sen and Nussbaum, and our vision is of professionals who can support the capability expansion of their clients by possessing the public-good professional capabilities that allow them to do so. When considering the lens the capabilities approach has on education, it should first be kept in mind that the advanced capabilities developed through education are founded on basic human capabilities which secure a reasonable quality of life so that individuals are not, for example, obliged to engage in daily struggles to find food or somewhere to sleep.

For Sen, then, the goals of education are threefold: instrumental (preparation for economic opportunities), intrinsic (for example, the acquisition of knowledge for its own sake), and social (oriented to pressing civic problems) (Dreze and Sen, 2002). Nussbaum (2000: 78) identifies a specific education capability of 'senses, imagination and thought' and she outlines three education capabilities: critical thinking, world citizenship and narrative imagination (understanding the experiences of others) (Nussbaum, 1997). Her central capabilities of 'practical reason' and 'affiliation' (see Chapter 4) further resonate as deeply educational (Nussbaum, 2000). Moreover, both Sen (2009) and Nussbaum (2011) connect the advancement of justice to inclusive democracy which depends on diverse people taking part in discussion and collective reasoning. The ability to take part in such debates implies having practiced in rich, dialogic and participatory pedagogical processes. From this perspective, the relevance of education in the capabilities approach is to highlight the processes as well as the opportunity aspect of freedom (Sen, 2004) – valuing particular capabilities without attending to the educational processes in place to develop them would jeopardize the achievement of capabilities accessed through educational processes. In a capabilities-oriented education process, education would aim to secure and distribute capabilities to all students, paying attention to the social arrangements in education (pedagogies, institutional culture, and education policy) and to barriers that might impede the development of opportunities and valued outcomes.

Our specific educational interest is in the production of professionals who both possess public-good capabilities capabilities and display public-good functionings. Sen defines a functioning below:

> A functioning is an achievement of a person: what a person manages to do or to be. It reflects as it were, a part of the 'state' of that person. It has to be distinguished from the commodities which are used to achieve those

functionings [. . .] it has to be distinguished also from the happiness generated by the functioning [. . .] A functioning is thus different both from (1) having goods (and the corresponding characteristics), to which it is posterior, and (2) having utility (in the form of happiness resulting from that functioning, to which it is in an important way, prior).

(Sen, 1987: 7)

Education has a special relationship to functionings in two specific ways, both of which are highly pertinent to our project. First, having the freedom to choose functionings is intrinsically valuable and, in this respect, the emphasis in the capabilities literature on a reasoned (informed, thoughtful, critical) understanding and choice of beings and doings implies having a formal education. Arguably, without some form of formal education it is difficult to make reasoned choices about values and how to lead one's life. Second, while education itself is often viewed as a capability (to be educated), educationally-based capabilities – any, for example, that involve reading and writing – require functioning (or practice) to develop and sustain capabilities. In Nussbaum's (2000: 92) words 'the more crucial a function is to attaining and maintaining other capabilities, the more entitled we may be to promote actual functioning in some cases'. We might argue that for students in professional fields, the opportunity professional education offers to develop the capability of being knowledgeable and skilful is crucial. Moreover, this capability is constituted of different functionings, many of which are the focus of educational assessment: observed functionings are proxies for assessing whether or not underlying capabilities have been formed. Thus, with regard to public-good professionalism, in a professional education department, it would be incomplete to educate for public-good values and practices without paying attention to how or if students are able to function as public-good professionals oriented to poverty reduction.

Agency is a concept central to the capabilities approach and to practices of public-good professionalism: agency and obligation. In the absence of a strong sense of personal efficacy and confidence, it is unlikely that professionals will be able to position themselves or sustain their positioning over time as public-good professionals. In the capabilities approach, agency is defined as the ability to act according to what one values or – in Sen's (1985: 206) words – 'what a person is free to do and achieve in pursuit of whatever goals or values he or she regards as important'. Consequently, 'people who enjoy high levels of agency are engaged in actions that are congruent with their values' (Alkire, 2007: 3).

In thinking about how a public-good professional would function (or act) we have paid especial attention to agency (freedom and power to act), which is a central concept to the capabilities approach and to the practices of public-good professionalism. First, there is a need for deliberation about what underpins agency in any specific context: 'What is needed is not merely freedom and power to act, but also freedom and power to question and reassess the prevailing norms and values' (Dréze and Sen, 2002 cited in Crocker, 2008: 11). Second is responsibility towards others. Responsible agency includes 'other-regarding' goals, meaning goals which concern the good lives of others and carry an obligation to use one's power to enhance human development. Sen (2008: 336) argues that being advantaged (which university-educated people are) 'inescapably' generates obligations to be responsible for promoting democratic values, social justice and fundamental human rights because 'capability is a kind of power, and it would be a mistake to see capability only as a concept of human advantage, not also as a concept in human obligation'. From Sen's perspective, if someone has the power to make a change that they can see will reduce injustice in the world, there is a strong social argument for doing so. Owing obligations to others arises from a view of ourselves as members of communities rather than as isolated individuals: collective acts might bind us to others to reform the institutions and structures that might guarantee equality beyond individual actions.

In theory then professional graduates have power (that is the capabilities) to contribute to society, and are obligated to do so. In South Africa 16 per cent of South Africans (mostly from richer socio-economic backgrounds) currently go to university while 84 per cent do not (Singh, 2011). This difference can be related to Rawl's (2001) principle whereby some inequalities are permitted if they are to the benefit of the disadvantaged. Thus the difference in life opportunities can be tolerated only if the knowledge and skills of more advantaged people are a common asset to benefit those less fortunate. Furthermore, research on social change by De Swaan *et al.* (2000) demonstrates that elites have played a decisive role in the development of Western European welfare states. In this work an elite is defined as controlling 'a much larger share of material, symbolic and political resources than the other strata of society' (ibid.: 46). The South African elite includes all professionals, who are substantially better off than the majority poor population, even if some professions earn more than others. De Swaan *et al.* (ibid.) further suggest that there are three basic attitudes to poverty among elites: indifference; concern based on self-interest accompanied by inaction and resignation to inequalities; and concern and confidence about their ability to act to bring about change. These attitudes hold inequality in place or challenge it. They argue that if elites are sufficiently socially aware, they can play a significant role in transformative development, both by contributions to good quality in public services, and by broadening civic participation and consolidating democratic reforms. If this is so, then universities can have a place in nurturing the social consciousness of elites.

Thus, while philosophically the capabilities approach supports an individual maximizing calculus ('what I have reason to value being and doing'), obligations to others directs this maximizing calculus to take into account the improvement of the well-being of others as a means to my own well-being. What I have reason to value as significant to my own good life then includes advancing the well-being of others, especially people living in poverty. University professional education can play a role in shaping ethically worthwhile, humanist and non-instrumental personal calculations, The notion of responsibility towards others chimes well with our interpretation of public-good professionalism, and the potential of particular kinds of professional education. Students should learn 'to deliberate about the possibilities for a [professional] life well lived [. . .] a kind of synthetic knowing that links self-conscious awareness to responsive engagement in projects in the world' (Sullivan and Roisin, 2008: 104), and lives of 'significance and responsibility' (ibid.: xv), combining knowledge and the power of vision and reflection.

The public-good professional that we envisage through the lens of the capabilities approach would ask such questions as: What are my clients or the communities I work with actually able to do and be? What opportunities do they have to be and do what they value? How do social arrangements have an influence on expanding people's capabilities? How do we build a profession that values creating capabilities for all? These professionals would be oriented to thinking about opportunities for clients to choose to live in meaningful, productive and rewarding ways. Where they found a failure of capabilities and valuable achievements for individuals, groups and communities they would ask what changes in structures, institutions, policies and practices might enhance people's flourishing. By influencing the thinking of professionals, the quality of professional education in universities might enable the poor and vulnerable – supported and empowered in part by professionals and their public service – to achieve valuable goals and to lead dignified and secure lives.

Defining public-good professional capabilities

The outcome of our research was the Public-Good Professional Capabilities Index. An essential element of our research and development approach was the decision to select professional capability dimensions which would capture individual- and other-regarding professional agency, and be normatively aligned with human development concerns and public good contributions. In relation to selecting a list of capabilities, there were differences in the approaches of Sen and of Nussbaum that we needed to resolve.

As a philosopher, Nussbaum (2000, 2011) formulates, justifies and defends a conception of the good life (Crocker, 2008). She argues that philosophy can identify valuable capabilities that ensure justice and human dignity, without recourse to discussions; and she stands by her central list of ten human capabilities (detailed in Chapter 4) all of which she judges as important and incommensurable for a life worthy of human dignity. For Nussbaum, removal of any of these central capabilities amounts to making life 'not worthy of human dignity' (2011: 31). All democratic nations should, she proposes, specify minimum thresholds for each of these capabilities for everyone. Such specification, she argues, defines justice by expressing at the level of governments 'some idea of what we are distributing, and we need to agree that these things are good' (Nussbaum, 1998: 314). Yet, she simultaneously claims that her list is tentative and revisable and that the ten capabilities constitute 'a minimum account of social justice' (Nussbaum, 2003: 40).

Recently, Nussbaum (2011) grounds her approach in the human dignity of each person. Any 'decent' plan 'would seek to promote a range of diverse and incommensurable goods, involving the unfolding and development of distinct human abilities' (ibid.: 127). Because human beings have dignity, 'it is bad to treat them like objects, pushing them around without their consent' (ibid.: 130). The question then becomes what kind of education plan 'permits human abilities to develop and human equality to be respected' (ibid.: 133). The norm of human dignity is tremendously attractive and relevant to professional education everywhere because it enables a moral judgement about a decent society and derives justice from this – a just society would treat every individual as a dignified human being.

By contrast, Sen's (2009) approach to identifying capabilities is deliberately incomplete. He accepts that there are some basic capabilities which could be agreed by everyone, for example those captured in the Human Development Index (for example, life expectancy at birth and mean years of schooling). But he argues that to specify a single list of capabilities is to change the approach into a theory, whereas he intends it to operate as a general framework for making normative assessments about quality of life. Therefore he does not stipulate basic human capabilities, nor how different capabilities should be combined into an overall indicator of quality of life. For him a 'workable solution' is possible without complete social unanimity being achieved. He is not against lists per se, but warns against 'one predetermined canonical list of capabilities, chosen by theorists without any general social discussion or public reasoning' (Sen, 2004: 77), and he includes Nussbaum's list in this criticism. For Sen (1999: 242), all the members of any collective or society should be able 'to be active in the decisions regarding what to preserve and what to let go'. The process of public discussion is crucial, with people as co-creators of development and change.

In response, Nussbaum (2003) argues that Sen's reluctance to make commitments about what capabilities a society ought centrally to pursue means that guidance in thinking about social justice is limited. In this vein, Unterhalter (2012) has recently argued that an open-ended approach (which includes focusing on comparative evaluations about whether one situation is more just than another [Sen, 2009]) may not work well if it comes up against erroneous common sense understandings: her example is of conceptions of gender equity which do not, in fact, advance expansive equality for girls and women, and which, rather, have the potential to constrain capabilities. Similar criticisms have been developed by Deneulin (2010) and by Robeyns (2012: 1) who argue that we need both transcendental (ideal) and non-transcendental theorizing of justice for 'justice enhancing action'. In our case, the ideal we argue for in the domain of professional work and education is public-good professionalism, it is the yardstick against which we adjudicate our practical 'justice-enhancing' efforts. (Though at the same time, as we shall show, we tested and developed our notion of composite capabilities with relevant stakeholders.) We cannot avoid moral reasoning and judgements about professional practice and we make these judgments in relation to deliberations about the 'best way to live' (Sandel, 2009: 10) or to be a public service professional. To develop personal powers through education is to have a view on which powers are worth developing (Crocker, 1995).

In our application of the ideas therefore, we bring together elements of public reasoning, the idea of a partial ranking – some professional capabilities which can be agreed are valuable for a comparative assessment of justice – and an ideal value of human dignity, which morally guides the right thing to do in concrete professional situations. We suggest that in thinking about professional education it is not possible to support any freely chosen capability and functioning, for example, to be able to treat poor clients with disrespect or for white professionals to treat black clients in a racist way, or to be professionally indifferent to suffering. Professional capabilities ought to be worthwhile and to capture worthwhile functionings. Here a list can provide guidance. We therefore opted for something of a middle way, steering a pathway between no list and one fixed list. There is a need for capability dimensions both to give some content to professional education, to work out what public-good professional education might look like, and to then consider how practice and reality accords with our ideal. Our thinking was that if one were to develop or evaluate professional education in universities in relation to contributions to poverty reduction, some evaluative tool was needed in order to judge whether things were more or less just and fair and indeed, effective. Moreover, without agreement on a multidimensional framework and procedure for identifying a valued and relevant professional capability set, 'multidimensional approaches to development are operationally vacuous and risk being misunderstood and misoperationalised by practitioners' (Alkire, 2002: 6).

The capabilities approach is a useful evaluative tool in educational settings because it is sensitive to diversity by allowing an analysis of how individuals in different contexts can convert available resources into functionings. Resources which contribute to functionings can include both financial and economic resources as well as non-market resources such as cultural capital (Bourdieu, 1990). For example, in South Africa, a working-class university student from an overcrowded school accepted into a law school may need more resources in the form of bursaries, academic support and access to networks which generate employment possibilities, than a student from a middle class and good-quality schooling background, with connections through family and friends to the legal profession. And how working-class students would fare in South Africa will not mirror how they fare in a different geographical context, such as the UK.

Clearly, the ability of an individual to convert resources into capabilities has a strong social element. Sen (1999) explains that the freedoms to lead different types of lives depend both on personal characteristics and social arrangements, while Nussbaum (2011: 21) describes 'internal' and 'combined' capabilities to capture the combination of personal abilities and the political, social and economic environment. Sen (1999) further elaborates five freedoms which allow human development: political freedoms (voting rights, participation, scrutiny of public policy, press freedom, right to dissent and so on); economic facilities (opportunities to utilize economic resources for consumption, production and exchange, fair distribution of resources); social opportunities (arrangements for education, health care, social welfare and so on, both for better lives and social and political participation); transparency guarantees (openness, social and political trust); and protective security (safety nets such as unemployment benefits or social grants). These freedoms strengthen one another and should be the means and ends of development and the resources for the expansion of individual capabilities to live more freely. We might argue that these freedoms should be present for students to be able to develop public-good professional capabilities. Questions, therefore, need asking about a university's arrangements and policies, for example does its funding policy enable all who qualify to access and participate in higher education? Are students in professional fields properly supported in dealing with difficult practical and ethical situations that they confront in the field, so that their knowledge, skills and values are strengthened?

To sum up we apply the discussion of the chapter to our case study in South Africa. The argument is that professionals for whom it is of value to work towards poverty reduction in South Africa are public-good professionals and need specific capabilities and functionings (that is, while specialized knowledge, skills and techniques are necessary, they are not sufficient). From the capabilities approach perspective, enabling people 'to live really humanly' is to reduce poverty. To reduce poverty by way of capability expansion is our version of public-good professionalism. For students who arrive at university valuing and motivated towards the potential to reduce poverty, professional education provides the means for realization. For students whose motivation towards poverty reduction is not strong professional education oriented to the public good and to the means of achieving it, might encourage a public-good direction. There is no guarantee that professionals will want or, indeed, be able to use the full range of capabilities their education and training bestow. For professionals, steering a path between cynicism or disillusionment and naive idealism might always be difficult. Nevertheless, a capabilities-based professionalism directs our attention and our actions to operationalize public-good ideals in a 'second-best' world (Sen, 2009). From this perspective, a professional education grounded in human development, capabilities' expansion and functioning achievements, can form rich human beings, and should be one site where we 'advance justice or reduce injustice in the world' (Sen, 2009: 337). There are both constraints and options in aiming for capabilities-based public-good professionalism, and hence grounds for optimism. Brighouse (2004: 162) tells us that all theories of justice emphasize 'that human beings have a high order interest in being able to exercise and develop their capacities for a sense of justice and conception of the good'. The hope, then, is to produce professionals who can act as agents for transformation in a society and in a world which faces serious political and social problems.

Having theorized a capabilities-based professionalism oriented to the poverty-reduction and the mitigation of inequalities, we move to Part 1 of the book in which we set out how we designed our study and operationalized the ideas we have discussed, the result of which is the Index which we used to explore specific professional-education sites (the subject of Part 3). The next chapter sketches the specific conditions for capabilities-based public-good professionalism in South Africa where our case study was located.

Part 2

Context, theoretical framing and methodology

3   History, inequalities and context
South African universities

Bitter knowledge.

(Jonathan Jansen, 2009: 114)

In Part 2 our aim is to explore how higher education functions in relation to the notion of capabilities and public-good professionalism, considering the context, the capabilities-based theoretical framing, and the methodology and methods for operationalizing both capabilities and context.

In the first of three chapters, we look at South Africa as one particular context of poverty and development challenges. In the next two chapters we develop the Index of capabilities with which to research contemporary South African higher education and training for a range of key professional groups significant to the country's transformation. At the same time we keep open the broader relevance and potential of capabilities to higher education in other contexts of poverty and development.

This chapter, then, contextualizes the possibilities and barriers to capability formation and human development as well as higher education and professional education in a dynamic relationship with history, political economy and one local context. We first sketch the South African political, social and economic context and provide background on the extent of poverty and inequality in South African society. We then consider developments in higher education and higher education policy in South Africa which have taken place since the change to a democratic government in 1994, outlining key policy values, goals and strategies and pointing to key shifts in policy formulation and implementation. We emphasize the importance of history: showing both the negative impact of the legacy of apartheid on the possibilities of creating capabilities, and equity achievements in society and in higher education.

From apartheid to democratization[1]

South Africa has been deeply affected by a history of political exclusion, racial and class discrimination, gender and other inequalities. These patterns of social relations had their roots in colonialism and were deepened by the form of economic growth in the mining and manufacturing sectors in the first half of the twentieth century and the way that labour was utilized to meet economic needs (Gelb, 2004). Racially-based discrimination and exclusion were further entrenched in government policy in the form of 'apartheid' when the Nationalist government came into power in 1948. A battery of apartheid policies were implemented in the 1950s in the political, economic, social and personal spheres. They aimed to restrict political power to whites and build up a white, especially Afrikaner, business and middle class. In addition, voting rights were restricted to whites, people were categorized into racial groups,[2] they were forced to live in areas segregated by these racial categories, were forbidden to marry across these racial lines, had restricted access to skilled employment opportunities, and mobility was controlled. Added to this was the introduction of massively under-resourced 'Bantu' education aimed at promoting an education for the African population that related to Afrikaner Nationalist perceptions of their inferior status in society and had the effect therefore of severely restricting the education hopes of generations of black youth. Migrant labour and influx control laws were implemented to control the number of Africans coming to cities. In turn, professional education was, not surprisingly, deeply racialized not only in high-status professions being restricted to whites, although with some access for black South Africans to teaching, nursing, medicine and social work.

Apartheid was, however, forcefully resisted through a long struggle, emanating from political and civil society organizations within South Africa, the trade union movement, the African National Congress (ANC) and other political groups such as the Pan African Congress (PAC), Black Consciousness (BC) and smaller left-wing groups. A combination of resistance by these groupings, together with international support and economic sanctions, led to a settlement which enabled a transition to a democratic government led by the ANC (Karis, 1997; McKinley, 1997; Rantete, 1998; Morris, 2004).

However, when apartheid officially came to an end with the democratically held elections in 1994, it left in its wake a pernicious legacy: described by Hall (2007) as a history of racial segregation and job reservation, and the racialization of economic marginalization, producing a population with vast inequalities across racial groups, and stark inequalities in provision of education, health and welfare services, as well as basic infrastructure, such as housing, water, sanitation and electricity (Seekings and Nattrass, 2005; Hoogeveen and Özler, 2006).

Democratizing times

At the time the research project began, the demography of South Africa looked like Table 3.1:

Between 1996 and 2001, inequality rose for all social groups, and national inequality rose sharply, from a Gini coefficient of 0.68 in 1996 to 0.73 in 2001 (Hall, 2007). 'The consequence,' writes Hall (2007: 3) 'is that, on all measures, South Africa is one of the most unequal countries in the world, and inequality continues to rise.' Citing Hoogeveen and Özler's (2006) combined evidence

Table 3.1 South African context: racial demographics in 2007

Population group	Africans	Coloureds	Indians	Whites	Total
Numbers (millions)	38	4.2	1.2	1.2	47.7 (approx)
Percentage	79.6	8.9	2.4	9.1	100

Source: Statistics South Africa (2007: 1)

from income and expenditure surveys and consumer price surveys, Hall (ibid.) notes that more than 58 per cent of South Africans were at or below the lower local poverty line in 1995, and were still there in 2000. By 2000, more than two-thirds of Africans lived in poverty and more than 40 per cent lived on less than $2 per day. Overall, the number of South Africans living on less than $2 a day increased by more than four million between 1995 and 2000, with almost two million more people living on less than $1 a day (Hoogeveen and Özler 2006 cited in Hall, 2007). Similarly, the 2000 UNDP country report on South Africa noted that over 60 per cent of South Africans could be considered poor (Taylor, 2000). Not surprisingly then, the South African Reconciliation Barometer of 2011 found that income inequality keeps South Africans more divided than race (Sapa, 2012).

In 2010 *The Economist* published a Special Report on South Africa, evaluating development in recent years. It cited 2008 Statistics from South Africa to show the gap in earnings among South Africans, heading their table as 'All right for some' (Table 3.2):

As *The Economist* pointed out, in 2008 three-quarters of South Africans had incomes below R50,000 a year. Of these, 83 per cent were black (who make up 75 per cent of the workforce) and just 6.5 per cent white (13 per cent of the workforce). Only 0.6 per cent of South Africans earned over R750,000, of whom three-quarters were white and 16 per cent (or about 30,000 individuals) black (see Table 3.1). A further 265,000 black people were earning R300,000–R750,000, and 1.6 million were getting R100,000–R300,000. That means, the article says, that nearly 2 million black individuals are now members of the newly emerging black middle class (*The Economist*, 3 June: 1). The middle classes, mostly white and increasingly also black, are doing well. The majority are not. The disparities make it very difficult to build an inclusive society, and raise important questions for the obligations that those with the privilege of professional education owe to the majority of South Africans, as we commented on theoretically in Chapter 2 and will consider empirically in the chapters which follow.

In the post-apartheid period, the official unemployment rate grew dramatically from 18 per cent in 1995 to 31 per cent in 2002 (Bhorat and Oosthuysen, 2006). It declined slightly to 25.5 per cent in 2007, but has more or less stuck at around 27 per cent (Hausmann, 2008; Treasury, 2008; Bimbassis, 2012). Moreover, these figures are based on a narrow definition of unemployment which excludes those members of the population not actively seeking employment, referred to as 'discouraged workers'. The parts of the economy that have grown the most,

Table 3.2 'All right for some': total working population aged 16 and above by income group and race by percentage 2008

	Total workforce %	Up to R50,000 %	R50,000– 100,000 %	R100,000– 300,000 %	R300,000– 500,000 %	R500,000– 750,000 %	Above R750,000 %
Black	75.3	83	65.9	47.1	29.9	20.3	16.3
Coloured	8.8	8.3	14.3	9	5.6	3	2.1
Indian/Asian	2.8	2.2	4	5.4	5.1	8.4	4.3
White	13	6.5	15.7	38.5	59.5	68.4	77.4
Total workforce	**100%**	**75.5**	**10.1**	**10.7**	**2.3**	**0.8**	**0.6**

Source: SAIRR, 2008 (quoted in *The Economist* 2010: 1).

such as finance and business services, demand a high level of skills, while there has been a relative decline in the agriculture, mining and manufacturing sectors which require larger numbers of low-skilled workers (Hausmann, 2008). Thus a serious shortage of highly skilled labour, together with a large excess supply of unskilled labour has emerged. Moreover, there is still a very high level of youth unemployment and unemployment in rural areas where only 29 per cent of adults are in work (Bimbassis, 2012).

To exacerbate an already bad economic situation, South Africa's incidence of crime is one of the highest in the world, and has a severely negative impact on the well-being of people in poor communities. Bhorat and Kanbur (2006) refer to a vicious triangle where poverty and income inequality have led to a high incidence of crime, which constitutes a barrier to economic growth, which in turn is needed to reduce levels of poverty and inequality. There is also, on the government's own admission, a severely high level of gender violence in the home and elsewhere, including rape, child abuse and abuse in schools (Gabara, 2012). Xenophobic violence in poor, black communities directed at immigrants from other parts of Africa has further exacerbated day-to-day livelihoods and security (*Mail and Guardian*, 2008, May 23–9). In addition to violent crime, there is increasing corruption in both the private and the public sectors, the impact of which is carried disproportionately by the poor in the shape of inadequate or non-existent service delivery and ineffective municipal services (Van Vuuren, 2006). As Saba and Van der Merwe report (2013), South Africa has a service-delivery protest every two days and people are angry and disillusioned.

The majority of Africans still suffer, Hall (2012b) suggests, in four of the quality of life domains: income and material deprivation, employment deprivation, education deprivation, and living environment deprivation. To add to this, South Africa has a high level of HIV infection, putting further pressure on public services, individuals and households. Hoogeveen and Özler (2006) argue that even were the government to achieve its projected growth rates, it should not be assumed that substantial reductions in poverty would follow. They argue that growth alone – without explicit poverty reduction strategies – is insufficient to address the problems of poverty and inequality in South Africa. The problem for the crucial sector of education in reducing poverty is its poor quality despite the government spending around 6 per cent of gross domestic product (GDP). By the government's own admission, they will be unlikely to meet their own goal by 2014 of ensuring quality, with the Basic Education Director-General admitting in parliament that '[i]n terms of access to meaningful education with quality outcomes, SA has done poorly' (Gernetzky, 2012: 3). Some 80 per cent of schools are regarded as dysfunctional (Seale, 2012: 1), with serious knock-on effects not only for entry to and success in higher education, but also for the likelihood of finding a job. In South Africa the correlation between more education and having employment is rising, for example, a graduate is five times more likely to find a job than someone without a degree (Keeton, 2012; Cloete, 2013). But those without education and without jobs face a vicious self-perpetuating cycle of poverty and social exclusion. Without formal education there are increasingly fewer chances of a decent job. Yet, as Sen (1999) has pointed out, a good education can make a dramatic difference to human abilities and achievements; it can transform individual lives and contribute crucially to social change.

Still, there are some hopeful indicators. The Constitution approved in 1997 enshrines the ideals of improving the quality of life of all citizens and establishing a society based on democratic values, social justice and fundamental human rights (Magasela, 2006). While there have been significant gains in 'first-generation' human rights – political and civil rights – there has not been equivalent realization of access to 'second-generation' socio-economic rights as outlined above (Robins 2006). Nonetheless, there have been important shifts in the redistribution of resources to address severe backlogs in social spending. There has been an increase in social service expenditure after 1994, with more resources being channelled to health, housing and social security, especially social grants which are now paid to around 16 million people (Keeton, 2012). Furthermore, there has been an increase in access of poor, black households to water, sanitation and electricity (Bhorat and Kanbur, 2006; Hoogeveen and Özler, 2006). These policies of redistributive social transfers and affirmative action to promote black economic empowerment (BEE)[3] have resulted in significant racial inclusion, even though the structure of overall inequality has persisted, including within-group income differentiation adding to persistent between-group inequalities.

Equality challenges for higher education: triple agendas

Turning now to higher education, in a society like South Africa undergoing rapid political, social and economic change, there is an urgent need for transformation of the higher education system, as an important aspect of social life. Higher education (in South Africa this means universities at the current time of writing) can be a powerful engine for transformation 'particularly suited to powering wider social change' (Jonathan, 2001: 37), albeit not without the contradictions confronting higher education everywhere as we discussed in Chapter 1. A central feature of South Africa's economic policy since 1994 has been the recognition that in order to achieve a high rate of economic growth, it is essential to develop the capacity to participate and compete in the global knowledge economy. Thus, one of the major roles that the higher education system has been required to play has been to develop highly skilled graduates in scientific, technological and business fields (Council on Higher Education [CHE], 2004).

However, higher education in South Africa can as easily reproduce privilege, albeit a privilege more evenly distributed than in apartheid days, and somewhat less racially aligned. As Jonathan (2001) explains, higher education is both a social good which delivers benefits for society and a private good which bestows economic, social and civic benefits on individuals. She comments:

> What is it about [higher education] which keeps alive our optimism in its socially transformative power and provides the preconditions for any socially transformative project, yet which also pulls in the opposite

direction – towards an ethos of individual competition and the reproduction of a hierarchy of social advantage?

(Jonathan, 2001: 48)

Thus, in South Africa some are concerned that while higher education has been shifting in the direction of greater responsiveness to societal needs, the shift has been defined narrowly in terms of the market (Singh, 2001). While Jonathan (2001) observes that the rightward shift in the global higher education climate reflects an individualistic/economistic vision of the public good described in Chapter 2, Singh (2001: 9) argued over a decade ago that transformation in South Africa 'in fidelity to its claimed radical roots must incorporate goals and purposes which are linked, even if indirectly, to an emancipatory and broad-based social and political agenda'. However, more recently Singh (2011) has argued that social justice has multiple interpretations and can be appropriated as a neo-liberal strategy for competitive knowledge economies. She argues that social justice is becoming increasingly 'elastic' and 'stretched' (ibid.: 482) depending on what policy goals are conceptualized and prioritized according to dominant political agendas, currently driven by human capital and economic growth (and see Walker, 2012).

The complexities are further complicated by the history of the higher educa-tion system under apartheid. It was differentiated along the lines of race and language, and designed to reproduce the social relations of white power and privilege and black subordination. There was an inequitable distribution of access and opportunity for students and staff along lines of race, gender, class and geography. Universities therefore comprise what are labelled historically white and advantaged and historically black and disadvantaged universities, based on a legacy of apartheid segregation from the 1950s. These descriptors signal not only racial designation of staff and students, but also broadly, social-class origins and institutional ethos, level of resourcing for the institution, and research capac-ity and outputs. They are not obviously descriptive of quality in teaching and learning though one might assume that large numbers of under-prepared black students, emerging from poor schooling provision, might strain quality.

Historically white or advantaged universities can be divided again into those in which the medium of communication and instruction was/is English and those which are/were Afrikaans. However, the division on language lines, while significant, is less important than the political divide signalled by language between those universities that supported the National Party Government and its apartheid university policies, and those that did not (Bunting, 2006a). The six white Afrikaans medium universities saw their support of the apartheid government as being essential to their survival as institutions (ibid.), training staff for the civil service and the professions. Knowledge, argues Bunting (ibid.), was regarded instrumentally in terms of its social, economic or political purposes, exacerbated by an academic boycott which cut universities off – especially the humanities and social sciences – from an international academic community until 1994. The intellectual agenda of Afrikaans universities, Bunting (ibid.) argues, were mostly determined by the perception that they had a duty to preserve the apartheid status quo, undertaking work with a local and national focus often for government, government agencies and the armed forces.

The four historically white English-speaking universities in South Africa took an anti-government stance to a greater or lesser degree, accelerating during the turbulent 1980s. As universities, they saw the need to maintain a critical distance from government and to locate themselves as part of an international academic community, albeit constrained by the impact of the academic boycott (Bunting, 2006a). Bunting (ibid.) suggests that they approached the post-1994 period with confidence, having seen their anti-apartheid stance vindicated. However, Mamdani (1998) has argued that historically these universities were never major agents for radical social and political change in South Africa; rather they were islands of white social privilege closely linked to capitalism and big business interests.

The eight historically black or disadvantaged universities comprised a group of African universities and the black medical school in Durban attached to the then white University of Natal, a university for Indians and one for coloureds, either in rural or peri-urban ('bush') locations. All these universities were established to operationalize apartheid policy in higher education and the distorted notion of equality of opportunity within a racial or ethnic group. They were intended to train students for roles in the apartheid state and schools (Bunting, 2006a). Their histories have been diverse, although all broadly became sites of struggle against apartheid in the 1970s and 1980s.

Overall, while some institutions were critical of the apartheid government, arguably all of them, as part of the system, were implicated in perpetuating the apartheid system of privilege and disadvantage, opportunities and barriers (Badat, 2004; Council on Higher Education, 2004). Nonetheless some universities more than others challenged apartheid laws to build and anticipate a different future.

The three universities selected for this project: one each from the group of white, English-speaking, white Afrikaans-speaking and black universities, therefore bring diverse histories. A brief overview of each of the selected universities is provided in Chapter 4.

Equity and development challenges

To this history must be added the higher education challenges that persist. In 2000 there were continuing discrepancies in the participation rates of students from different population groups: 58 per cent of university students were African, 5 per cent coloured, 7 per cent Indian and 30 per cent white (Soudien Report, 2008: 147). The average participation rate was 17 per cent (Bunting, 2006b: 106) and by 2009 had declined to 15.9 per cent (Council on Higher Education, 2009). Transformation of universities, even in numbers terms, looked remote.

Since 1994 all policy documents and proposals have also struggled with a fourfold problematic: how to reconcile equity, efficiency, democratic participation and development (Cloete, 2011). The transformation project in South Africa has been premised on the goals of economic development on the one hand, and social equity and redress on the other (Jonathan, 2001: 37). Badat (2001) points to the tension between these goals, and emphasizes that they need to be pursued simultaneously – which is difficult because it is a tension exacerbated by the historical context of inequalities, uneven development and the challenge of economic growth. Thus, South African higher-education policy formulation in the mid-90s was framed by the relationship and tensions between the objectives of equity, reconstruction and development and participation in the global economy, and above all, by the trade-offs of equity and development (Badat, 2001).

Within this frame Badat (2004) identifies three periods of policy activity in higher education. The first period was from *1990 to 1994* in anticipation of the change of government. During this period the predominant concerns were with formulation of principles, values, visions and goals for higher education policy in a process of, as yet, symbolic policy formation. The second period was from *1995 to 1998*. The new ANC-dominated government set up processes to construct an overall policy framework for higher education transformation, culminating in the White Paper on Higher Education (DOE, 1997) and the Higher Education Act of 1997. The White Paper mapped out a broad transformation agenda underpinned by core principles of equity (of access and the distribution of success along lines of race, gender, class and geography), and redress of past inequalities. It declared that higher education was to be transformed to meet the challenges of a new non-racial, non-sexist and democratic society committed to equity, justice and a better life for all. Equity of access was to be complemented by a concern for equity of outcomes:

> [An] enabling environment must be created throughout the system to uproot deep-seated racist and sexist ideologies and practices that inflame relationships, inflict emotional scars and create barriers to successful participation in learning and campus life. Only a multi-faceted approach can provide a sound foundation of knowledge, concepts, academic, social and personal skills, and create the culture of respect, support and challenge on which self-confidence, real learning and enquiry can thrive.
>
> (DOE 1997 quoted in Badat, 2008a: 12)

The White Paper (DOE, 1997) located the purposes of higher education in South Africa within the frame of contributions to multidimensional transformation: social, economic and educational. Higher education was seen as an important vehicle for achieving equity in the redistribution of opportunity and achievement among South African citizens. It needed to equip people to contribute to the social, economic, cultural and intellectual life of the society. Higher education was to provide access to learning and the fulfilment of human potential through lifelong learning, as well as laying the foundations of a critical civil society with a culture of debate, tolerance and critical engagement. It was also expected to address the human resource needs of a developing society, providing the labour market with the high-level skills needed for participation in the global economy. As an education transformation project, higher education would produce, disseminate and evaluate knowledge, and foster academic scholarship and intellectual inquiry through research, learning and teaching. Higher education would address pressing local, regional and national needs and challenges of the broader African context.

The third period of policy making, which began in 1999, was characterized by the attempt on the part of the education ministry to assert stronger state-steering of the process of higher education transformation. The National Plan for Higher Education released in 2001 reaffirmed the key policy goals of the White Paper of 1997 (and the Act of 1997). It established targets for the size and shape of the higher education system. These included: a medium-term increase in the participation rate from 15 to 20 per cent; graduation rate benchmarks to ensure access and success; shifting the ratio of enrolments in disciplinary fields, with the effect of lessening enrolments in the humanities and increasing enrolments in business and science, engineering and technology; and achieving student and staff equity targets (Council on Higher Education, 2004). However, higher education after 1997, in addition to meeting equity goals, was expected to be more responsive to social needs and the demands of a high skills technologically oriented economy in global times (Cloete, 2006b). There was also a rapid proliferation of the power and influence of the market on the sector (Kraak, 2001; Council on Higher Education, 2004). Universities now needed to seek new sources of income because of the unwillingness of the state to increase their subsidy allocation in the face of competing health, welfare and compulsory schooling demands. Some universities were quick to take up the call for responsiveness to economic needs, forming interpretations of what skills were needed by the market, and taking up a range of entrepreneurial strategies. Yet shifts made by institutions were 'not necessarily responses to national socio-economic priorities, [but were often] merely forms of opportunistic competition between institutions trying to capture key market niche areas' (Kraak, 2001: 108).

Although tabled after the end of the research project, the *National Development Plan: Vision for 2030* released in 2011 shapes the environment in which professionals will be trained and in which they will work. It is therefore relevant to our account here. The Plan proposes to address the key problems of inequality and poverty through a mutually reinforcing cycle of growth and development. According to Cloete (2011), the education section for the first time acknowledges higher education explicitly as a major development driver in the information-knowledge system. The Plan states:

> Higher education is the major driver of the information-knowledge system, linking it with economic development [. . .] Universities are key to developing a nation. They play three main functions in society. Firstly, they educate and train people with high-level skills for the employment needs of the public and private sectors. Secondly, universities are the dominant producers of new knowledge, and they critique information and find new local and global

applications for existing knowledge. Universities also set norms and standards, determine the curriculum, languages and knowledge, ethics and philosophy underpinning a nation's knowledge-capital. South Africa needs knowledge that equips people for a society in constant social change. Thirdly, given the country's apartheid history, higher education provides opportunities for social mobility and simultaneously strengthens equity, social justice and democracy. In today's knowledge society, higher education underpinned by a strong science and technology innovation system is increasingly important in opening up people's opportunities.

(National Planning Commission, 2011: 262)

Cloete suggests that this direction of policy travel encapsulates trade-offs between knowledge production, skills training, efficiency and equity. While equity remains a key goal, it has dropped to third place, with the first being higher education as the driver of the information-knowledge system, and the second as the producer of knowledge for a society in constant change. On the other hand, notwithstanding this recent policy shift – the impact of which we do not yet know – there is evidence of equity achievements.

Equity achievements in universities

Significant for the development of professional education is the expansion of the undergraduate population and its changing demographics, so that more diverse students now enter higher education and professional studies. While change in the higher education sector has been uneven and African staff and student numbers remain low, there have nonetheless been achievements in the transformation process since 1994. By 2011 there were 899,120 students at the 23 universities in South Africa, up from 495,356 in 1994 (DHET, 2012: 37). In 2008, 38,820 students graduated in science, engineering and technology; 33,788 in business or management; 35,532 in education; and 34,517 in 'other humanities' (ibid.: 38). Thus, in 2008, South Africa graduated a total of 133,171 students, from whom the pool of professionals could be drawn (ibid.).

There have been positive developments towards attaining the goal of equity in some areas, with significant shifts in the racial profile of student enrolments in many institutions. During apartheid, as mentioned earlier, there were skewed and inequitable participation rates in higher education according to race and gender (Cooper and Subotzky, 2001). In 1994, 55 per cent of students at public universities were black (African, coloured and Indian), 43 per cent of these were African and 55 per cent were male. By 2010, 80 per cent were black, 67 per cent African and 43 per cent male (DHET, 2012: 37, see Table 3.3).

Nonetheless, as the Green Paper notes, while the proportion of Africans has increased substantially, the level is still dramatically smaller than the proportion of Africans in the overall population. Thus South Africa's participation rate (enrolment as a percentage of 20–24-year-olds in the overall population), estimated in 2005 as 16 per cent overall, is uneven, with whites accounting for

Table 3.3 Headcount enrolment and growth by race 2000–2010, with three years highlighted

	2000	*2008 (Research project is mid-way)*	*2010*	*Average annual increase (%)*
African	317,998	515,058	595,963	6.5
Coloured	30,106	51,647	58,219	6.8
Indian	39,558	52,401	54,537	3.3
White	163,004	178,140	178,346	0.9

Source: DHET (2012: 38)

60 per cent participation rate, and Africans and coloureds 12 percent. A report by Badsha and Cloete (2011) for the National Planning Commission shows the participation rate increasing to 13 per cent African students, with white participation rates dropping to 56 per cent in 2008. The change in enrolments of black students has been notable, in particular of African students, previously the most marginalized: in 2010 the percentage of enrolment of African students was 67 per cent and black students overall 80 per cent (DHET, 2012). While 57 per cent of undergraduates are female, there have continued to be inequalities in the distribution of female students across academic programmes, with most in humanities and teacher education, but fewer in science, engineering and technology and in business and management (ibid.). This has some implication for professional education in that some professions are more likely to attract male students (engineering in our study) and some professions to be female-dominated (social work in our study).

When assessing achievement of equity goals, there needs to be consideration not only of equity of access, but also to equity of opportunity to succeed and of outcomes (Badat, 2008a). Recently, there has been serious concern about the unsatisfactory throughput and graduation rates of students in higher education institutions (Scott *et al.*, 2007). Given the historical problems with inequalities of school education which are still impacting on the quality of education at a higher level, higher education institutions need to provide supportive contexts and academic development and foundation programmes to provide equity of opportunity to succeed. The recent Green Paper (DHET, 2012: 40) emphasizes that '[w]hatever else they do, all universities in South Africa must offer a high quality undergraduate education. This should be the first step in overcoming historical injustices inherited from apartheid'. This has particular relevance for Chapter 7 in which we consider the educational arrangement in our case study professional departments and universities.

Transformation difficulties

Overall student numbers show significant progress towards transforming universities in relation to student equity and redress. However, South Africa's overall gross participation rate based on a percentage of the 20–24 age group enrolled in some form of higher education is low, as noted earlier, only 16 per cent in 2005 (Scott and Yeld, 2008). The overall graduation rate stands at only 15 per cent (Letseka and Maile, 2008: 1). Thus, Cloete (2006b: 271) suggests that the 'equity improvements' (for the student population) are 'not unambiguous':

> The equity objective in the post-1994 period has not been fully met. Instead changes resulted in a more elite public higher education system: while the student population became dramatically blacker, this was against an overall decrease in participation rates. Effectively this meant that while the complexion of the elite had changed the gap between 'those with' and 'those without' higher education had not decreased.
>
> (Cloete, 2006b: 273)

More individuals are gaining access to higher education but, in the case of most universities, not enough has been achieved to redress the systemic imbalances between historically disadvantaged and historically advantaged institutions (Cloete, 2006b). Relative levels of resourcing were unchanged. Moreover, discourses of development have shifted as outlined above from the early emphasis on equity to 'effectiveness and efficiency challenges' articulated by the CHE (an independent statutory body that advises the Minister on higher education policy) in 2000, followed by the emphasis on 'human resource development' in the National Plan for Higher Education in 2001 issued by the Department of Education (Cloete, 2006b), and then the emphasis on knowledge production in the 2011 Plan (Cloete, 2011). This trend is accompanied by a requirement for greater accountability to the state as primary funder (Jansen *et al.*, 2007).

Some key commentators have therefore suggested that the transformation project in higher education has 'come to be widely seen as a disappointment' (Muller *et al.*, 2006: 289), with an 'apparent loss of virtuous course'. That there have been far-ranging changes is not in doubt, but there have also been 'disconcerting continuities', for example, in the continued domination of senior appointments by white men, in uneven research productivity, and in institutional cultures which still bear their historical traces (Jansen *et al.*, 2007). Muller (2006) and his fellow critics point to what is seen as the common cause, the shift to a growth-based macroeconomic policy, away from earlier more egalitarian redistributive measures in the immediate post-1994 years.

However, they suggest, economic policy alone cannot explain the faltering of the project of transforming higher education. The picture is more complex, they argue, with limits to the transformation project shaped by: the need for trade-offs in policy priorities; different types of institutions; and diverse governance regimes at universities. They point out that transformation of universities was never envisaged as radical, given the 'sophistication and fragile nature of higher education' according to Sibusiso Bengu, the first minister of education (quoted in Muller *et al.*, 2006: 293). Policy was envisaged more as a symbolic break with the past and the signalling of a new direction concerned initially with more equity and democracy in the sector (Muller *et al.*, 2006).

There have been trade-offs in keeping the higher education show on the road, as it were. A key trade-off has been that the sector continues to be stratified along lines of colour and social class, while various commentators argue that market-led values of efficiency and productivity have come to supersede participation, equity and justice and have 'pushed higher education into the market' (Muller *et al.*, 2006: 306). Shifting from the macro to the meso level of change, Higgins (2007), argues that a concern with 'whiteness', in this case at the University of Cape Town, underestimates social class as an element in the dilemmas and experiences described by students and pedagogical encounters which might be understood in Bourdieu's terms as struggles for distinction where the 'naturally distinguished [privileged] merely need to be what they are in order to be what they have to be' (Bourdieu 1990 cited in Higgins, 2007: 111). Higgins further notes the dangers of equity policies that may end up perpetuating and solidifying thinking in terms of race. Taking this into account and mapping it against the problematic of social class, Higgins proposes a more modest and more targeted micro-level focus on pedagogical culture and its transmission, and the uneven distribution of cultural capital among diverse students.

Alongside these shifts is the claim by Chetty and Webbstock (2008) that students are increasingly choosing study on the basis of what is going to bring the greatest financial rewards and status. They suggest that students (and staff) ought to be addressing challenges other than those of money and prestige:

> How can we create a more caring and compassionate society, one that is more responsive to the needs of the poor and less fortunate, one that is more efficient in the use of limited resources, one that is more respectful of our delicate environment, and one that is committed to leaving this world in a better state than we found it? How can we build an ethically and morally binding society? How can we use our skills in our niche area to achieve this?
> (Chetty and Webbstock, 2008: 2)

The implications for professional education

For our project the answer to these questions lies in grappling with the implications and challenges of university-based professional education in Chapter 7. Badat (2008b) has criticized the lack of 'visibility' of South African universities in relation to problems of economic and development challenges and contributions to social transformation. For example, writing of the University of Pretoria (an historically white and Afrikaans-speaking university), Jonathan Jansen, then dean of education, comments that in 2001 he found 'a lack of critical discourse [. . .] with respect to pressing social and human problems' (quoted in Bunting, 2006a: 40). For his part Badat (2008b: 2) argues for the importance of critical scholarship in investigating a range of crucial issues, including poverty, unemployment and other inequalities so that universities live up to 'the responsibility our

Constitution has given the country's universities'. He points out that the arrival of democracy is not in itself 'a sufficient condition for the erasure of the structural and institutional conditions, policies and practices that have for decades grounded and sustained inequalities in all domains of social life' (ibid.: 5). But, he writes, '[i]t is precisely this reality that gives salience to the idea of redress and makes it a fundamental and necessary dimension of higher education transformation and social transformation in general' (ibid.). We grapple with redress in our project not in relation to access to the professions (although this is hugely important, but beyond the scope of our project), rather we translate it into the formation of other-regarding obligations on the part of any university graduate (see Chapter 2).

Shifting to the micro level of concern for students, Badat (2008a) rehearses the importance of what it is that universities ought to do in their formation. Students ought to learn to: think effectively and critically; achieve depth in a field of knowledge; have a critical appreciation of the ways in which they gain knowledge and understanding of the universe, of society, and of themselves; have a broad knowledge of other cultures and other times and be able to make decisions based on reference to the wider world and to the historical forces that have shaped it; have some understanding and experience of thinking systematically about moral and ethical problems; and be able to communicate with precision, cogency and force. At stake, says Badat, is the importance of producing graduates who can contribute to the economic and social development of South Africa. He reminds us of the importance of inclusive institutional cultures and quality in teaching and learning environments, which are all vital if diverse students are to succeed and graduate with the relevant knowledge, competencies, skills and attributes that are required for any occupation and profession, to be lifelong learners and function as critical, culturally enriched and tolerant citizens. Moreover, rigorous scholarship is necessary to protect our freedoms and deepen democracy in South Africa (Badat 2008a). It is needed to 'investigate the theoretical foundations and the empirical analyses that define the country's direction' (ibid.). More specifically, universities could contribute to development and poverty alleviation through relevant research drawing on different disciplines within universities (see Hall, 2007).

This chapter has sketched the historical and macro social arrangements and context within which our participating universities are located. Clearly there have been huge political changes: the formal ending of the apartheid regime, the ushering in of parliamentary democracy, a robust Constitution and Bill of Rights, as well as redistributive measures in society, and genuine equity gains in higher education. Significant problems remain, as we acknowledge in this chapter, for the quality of life and well-being of South Africans: crime, poor public health, poor schooling, political corruption and growing inequalities, together with the persistence of patterns of race, class and gender carried over from the past. We are deeply worried by the recent World Bank Report which describes inequality in South Africa as 'corrosive' and the country as 'a complete global outlier in terms of inequality' (quoted in Isa, 2012: 1). Returning also to Sen's instrumental freedoms – political, economic, social, transparency guarantees and protective security – and the part they play in creating and sustaining capabilities, a 'scorecard' for South Africa would be extremely mixed along all his dimensions. This is seriously compounded by the continuing poor quality of schooling. South African primary schools were placed 132nd out of 144 countries with regard to quality teaching, in the recent World Economic Forum (WEF, 2012) Global Competiveness Report 2012/2013. With regards to the quality of mathematics and science education South Africa was placed second last.

More positively, South Africa's Higher Education and Training sector as a whole was placed at 84th position. At issue is that universities both form and are formed by social relations, as we explained in Chapter 1. Certainly, our research project assumed that South African universities could contribute through quality teaching and learning by developing the capabilities of students to contribute to transforming society. They are instrumental in improving the quality and skills level within public services, such as schooling, health care and welfare at national, provincial and local levels, including the ability to critique, monitor and evaluate implementation of policy. Similarly, Jonathan (2001: 22) argues that because each of us must make continuing choices between personal advancement and social benefit, 'one among several of the influences on such choices is the impact on students of their academic experience'. Universities are 'social institutions properly governed by conceptions of service: to disciplinary areas, current students, and the wider society' (Jonathan, 2006: 47). Jonathan (2001) points out that although removing inequities from the higher education system would not in itself deliver social equity, it would enhance the life chances of large numbers of previously disadvantaged individuals. In this way, higher education could improve the life chances of people who are not able to participate in higher education but who are in need of high-quality professional services to make their lives go better.

Recent comments by Trevor Manuel, at the time Minister in the Presidency, call for young people to develop a service ethic. In his speech he pointed out South Africa has large numbers of young people (and for our purposes some of them will be studying professional education):

> I am also asking you to work hard at what you do, not only in your immediate occupation but in the service of others. Service is not about income; it is about placing your skills, knowledge, time and other attributes at the disposal of others and in their interest [. . .] Societies develop and sustain momentum because of service [. . .] Do something that will make a difference.
>
> (Manuel, 2012: 31)

The question which follows and one that informs our study is: What obligations are then owed by young professionals and what contributions through professional education should universities be making to improve the lives of the majority of South Africans? We think the lives of the majority of South Africans are exemplified in the account of Unabantu Mali in Chapter 1 and in the stories here, taken from *The Economist* of Tebogo and Lindiwe.

Tebogo, aged 25, is a security guard in Johannesburg, earning just R11.38 an hour. Improperly classified as 'self-employed', he gets no paid holiday, sick leave or other benefits. By dint of working a 12-hour day, 25 days a month, he manages to earn R3,400 a month. Out of this he has to pay R250 rent to a friend who allows him to live in a one-room shack in his yard, next to seven others. Their 15 occupants share a single pit-latrine and outside water tap. Tebogo pays his employer R390 a month for transport and R98 for the uniform he is obliged to wear. Another R350 a month goes on maintenance for his six-year-old daughter. He also gives about R800 a month to his parents, who have no other source of income. In a good month that leaves Tebogo with about R1,500 for himself and his studies. He would like to become a radio journalist one day.

Lindiwe is a 58-year-old cleaner for a block of offices. For an eight-hour day, five days a week, she earns a basic R1,500 a month, which with tips bring it up to R2,100. That has to keep her, her unemployed husband and two grandchildren whom she looks after. Having inherited her parents' home, she pays no rent, but spends around R55 a month on electricity, R30 on water and R300 a month on her one-hour bus journey to work. During apartheid, she used to work as a domestic servant for a white family, living in a one-room shack at the bottom of the garden and working 13 hours a day, seven days a week. On her one weekend off a month she would try to visit her two children who were being brought up by her mother in Soweto, a sprawling African township south of Johannesburg.

(*The Economist*, 3 June 2010: 1)

Sen (2009) is always concerned with justice in these actual lives. What kind of professional education is then needed so that graduates are more likely to turn to public service for Unabantu's family and for Tebogo and Lindiwe and thousands like them, working to expand their capabilities?

In the chapters which follow we build on our account of higher education in the world and in the particular case of South Africa, to consider the specificity of professional education as a potential contribution to social transformation in conditions of poverty and inequality. We show how we operationalize our theoretical framework from human development, capabilities and public-good professionalism to take up the challenges outlined in this chapter and the kind of professionals South Africa needs universities to educate.

4 Professional capabilities, educational arrangements and social conditions

A new research design

> Practical wisdom is of the ultimate and the particular [. . .] the sort of perception by which we grasp that a certain figure is composed in a certain way out of triangles.
>
> (Aristotle, quoted in Nussbaum, 1990: 74)

The next two chapters of Part 2 explore in detail the ways in which we developed and operationalized the concept of a capabilities-based, public-good professionalism described in Chapter 2 within the context of South Africa detailed in the previous chapter. The Public-Good Professional Capabilities Index that we finally produced was intended as a 'prospective analysis' (Alkire, 2008: 32) of professional education in the sense that the final interest of the project was to develop a tool for future use in professional education and training.

It is important to note that, in Nussbaum's (1990: 72) terms, the Index that has been produced is not 'the precise final word', rather, it is a general outline offered as a 'way of rendering the concrete, putting all the variety, messiness, and indefiniteness of the matter of the practical into words that will not debase its value or simplify its mystery' (ibid.: 104). There might be elements in the South African case which, in a different context, do not occur, and nothing is fixed. Developing policies, curricula, pedagogy or reshaping institutional cultures take place in particular contexts influenced by professional fields, existing departmental/ department/university cultures, and broader societal change processes, which are themselves contested and in flux in South Africa and elsewhere. Nevertheless, while we attended carefully to the particular and the concrete, the theoretical underpinnings in human development, capabilities and theories of professionalism yielded the principles according to which successive versions of our Index were designed and implemented.

We focused on change and transformation in South Africa as a form of 'social science that matters' (Flyvbjerg, 2001: 166). In this chapter we make explicit the research design and process for choosing particular professional capabilities dimensions in order to enable open discussion and critical scrutiny. We outline the broadly critical, reflexive and dialogical research approach; clarify why and how research sites were selected; and explain the combined processes of consultation, data collection and analysis which helped us develop what we call a Public-Good Professional Capabilities Index. In this chapter we present an overview of the selected universities and professions, together with the first phase of generating the Index based on capabilities theorizing. In Chapter 5 we show step by step how the Index was constructed deliberatively from our data and in dialogue with colleagues at the participating universities. We aimed both for a product (the Index) which would be practically meaningful and oriented towards the public good, and explore example of professional education which could encompass – across professional fields – orientation towards the well-being of others.

South Africa's goal of social transformation relies on poverty reduction, described in Chapter 3, and poverty reduction is conceptualized as capability-expansion in our study. Theories of professionalism were combined with the capabilities approach to theorize questions of social justice in relation to professional education in universities. In Chapter 2, we described how capabilities places centre stage an evaluation of each person's achievements and freedoms to do or be what each person has reason to value being and doing. We proposed that professional work can link personal satisfactions with making contributions to the public good because the intrinsic value of the work, to which professionals are often attached, is the improvements of the lives of others. Doing professional work well and ethically, therefore, contributes to the well-being of professionals themselves, beyond the remuneration and prestige they might enjoy. By making elements of public-good professionalism explicit we shall show how a capability framework both strengthens the well-being of the individual professional and professional collectives and increases the opportunities for well-being and agency of the individuals and communities with which professionals work. From this perspective, the responsibility of university-based professional education in South Africa could usefully be reconceptualized as imparting the knowledge, ethics, skills and competences which constitute the functionings of professionals working for social transformation.

So the broad focus of our research project is the transformation of higher education in South Africa to meet the challenges of professional contributions both to alleviating poverty and enhancing human talent and well-being. We wanted to develop a capabilities set which would align professional practitioners with social justice and which could be applied to educational policy and practices. The research questions we formulated were:

1   How can a human development and capabilities conceptualization of professionalism and its practical realization in professional education in universities contribute to poverty reduction?

2   How might professional education foster the values and expand the capabilities and functionings of students to make contributions to human development by practising professionals?

3   How can a professional capabilities yardstick contribute to policy and practice in relation to teaching and learning in university-based professional education?; and

4   How can capabilities theorizing be operationalized as a method for higher education research?

To address these questions we investigated professional education in five professional fields (engineering, law, theology, social work and public health) working with departments in three different types of South African universities.

It is worth noting how our particular study might have general applications across professional groups and countries. We make three specific claims: the first is that professionalism for the public-good is of perennial interest (the long-standing and wide literature about professions and their role in society suggests that this is so); the second is that capability lists have a potential to be taken up for systematic analysis, evaluation and adjustment in a range of contexts (Robeyns, 2005); and the third is that the participatory and iterative research process whereby groups interested in professional education can come to agreements can be replicated.

As noted in Chapter 2, we planned to select valuable professional capabilities to give substance to our concept of the public good. The method of selection for what is included on a [professional] capabilities list requires transparency and justification. Any list should further be open to public scrutiny and revision where justified through public reasoning (Sen, 2009). Robeyns (2003: 70–1) suggests the following five criteria as a method for the selection of capabilities; we used this as a process guide, not necessarily working in this sequence:

1   *Explicit formulation* – a list should be 'explicit, discussed and defended'.
2   *Methodological justification* – clarifying and scrutinizing the method that has generated the list and justifying its appropriateness.
3   *Sensitivity to context* – taking into account audience and situation so that, in some contexts, the list might be more abstract or theory-laden than in others.
4   *Different levels of generality* – involves drawing up a list in two stages, where the first stage involves an 'ideal' list and the second a more 'pragmatic', second-best list, taking actual constraints into account.
5   *Exhaustion and non-reduction* – the listed capabilities should include all important elements and the elements should not be reducible to each other, although there may be some overlap.

Our research practice was to move iteratively and dialectically between capabilities, Robeyns' guidelines, and empirical data. We asked ourselves if our capabilities were non-commensurable. Had we attended to context and were we explicit? Could we justify our method, and so on? The list we developed was a combination of ideal theorizing (what a public-good professional ought to do and be in conditions of inequality) and pragmatic grounding in people's reality in their everyday lives (what could a public-good professional actually do to reduce poverty). The idea was both to embody ideals and to produce a workable tool for those teaching, working and studying in the professional fields.

Furthermore, attention to context requires that professional capabilities are embedded in educational and social arrangements to capture Sen's (1999: 31) concern that 'there is a two-way relation between (1) social arrangements to expand individual freedoms and (2) the use of individual freedoms not only to improve the respective lives but also to make social arrangements more appropriate and effective'. Further, as Sen explains, while the exercise of freedom is mediated by values (public-good values in our case), these values are influenced by public discussions (in professional associations, professionals working alongside civil society, and so forth), which are influenced by participatory freedoms. The Index we have produced and the processes by which it was produced is intended to capture the connections between values, discussion and freedom.

A dialogical methodological approach

Here we outline the methodology, the selection of university and professional sites, and describe the first phase, which involved us identifying a specific list of professional-good capabilities. While in Chapter 2 we offered a rationale for selecting capabilities, we now show the dialogical processes by which we worked towards our actual list.

Our concern with research that informs justice-enhancing actions led us to describe the process as 'phronetic' from the Greek phronesis, meaning practical wisdom:

> [phronetic social science] explores historic circumstances and current practices to find avenues to praxis. The task [. . .] is to clarify and deliberate about the problems and risks we face and to outline how things may be done differently, in full knowledge that we cannot find ultimate answers to these questions or even a single version of what the questions are.
>
> (Flyvbjerg, 2001: 140)

This cast of social science research further focuses on variation, the specific, and the non-universal (Flyvbjerg, 2001). Closely aligned with these intentions has been our aim to conduct research aimed at generating practical insights and judgements about professional education in particular circumstances. We thus do not seek a totalizing explanation about professional education and social transformation; rather we acknowledge that our answers are partial, historically situated and contextual. The empirical accounts which follow in Chapters 6, 7 and 8 add context, history and detail to more generalized interpretations of capabilities theorizing which, in turn, benefits from these concrete interrogations.

Dialogue in the research process was aligned with the capabilities approach, because social evaluation of the kind we attempted 'is not just a matter of separated and sequestered individual reasoning' (Sen, 2009: 18). Thus our broad approach was reflexive and participatory in that we examined the adequacy of our own ways of thinking in the light of participants' interpretations, and it was in the critical tradition which attempts connections between everyday lives and social structures that influence ideas and actions. Chapters 1 and 2 established a conceptualization of capabilities-based public-good professionalism as a basis to the research, the participatory approach guarded against allowing a theoretical approach to over-determine our analysis. Collaborative reflection in team discussions was central. The sometimes sceptical responses from participants in South Africa about capabilities as an approach engaged us in a constant process of argument and clarification about the potential of the capabilities approach to do analytic and knowledge-producing work and led us to explore the potential of other theories.

The study took the form of an inquiry into 'the particularity and complexity of a single case coming to understand its activity within certain circumstances' (Stake, 1995: xi). The single case was the domain of university professional education, and it comprised subsets of five professional fields across three different university locations. We aimed to collect multiple narrative-based perspectives in order to capture complexity across university sites and professional departments, the particularity of each professional field, and real lives. Furthermore, we wanted to collect vivid qualitative accounts of public-good capabilities in order to catch the attention of policy makers and practitioners.

We recognized that research practice is always subject to the effects of power, and following Burawoy (1998) we noted resistance or domination as we encountered them. For example, access is a common problem for researchers: in the study, the process of mobilizing contacts in South Africa to identify university sites and the subsequent email contact with possible sites extended over several months. In some cases the site was secured after the research had begun. Being funded in the UK, being led from there and being tightly accountable to the UK funder circumscribed the fully equal research relationships which we and our university participants would have preferred. However, the participants in all groups (with the exception of students) advanced clear and confident views and indeed were in control of the university and practice contexts. Moreover students, who by virtue of their position are less powerful than their teachers and those already working in the field, are often not consulted in higher education research. Here they were given an opportunity to express their views about what it meant to them to be a professional in their chosen field. We did not speak directly to people living in poverty; but we did use the perspectives of professionals working with people living in conditions of poverty as an imperfect proxy. The respectful and convincing accounts of these professionals about their clients gave us access to the stories of individuals and communities living in poverty.

Selecting university sites

We now outline the basis for the selection of universities and professional fields. The selection of universities and case study professional education departments was purposive rather than random, drawing on personal contacts and suggestions, while adhering to the principle of diverse professions. We choose three universities because each has a different historical genesis and trajectory in relation to educational and social transformation (also see Chapter 3). Each was given a pseudonym. Silvertree is historically white and English-speaking, Fynbos is historically black, and Acacia is historically white and Afrikaans-speaking. Given diverse histories we were interested in the policy environment the universities provide – the mission and the rhetorical approach to transformation.

Provided below is some detail on each university, and its student intake. To mitigate the chances of the universities being identified, we have resisted definitely identifying or naming each of the universities in their own public documents, even though the universities were known to each other and willing to be named. Nonetheless, given the small size of the university system in South Africa, these universities will be recognizable to those in the country, so we acknowledge the ethical compromise made, but think it is necessary for readers to make sense of the research processes. The identity of the universities will be less obvious to those reading outside South Africa.

Acacia University

One of South Africa's oldest universities, Acacia, is a comparatively advantaged university, historically white and Afrikaans-speaking. The campus is spread out, filled with historic and well-designed newer buildings, and set in a charming historical town. Its original resourcing by the state and the accumulation of further state and alumni resources over the years make it one of South Africa's richest universities. The University played a significant political and intellectual role in apartheid, educating the Afrikaner political elite and leading civil servants and providing philosophical underpinnings for segregation. Currently, it has a high reputation across many disciplinary fields, has a successful track record in attracting funds for research and is one of six productive research universities in the country, while its graduates generally have a high reputation among employers. Recent years have seen a significant, if still limited, shift towards a more racially diverse student and staff body. In 2007 the University enrolled 23,439 students (including 7,741 postgraduate students, who make up over 30 per cent of the student body). A total of 16,528 (70.5 per cent) of these students were white. In the same year, the University employed 2,319 permanent personnel, of which 786 were instructional/research staff. Of these, 85.1 per cent were white, 10.3 per cent were coloured, 1.8 per cent were Indian and 2.8 per cent were African (Acacia University, 2007). The University's Division of Institutional Research and Planning issues targets for enrolment and performance, with specifications by subject, as well as racial and gender equity goals. The University now has a black vice-chancellor and rector. While the proportion of African students grew after the transition to democracy, after almost 20 years after the advent of democracy, Acacia remains the institution with the smallest number of African student enrolments and staff appointments in the country.

Institutional reforms which have been explicitly concerned with social justice occurred at a later date at Acacia than at the other two case study universities. Nonetheless, they are occurring. An Institutional Forum was established in 1999 on policy matters affecting the University, and operates via three task groups: institutional planning, institutional culture, and equity and diversity. In 2000, the University published its *Strategic Framework* to guide future planning of initiatives and programmes. Many of the ideas relating to how the University sees its role in social justice are contained in this document, with the *Strategic Framework* outlining the University's mission, vision, commitment and values, subsequently clarified in its *Vision 2012* in 2003. The University 'acknowledges the need for development and service in communities and areas previously and currently disadvantaged in the provision of services and infrastructure' and 'commits itself to carry through appropriate redress and development actions on a continuous basis' (Acacia 2000). The concern with Acacia's previous contribution to social and economic inequalities under apartheid continues to be highlighted in management-level discourse, for example, being raised publicly in 2007 by the current vice-chancellor, 'as far as we as an institution are concerned: we know that we cannot apologize enough'. Thus, the *Strategic Framework* speaks of 'a responsibility to serve the well-being of the community' (2000). The *Strategic Framework* demonstrates, particularly through the sections outlining the University's vision, mission, and values, that social justice issues in wider society are to be considered alongside (and as part of) the University's research and teaching responsibilities.

Beyond the *Strategic Framework*, one of Acacia's main university-wide activities which engages with social justice issues is a service/community interaction programme established in 2006, which encourages departments to 'play a bigger role in addressing the development needs of the society' (Acacia, 2004). What cannot be ascertained from the outside is the level and nature of contestations around these policy changes. Not surprisingly, the public forum of the website presents a united front and support for these developments, which might or might not reflect reality.

Silvertree University

Silvertree is also an advantaged university. It has accumulated significant resources over many years, and like Acacia, it has the benefit of a stunning urban setting, with both historic and extremely attractive new buildings and extensive landscaped grounds. After 1957, apartheid legislation applied to universities meant it developed as historically white and English-speaking. It was, however, known for its opposition to apartheid, while sustaining its reputation as a leading national and international research institution. In 2006 there were 21,562 students (15,413 undergraduates and 6,149 graduates). At undergraduate level, 51 per cent of students were women and 49 per cent men. In 2005, there was 730 permanent or full-time academic staff. In terms of proportions of black students, the first small group of black students was admitted in the 1920s, but the number remained low until the 1980s and 1990s when the University committed itself to a deliberate and planned process of transformation. From the 1980s to the early 1990s, the number of black students admitted to the University rose by 35 per cent. It has undergone further changes in its student body and curriculum in recent years since South Africa's transition to democracy in the 1990s. The University now sets annual admissions targets to ensure a 'reasonable level of diversity'; in 2006 there was a 50:50 balance between black and white students (Silvertree, 2007). Not all of the black students are from poor backgrounds, indeed many now come from comparatively advantaged homes and from the better (formerly white) schools (PVC interview, August 2008).

The University's understanding of poverty and its role in poverty reduction can be seen through both institutional provisions and in texts which explain the University's activities and mission. In 2001 Silvertree issued a statement of values. This statement included the following values: integrity in both academic and other work, and in all personal and institutional relationships – compassion, generosity and concern for the needs and aspirations of others, and in particular for the challenges faced by the less privileged in our society; respect and tolerance; intellectual honesty, vigour in debate, openness to alternative ideas and respect for other views, beliefs and opinions; and commitment to the pursuit of excellence. An official Transformation Office was established in 2003 to support policy development, and to monitor and advise on transformation activities. Further, since 2004, the University has been reporting on activities which are socially responsive and the University senate directed that 'all academic staff are expected to exhibit some level of social responsiveness through teaching and learning, research or leadership' (Silvertree, 2007). Notions of social justice feature heavily in Silvertree's descriptions about its own aims, goals and role in South Africa's future.

'Transformation' is prominent within the University's self-narratives, chiefly used to describe how it should change and reorient itself in order to reflect and contribute to the wider changes in South Africa. Yet while the transformation agenda largely refers to strategies to be adopted within the University, there is also some sense that it should directly contribute externally to South Africa's development. One of the most notable features of the transformation agenda has been changing the composition of the student and staff bodies to better reflect the demographic proportions in South African society. Central in the mission statement is that Silvertree should 'strive to transcend the legacy of apartheid in South Africa and to overcome all forms of gender and other oppressive discrimination'; and likewise, 'promote equal opportunity and the full development of human potential'. The transformation website states, 'transformation at Silvertree must be about the teaching, learning and research environment and activities'. A social responsiveness community engagement programme for students has been established to foster conscious reflection and critical self-analysis. This, it is claimed in the University's own Social Responsiveness Report of 2008, often leads students to realize positively that community engagement contributes substantially to their own personal development.

Fynbos University

Fynbos is a comparatively disadvantaged university. Although now a very attractive campus, its early buildings are ordinary and unimaginative, at the time of its establishment the out-of-town setting was rather bleak, not well served by safe public transport, and obviously not resourced at the same level of the advantaged universities. It was established under apartheid laws as a college for black [coloured] students only, offering training for low- to middle-level positions in schools and the civil service. It began as a small institution, starting with 166 students and 17 teaching staff. In 1970 the institution gained university status, enabling it to award its own degrees and diplomas. For the first 15 years after its foundation, teaching staff were primarily white, with many lecturers coming from Afrikaans universities; the language of tuition was Afrikaans. However, the University had already become an integrated and multi-racial institution some time before the end of the apartheid regime in 1994. The first black rector was appointed in 1975, giving way to a more liberal atmosphere in the following years; it was in this decade that the University shifted its identity to an institution associating itself with the democratic struggle. In the 1980s it began to admit black African students in defiance of government policy, and in 1982 issued a mission statement in which it formally distanced itself from the apartheid regime and adopted a firm commitment to the development of disadvantaged communities in South Africa. In 1983 the University gained the same level of autonomy as white universities. After 1987, institutional shifts included reform of curricula and outreach projects, with the University striving to implement its mission of providing opportunities for lifelong learning since 1997 in particular. It has a long-standing record in this area: from early on it sought to accommodate adult learners through evening classes for teachers and other civil servants, and its part-time studies programme was established around 1970.

In 2006/2007, 14,823 students were enrolled, of which 2,724 (18.5 per cent) were postgraduates. In 2005, 50 per cent of the student body was coloured, 31 per cent African, 5 per cent white and 2 per cent Indian. Fynbos has a staff complement of approximately 1,900, of whom 1,185 are permanent staff, with 390 of these being permanent academic staff. In terms of home languages, 31 per cent of students spoke African languages, 18 per cent spoke Afrikaans, and 37 per cent spoke English (Fynbos, 2008).

On its website, Fynbos foregrounds its history in the struggle against oppression and discrimination under apartheid, and the role of academia in working against systems of disadvantage. It states that its concerns with access, equity and quality in higher education today have their roots in 'extensive practical engagement in helping the historically marginalized participate fully in the life of the nation'. It has been commended for its level of community engagement. The recent *Strategic Plan* identifies that the key words to describe the new strategic direction are inclusivity and opportunity; it requires that the University become more flexible and efficient in order to serve a wider range of clients; and it requires that the University ensures that it is providing precisely those opportunities that are most sought after by the students who, Fynbos claims, are being denied them elsewhere. This is to occur through establishing more links with employers, 'so that access into Fynbos becomes associated with increased access into work, thereby making the University a more attractive option' (Fynbos, 2000).

Selecting the professional fields

The five professional educational departments – Engineering, Law, Social Work, Theology and Public Health – are described fully in Chapter 6, together with a contextualization of each profession in South Africa. Here we note that selection was both theoretical and pragmatic. A priority was to investigate variation: so the professional fields to be scrutinized included some which might be considered lower-status professions working at the interface of poverty, and others with greater social prestige and financial rewards. We decided that the primary focus on professional capabilities was better served by examining a diversity of professions, even though we inevitably sacrificed some of the richness of an institutional or single profession account.

We also considered Bernstein's (2001) characterization of professionals as agents in fields of symbolic control. He suggests six categories of professional agents: regulators, repairers, reproducers, recontexualizers, shapers and executors. Our five professions included 'regulators' (law, with some crossover with 'executors' in so far as some law graduates will take up posts in the civil service and government); 'repairers' (social work, public health, theology, again with some crossover with 'executors' for social work and public health professionals employed in government departments), and, a 'shaper', engineering (Larson [2013] points out that engineering improves the lives of collectivities). Of course, the categories are not determining or tightly bounded. Nor do we think there is any necessary correlation between each category and its reproductive or transformative role; actual policies and practices are likely to encompass both and might inflect towards either or, indeed, both. In all, there were spaces for change and transformation which could be exploited if professionals and professional bodies choose to operate with them.

In addition to these considerations, our final selection was also determined by access – who would work with us. We had wanted to work with engineering, law and social work, but had not set out to include theology before we discovered the special emphasis on tackling the legacies of a divided church under apartheid and on poverty-reduction in the department, and agreed it would be a generative site. Public health was something of an 'outlier' in our set of sites because it is a graduate programme for people already working in the field, the reason it was included was that the South African university co-ordinator of the project was keen, and we agreed that public health is of special importance in the South African context. We obtained letters of support from a senior manager at each university prior to applying for funding, which gave official sanction for working in the university. Then access to each professional case department was separately negotiated with the relevant department.

Table 4.1 Summary of university faculties or departments and their student intake

University	Faculty	Student intake	Degree
Acacia Historically white, predominantly Afrikaans as language of instruction	Engineering	Mostly male, white, middle-class and Afrikaans-speaking, very few women	Undergraduate four-year Bachelor of Engineering
	Theology	Racially mixed, social-class origins mixed, balance of men and women	Undergraduate four-year Bachelor of Theology
Fynbos Historically black, predominantly English as language of instruction	Law	Predominantly black (coloured) students, bilingual in English and Afrikaans, diverse social class origins (many students are quite poor), balance of men and women	Undergraduate four-year Bachelor of Law
	Public Health Department	Black mature students, many from other parts of Africa, mixed social origins, predominantly women, English-speaking	Masters in Public Health, part-time distance degree with contact summer and winter schools
Silvertree Historically white, English as language of instruction	Social Work Department	Mostly white students but with some South African black students and black international students from elsewhere in Africa, mostly middle class, English-speaking	Three-year undergraduate degree plus fourth postgraduate honours year (from 2007 an integrated four-year degree)

The engineering and theology departments were located in Acacia, which attracted mainly middle-class Afrikaans-speaking students to engineering, but had a more varied intake to theology. The law and public health departments were at Fynbos which had mainly working-class students in law, although public health was more mixed, both groups were predominantly English-speaking or fully bilingual. The social work department was at Silvertree and had a more middle-class English-speaking intake than might be usually expected for social work. In other words, the type of the university intersected with the nature of the professional group to shape who comes into each professional department (see Table 4.1).

It is worth commenting here on how we dealt with the specificity of professions. As noted in Chapter 2, professions have histories of struggle for autonomy and prestige, some professional fields gain more power in relation to the state and to the public than others. It has not been possible to come to definitive conclusions about whether a powerful or less powerful profession is more or less likely to engage with poverty and disadvantaged people. We did not embark on drawing up detailed histories of particular professions pre- and post-apartheid in South Africa (but see Breier and Wildschut, 2006; Earle, 2007; Breier *et al.*, 2009; du Toit and Roodt, 2009). Nevertheless, we are cognizant of them and have contextualized our empirical accounts (in Chapters, 6, 7 and 8) in a reading of the professions' relationship to South Africa's transformation agenda and its responses to apartheid's legacy.

Our concern then has been both with specific occupational milieu and with the university conditions that may have shaped the departmental professional education. As we talked to our respondents about what kind of professionals they thought South Africa needed and about their experiences, we were interested in such questions as: What did it mean to be a social work or engineering professional in South Africa? How did the socio-economic–political–educational context shape possibilities, obstacles and expectations of appropriate service and behaviour both on the part of the profession and the professional school or department? How did a specific socio-political context get taken up in professional education in terms of what kind of social worker, engineer or lawyer was being educated, with what values, knowledge and practical skills? To what extent did the existing structure of occupational practice (for example, the domination of engineering by white men) determine whether poverty was addressed? And how, if at all, was a professional status quo challenged and reframed by the professional education department seeking to educate a new kind of engineer, lawyer, church minister, public health professional, and social worker, with different personal and social motivations?

First phase: designing a capabilities index relating to the public good

In designing our project, we wanted to tie the generalities of educational possibilities for influencing individual motivations, values and knowledge to the specificity of particular professional work. Lecturers, students, alumni, and practitioners in all fields were involved at each stage in negotiating what became the final Index. We identified a list of comprehensive capabilities theoretically, and then we took the list to the universities and the NGOs for discussion during interviews. The respondent groups were in broad agreement with the capabilities required for a fully human life, so the 'comprehensive' list did not change. We then posed the further question: which of these capabilities and functionings should inform what professionals ought to be and do to work for social transformation and hence which capabilities should be incorporated as broad goals in professional education and training? In the sections below we introduce first the comprehensive capabilities and then describe the processes of coming to agreement about the public-good professional capabilities which framed our research.

Comprehensive capabilities

In our perspective, universities can contribute to poverty reduction through expanding the capabilities and functionings of students in professional education so that they are able to expand the capabilities of disadvantaged individuals and communities. So as a foundation of such professional education we first needed agreement among our participants about the capabilities everyone needs for full human flourishing.

We had helpful resources. There is the extensive work by Narayan and Petesch (2000) which captures the voices and aspirations of some 60,000 people living in poverty across the world. What emerges is that the people interviewed value the plural dimensions of well-being, including the following: material assets; bodily health and integrity; social belonging; self-respect and dignity; peace, harmony, good relations in the family/community; personal physical security; security in old age; confidence in the future; psychological well-being; harmony (including a spiritual life and religious observance); information and education; and political representation. These dimensions aligned with the 10 universal human capabilities identified by Martha Nussbaum, as well as a further three human capabilities generated by the research on disadvantage by Wolff and De-Shalit (2007), which relate well to the specificity of the South African context. We list them below because they influenced our thinking about the purpose of public-good professional capabilities. They show, too, how capabilities offer guidance about what well-being and quality of life for all ought to comprise:

Martha Nussbaum's central human capabilities

1 *Life.* Being able to live to the end of a human life of normal length; not dying prematurely, or before one's life is so reduced as to be not worth living.
2 *Bodily health.* Being able to have good health, including reproductive health; to be adequately nourished; to have adequate shelter.
3 *Bodily integrity.* Being able to move freely from place to place; to be secure against violent assault, including sexual assault and domestic violence; having opportunities for sexual satisfaction and for choice in matters of reproduction.
4 *Senses, imagination and thought.* Being able to use the senses, to imagine, think and reason – and to do these things in a 'truly human' way, a way informed and cultivated by an adequate education, including, but by no means limited to, literacy and basic mathematical and scientific training. Being able to use imagination and thought in connection with experiencing and producing works and events of one's own choice, religious, literary, musical, and so forth. Being able to use one's mind in ways protected by guarantees of freedom of expression

with respect to both political and artistic speech, and freedom of religious exercise. Being able to have pleasurable experiences and to avoid non-beneficial pain.

5 *Emotions.* Being able to have attachments to things and people outside ourselves; to love those who love and care for us, to grieve at their absence; in general, to love, to grieve, to experience longing, gratitude, and justified anger. Not having one's emotional development blighted by fear and anxiety. (Supporting this capability means supporting forms of human association that can be shown to be crucial in their development.)

6 *Practical reason.* Being able to form a conception of the good and to engage in critical reflection about the planning of one's life. (This entails protection for the liberty of conscience and religious observance.)

7 *Affiliation.*

   (a) Being able to live with and toward others, to recognize and show concern for other human beings, to engage in various forms of social interaction; to be able to imagine the situation of another. (Protecting this capability means protecting institutions that constitute and nourish such forms of affiliation, and also protecting the freedom of assembly and political speech.)

   (b) Having the social bases of self-respect and non-humiliation; being able to be treated as a dignified being whose worth is equal to that of others. This entails provisions of non-discrimination on the basis of race, sex, sexual orientation, ethnicity, caste, religion, national origin.

8 *Other species.* Being able to live with concern for an in relation to animals, plants and the world of nature.

9 *Play.* Being able to laugh, to play, to enjoy recreational activities.

10 *Control over one's environment.*

   (a) Political. Being able to participate effectively in political choices that govern one's life; having the right of political participation, protections of free speech and association.

   (b) Material. Being able to hold property (both land and movable goods) not just formally but in terms of real opportunity; and having property rights on an equal basis with others; having the right to seek employment on an equal basis with others; having freedom from unwarranted search and seizure.

(Nussbaum, 2000: 78–80)

Jonathan Wolff and Avner De-Shalit's additional three human capabilities

1   *Doing good to others.* Being able to care for others as part of expressing your humanity. Being able to show gratitude.
2   *Living in a law-abiding fashion.* The possibility of being able to live within the law; not to be forced to break the law, cheat, or to deceive other people or institutions.
3   *Understanding the law.* Having a general comprehension of the law, its demands, and the opportunities it offers to individuals. Not standing perplexed before the legal system.

(Wolff and De-Shalit, 2007: 48)

These 13 items constitute all the capabilities each person would need for a fully human life and provide a blueprint for professionals thinking about what it might mean in their particular circumstances to expand their clients' capabilities.

Professional capabilities

Assuming an underpinning comprehensive list of human capabilities for the general population, we set out to develop a subset of distinctively professional capabilities so that capability expansion could be enabled through the availability of high-quality professional services to the public. We envisaged that professional capabilities would align and integrate an individual professional's well-being with commitment to the well-being of others. Without such a synthesis, we would not have the kind of professionals with the capacities and dispositions to bring about social change for justice in South Africa.

Under Nussbaum's (2000) description, capabilities should be 'thick', that is philosophically meaningful in relation to a life of full human dignity, and 'vague' (ibid.), that is, not over specified or derived too precisely from a particular metaphysical worldview (e.g. secular or religious). More practically, Alkire (2002: 183–84) proposes five methods for selecting professional capabilities which we used:

1   *Use existing data:* for example, we made use of secondary literatures on South African higher education, newspapers and webpages;
2   *Propose normative assumptions:* we theorized from human development and the capability approach from professionalism, and from key concepts such as 'transformation';
3   *Attend to public consensus:* we drew on Nussbaum (2000) and the research conducted by Wolff and De-Shalit (2007), and checked how the large-scale study by Narayan and Petesch (2000) produced dimensions aligned with Nussbaum;

4   *Use a deliberative process*: during the project we had discussions with universities and departments in interviews and in working groups; and
5   *Collect empirical evidence*: we collected interviews from diverse groups on their perspectives on professional values, professional education and professional actions.

Across Phase 1 and Phase 2 of the research process, we kept Robeyns' criteria, introduced above, in mind: be explicit, justify your method, be sensitive to the context, produce an ideal and non-ideal list, and generate incommensurable dimensions. More specifically, in the first phase we attended to normative assumptions, to public consensus and initiated a deliberative process. Our first iteration of professional capabilities drew on Nussbaum (2000), applied the ideas to professional education, and was not data- or dialogue-driven (items 1 and 5 on Alkire's list). We initially conceptualized professional education as enabling students to clarify their own conception of the good and to form justice-enhancing relationships with others. In Nussbaum's list, the capability is 'practical reason'; and the corresponding functioning is clarifying a conception of the good. We worked out more functionings by combining the concept of 'practical reasoning' which is transformative, critical, and attentive both to acquiring knowledge and to being oriented to taking responsible action in society. Examples that we worked out from capabilities theorizing applied to professionals and professional education in the early stages of the project before data collection began are sketched in Table 4.2.

An assumption of the project was that educational environments can foster public-good professional capabilities, and so we also proposed an alignment of university arrangements for fostering public-good capabilities (distinct from the educational arrangements in departments). We selected university arrangements based on our current knowledge (from literature and experience) of the possible roles of universities in society. One of the examples we developed was 'connectedness': a South African university which is connected to a transforming society through attention to poverty reduction would support and reward professional departments in pursuing these goals (see Table 4.3).

In this chapter we have outlined the broad dialogic approach to our research, and we have made an important distinction between comprehensive capabilities for all and a distinctive but related set of professional capabilities. We have made explicit and justified the selection of our case study universities and professions and outlined a first phase normative and conceptual approach to selecting professional capabilities. We have identified educational arrangements to consider what already expands certain (professional) capabilities and what changes to existing arrangements would be helpful (Alkire, 2008).

However, to produce a prospective (futures-looking) application of the capability approach, we also needed to evaluate what is the current configuration of professional education in South Africa and whether a list of public-good capabilities had relevance and use. Thus the next chapter outlines how the public-good professional capabilities were refined, which were valued by diverse

Table 4.2 First iteration of professional capabilities, functionings and education

Capability*	Professional functionings ('beings' and 'doings')	Possible indicators in professional education
Practical reason	Forming a conception of the good Critically reflecting in planning one's life Being knowledgeable about both South African society and global society Having knowledge base of the profession Integrating theory, practice and professional values	Exposed to and engaged in socially relevant, critical scholarship An up-to-date curriculum of professional and subject knowledge which also integrates theory, and practice Learning how to identify and listen to the 'better' argument Being prepared for active citizenship Debates about what it means to 'act rightly' as a professional
Control over one's environment – political	Participating effectively and confidently in political choices that influence one's professional life	Opportunities to have a voice in curriculum development, pedagogy and assessment Opportunity to openly and critically debate the role of the profession as it is now and as it ought to be to contribute to social transformation Learning to communicate effectively
Affiliation	Imagining and understanding how the world is experienced by different 'others' Respecting each person's identity and dignity Working collectively with fellow professionals for transformation Identifying with the role of contributing to 'pro-poor' professionalism beyond your own professions Acting in an ethical way	Pedagogies of discussion, dialogue, deliberation and collaborative work Respectful relations between staff and students, and students and students Learning to live with and value diversity; learning how to act/be interculturally aware and competent, and to act and communicate in an anti-sexist and anti-racist way

Source: *(from Nussbaum 2000).

Table 4.3 First phase iteration of university dimension

Dimension of university transformation	Evidence
Connectedness	University is connected to society and society in turn is connected to the university, change in one influences change in the other.
	Both critical scholarship and public intellectuals.
	Research and teaching address the 'moral urgencies' of poverty in the city, region and country.
	Leadership 'speaks truth to power'.

individuals and groups across five professions, and which policies, practices and institutional cultures would promote capability expansion. The case study narratives (drawn on for Chapters 6, 7 and 8) therefore are *both* forward-looking to what could or ought to be, *and* evaluations of cases of professionalism against the framework list of capabilities. We describe next how we fleshed out an emergent Index in the second phase of our research, that is, when we were collecting data, in dialogue with university departments about its interpretation, and analysis.

5   Dialogic stages of the Public-Good Professional Capabilities Index

> The professions have become responsible for key public values.
>
> (William Sullivan, 2005: 4)

This chapter builds on Phase 1 described in the previous chapter. Phase 2 of building a Public-Good Professional Capabilities Index combined dialogue and data to operationalize capabilities. The empirical stages of Phase 2 were: conducting of interviews with diverse stakeholders in professional education; iterative coding of data sets; analysis and discussion; working at first with the social work data to generate public-good professional capabilities; finally, testing the capabilities against the other four data sets and in dialogue with the universities by way of research working groups in each university. At the same time as we were identifying capabilities in the data, we considered educational arrangements and social conditions for public-good professionalism. These multilayered considerations were brought together as the Index.

The data collection aimed to test and operationalize theoretical ideas about capabilities-based public-good professionalism in order to establish more precisely which professional capabilities were valued and why; the form and purposes of professional education in the selected case study sites; the overall university ethos in relation to poverty reduction; and what might put constraints on or enable public-good professionalism. Dialogue with three research working groups [RWGs] and debate in public seminars in South Africa and internationally provided formative feedback. We used the feedback to refine the emerging list and to inform continuing questioning about the usefulness of the capabilities approach. A complex account emerged in which the capabilities are potentially widely applicable as long as they remain 'vague' and 'thick', while the functionings are contextual and specific and will vary according to profession.

The second phase: collecting data and consulting

The challenge in the second phase of our research with the three South African universities was to find a way of operationalizing and testing the ideas described in the previous chapter. We bore in mind that the process of specification of capabilities and dimensions should be participative, transparent, and revisable (Alkire, 2002), and subject to ongoing scrutiny. The stages in our data collection and analysis were iterative, rather than linear. Nonetheless, we outline below the chronological sequence of events underpinning our analysis and synthesis into an Index.

Empirical research stages

Stage 1 (August–October 2008): Interviews with students, lecturers, university leaders, alumni, professional bodies, NGOs. Discussion with a research working group [RWG] at each university. Initial draft and circulation of Professional Capabilities Index (and see Walker *et al.*, 2009).

Stage 2 (December 2008): Coding of social work data by research team to agree nine themes (drawing on theory and data). The themes were: transformation; poverty; contribution to poverty reduction (positive); contribution to poverty reduction (negative); capabilities of the poor; professional capabilities; lecturer capabilities; educational contribution (positive); educational contribution (negative).

Stage 3 (by mid-March 2009): Coding and 'chunking' of student, lecturer, alumni data using agreed categories of professional capabilities, educational arrangements, and social constraints, followed by professional bodies and NGOs, and university leaders.

Stage 4 (March 2009): A summary narrative produced for each case study.

Stage 5 (March 2009): Further responses from research working groups.

Stage 6 (March 2009): Revision of professional capabilities tables across all five case studies, and indexing of educational arrangements, institutional conditions and social constraints, drawing on summary narratives and RWG inputs.

Stage 7 (July–September 2009): Further iterative adjustment of these four tables after feedback from RWGs.

Stage 8 (by December 2009): Drafting of expanded case study for each professional site, including discussion and feedback from each participating department.

Stage 9 Ongoing review of the Index.

In addition to making our process visible, our claim to validity for the Index is grounded in a checklist suggested by Maxwell (2010):

1   *Rich data* was generated (especially through intensive interviewing);
2   We arranged *extended involvement* (over 18 months and beyond in the site and project);
3   *Respondent validation and feedback* was sought from research working groups (on the analysis and the Index);

4   We searched for *discrepant or negative cases* (across the professional sites and universities in relation to the capabilities and functionings asking repeatedly whether any capability on the list failed to hold or appear in every professional case study);

5   We practiced *triangulation* using multiple data sources and individuals for feedback;

6   We employed *quasi-statistics* to test how often a capability appeared in each professional site and how strongly or weakly it was framed; and

7   We made *comparisons* across the professional cases and the universities.

We collected empirical data from a range of stakeholders; and the interviews with people on the ground in professional education and practice were highly influential – the Index is embedded in realities as they were told to us, and as we observed for ourselves. Discussion and dissemination began in October 2008 and continued through to December 2009; presentations and working papers were placed on the project website to disseminate evolving thinking about key aspects of the project. Iterations of the Index were developed at four key points: July (2008 as explained in Chapter 4), October 2008, March 2009 and September 2009, and have been subject to further review subsequently, including in the writing of this book.

This iterative process is described now and mapped against empirical data in Chapters 6, 7 and 8.

A consultative and deliberative process

The interviews were the core of the data base and revealed to us which professional capabilities were valued by diverse individuals and groups in professional education and practice. We conducted semi-structured interviews with university leadership, selected academic staff and student focus groups, as well as graduates, NGOs and professional bodies (see Chapter 6 for details of all interviewees). In engineering, law, social work and theology it was decided to interview undergraduate students in the fourth and final year of their degrees so they had been exposed as much as possible to their university-based professional education. The public health students were taking postgraduate courses on a part-time basis and were working in different fields of public health. Students were interviewed in focus groups of black and white students, and we bore in mind the salience of race in understanding transformation in South Africa. In addition, we interviewed individually a Dean or Deputy Dean and Head of Department and one or two lecturers in each department, as well as a university leader. Again these included people from different racial groups. Non-governmental organizations [NGOs] were selected on the basis of the focus and relevance of their work to particular professional groups. In total 120 people were interviewed: 23 in social work, 19 in engineering, 25 in theology, 27 in law and 26 in public health. Interviews were tape recorded with permission and fully transcribed.

The interviews explored experiences of and perspectives on professionalism and professional education, and university initiatives to transform professional education. The participants were asked about their views on the role of higher education, and about their understandings of the barriers and bridges to professional education for poverty reduction. Students were asked about what they thought it meant to be a health worker, lawyer and so on, about their future plans and about their experiences of learning and professional identity formation (see Appendix A for the interview questions). This qualitative data is highly significant because it enabled us to listen carefully to the voices of a range of people involved in professional education and in professional work. Generally, interviews generated rich and nuanced data on desired capabilities and experiences of university education and social change. Variation of professional capability emphasis and career paths across the universities and professional sites was particularly informative.

As noted in the previous chapter, we were not able to speak directly to poor and vulnerable service users for reasons of access and ethics, instead, in addition to practitioner interviews, we used news reports and secondary literatures for information about what the users might value for their own lives and their interactions with professionals.

Although each professional-field interview data set is not homogenous, including as it does lecturers, students, alumni, NGOs, professional bodies and university leaders, we found each subset to be sufficient for our analysis and the saturation of the capability dimensions which emerged (Guest *et al.*, 2006). We assumed that all interviewees were competent to comment in their specific area (for example, student experiences, curriculum, professional practice, and so on), and each group was asked a similar set of questions.

Documents and literatures were scrutinized which related to: international agencies and national higher education policies; university teaching and learning and equity policies; quality reviews; student evaluation forms; and programme, course and module descriptions. Existing university statistics relating to diversity of race and gender of students were collected to ascertain the gender and race profile of students, staff and alumni interviewees, and the impact of each within and across the universities and professional fields. Finally, relevant media stories during and after the life of the project were collected.

Data analysis was ongoing, beginning early in the project as documentary and statistical data was collected, continuing as qualitative interview data was gathered, and therefore developing and building throughout the project.

University research working groups [RWGs]

The research project involved a three-person RWG at each site, comprising someone from a participating department, a Head of Department or a Dean, and someone in senior management such as a Pro Vice-Chancellor (PVC) or Director of Teaching and Learning. It was to these groups at the participating universities that we circulated our first phase ideas as a basis to begin work with

Table 5.1 Process of consultation and discussion

Date	Form of consultation
August 2008– November 2008	Interviews and focus groups: 120 people consulted on valuable professional capabilities Three universities, five professions Students (black and white, men and women, working and middle class) Lecturers Heads of departments University leaders Alumni NGOs Professional bodies
August 2008 October 2008 March 2009 October 2009	Research working group (RWG) face-to-face meeting or workshop 1 in each University. Each included one person from the participating professional department and two other members with Faculty and/or University wide roles. The two key tasks of the RWGs were: to respond to the data and emerging analysis; and to discuss how transformation might be understood in relation to human development and poverty reduction.
August 2008/October 2008/June 2009	Open seminars in South Africa on the research
October 2009	A final seminar at each university
November 2009	Kenton education conference

the departments to refine and revise our draft professional capabilities. We kept notes of: three face-to-face meetings with each group in August and October 2008; a joint workshop in March 2009 which included all RWGs and the full research team; and a final meeting with each RWG in October 2009. There was also regular email communication with each RWG co-coordinator.

Our process of consultation is summarized in Table 5.1.

Iterations of professional capabilities

For the second iteration of professional capabilities (the first iteration was described in the previous chapter) we brought theory into play with dialogue and practice. After our visits to South Africa in August 2008 and October 2008, we drafted two core capabilities (Table 5.2) – the capability to be a change agent and the capability for affiliation – which had emerged from our early discussions in South Africa.

For the third iteration we moved from fieldwork to producing a case record by selective editing of the case data (Stenhouse, 1978). We initially selected social work as a 'critical case' (Flyvbjerg, 2001: 79) to test a public-good capabilities

Table 5.2 Second iteration of professional capabilities (August–October 2008)

Professional capabilities	Examples of functionings
Capability to be a change agent	Being able to form a conception of the good
	Having 'public-good' professional values; valuing human beings and their human dignity
	Having critical theoretical knowledge, but also able to integrate theory, practice and professional values
	Leadership skills and confidence to speak/advocate
	Able to mobilize resources for change
	Strong sense of their own effective agency
Capability for affiliation	Showing concern for others; imagining and understanding how the world is experienced by poor persons
	Respecting each person's identity and dignity
	Acting in an ethical way
	Ability to work effectively with other agencies; working collectively with fellow professionals for transformation
	Contributing to pro-poor professionalism beyond own profession

framework. Social work is a profession working directly at the interface of vulnerable lives, so if the list of public-good capabilities focusing on poverty reduction was not valid in this case, it was unlikely it would be valid in professions further removed from working with people living in poverty. We first generated nine analytical codes: transformation, poverty, contribution to poverty reduction, non-contribution to poverty reduction, capabilities (of people living in poverty), professional capabilities, lecturer capabilities, educational contribution, and educational non-contribution. Analysing these codes generated four central capabilities which were extrapolated from the significant functionings that emerged from the social work data. We described these professional capabilities as vision, professional agency, affiliation and resilience. For example, data from one social work alumnus for contextual functionings and the corresponding professional capabilities included those listed in Table 5.3.

We began to build case studies of each profession working from these initial four empirical capabilities, together with the nine codes. We now analysed the data bearing in mind three themes: the integration of macro/meso and micro levels; what kind of professional is envisioned; and what is actually going on in professional education at each site. Working systematically across our coded interview data sets, we organized data from lecturers, students and alumni and NGOs and professional bodies, under three analytic categories of: *Professional capabilities*, for example, 'making a difference'; *Educational contributions*, for example, not enough practical education; curriculum; and *Constraint*, for example, changing student values; failures of the law. We compared and contrasted diverse groups in each profession, and then across different professions.

Table 5.3 Third iteration of professional capabilities derived from functionings in social work evidence

Capability	Functioning (contextual)
Vision	'Not to be deluded about the situation and not to romanticize it, but to know that humans can change, countries can change, but you've got to be there for the long haul' and, 'You've got to have a commitment, first of all to this country and the change that the country needs, the human change it needs.'
Resilience	'You've got to be prepared to be committed and to persevere. It's so easy to give up and there are reasons to give up. There is burnout, case loads are incredibly high, turnover is really high, and there are too few social workers and too many problems. But if you stick long enough and you're committed enough . . . I think that's what a social worker needs.'
Affiliation	'Our ethos is relationships before projects.'
Professional agency	'I can do stuff. I can make a difference.'

We continued to generate capabilities until the data was exhausted and used new capabilities to revisit previously coded data. Variation within and across case sites and informant groups was looked for, as well as any negative cases (a capability which did not appear in a profession).

This yielded evidence-based tables organized around three key categories: human development professional capabilities; educational arrangements (including institutional conditions); and, socio-historic constraints for each case study. We then wrote five summary narratives, one for each profession. Appendix B shows the initial coding and categorizing of functionings in the social work data. (See B.1 Professional capabilities from social work data; B.2. Educational arrangements, social work data;, and B.3 Social constraints). The Index then emerged from across the functionings evidence in all five data sets.

The data was interrogated to construct narratives about how public-good professionals were being educated in universities, notwithstanding tensions, contradictions and constraints of change and transformation. While we looked for a consistent educational philosophy, for example, the importance of human dignity, we did not expect to find a homogenized vision, rather we expected a plurality of strategies, locations and underpinning themes. Nevertheless, we sought an iterative thread for each professional site in order to tell a reasonably coherent story about educating professionals. Thus, if evidence was found of public-good professionalism in alumni and students, we assumed it had some connection to their professional education and so expected to find evidence from discussions or in documents that would support the assumption. As we proceeded, we made connections the emerging list of valuable professional capabilities, which were intended to be broad and vague enough to hold across all five professional groups.

Eventually, a list of eight normative professional capabilities emerged which we thought could realistically be developed through professional education in universities. We further extrapolated four distinctive professional meta-functionings from the data (which come close to constituting an ideal list and hence for our purposes are also normative):

1   recognize the full dignity of every human being;
2   act for social transformation and to reduce injustice;
3   make sound, knowledgeable, thoughtful, imaginative professional judgements;
4   work/act with others to expand the comprehensive capabilities ('fully human lives') of people living in poverty.

Within this process we worked from data in which some functionings were repeatedly named as valuable, and the capabilities and meta-functionings identified were refined in discussions with the RWGs. For example, the capability of *social and collective struggle* (at the time missing from the Index) was suggested during workshop discussions in March 2009. We returned to the data after the discussion to identify how much evidence in the form of functionings there was for the new capability (it was present, even though we had not coded it as such without having our attention drawn to it by our colleagues). To take another example, in our data the emotional content of professional work is often faintly heard; however, participants in the RWGs were adamant that being able to reflect on and manage emotion is central to professional work. Their argument was based in their own experiences and it aligns theoretically with Nussbaum who argues that emotions are valuable reminders of our common humanity and are essential to a 'decent' society (Nussbaum, 2001: 350). We therefore decided that the phrase 'emotional reflexivity' (Zymbalys, 2008) captured the capability.

The capabilities and examples of functionings from our data are set out in Table 5.4.

As noted above and demonstrated in Table 5.4, each of the capabilities can be traced back to functionings discussed in the data. While the capabilities are normative and should hold across contexts, the functionings depend on contexts and will vary from case to case or country to country. Importantly, the list is multidimensional – for the conceptualization of a public-good professional that we propose all the professional capabilities identified are important and incommensurable (the presence of one cannot make up for the absence of another). For example, informed vision (number 1 on the list) without knowledge and skills (number 8 on the list) would not make for a public-good professional as we understand it, equally knowledge and skills without informed vision would be insufficient (even if forced to choose we might prefer knowledge and skills in a professional). Each capability contributes to the building and strengthening of the others.

Nonetheless, it is important to emphasize that the acquisition of a high level of specialized knowledge and technical skills are a *sine qua non* of public-good professionalism – that is without them these meta-functionings cannot be realized

Table 5.4 Public-good professional capabilities derived from functionings in the data

Functionings	Professional capability
Understanding how the profession is shaped by historical and current socio-economic, political context national and globally; understanding how structures shape individual lives; being able to imagine alternative futures and improved social arrangements; commitment to economic development and equitable economic opportunities; environmental awareness	1 Informed vision
Accepting obligations to others; care and respect for diverse people; understanding lives of poor and vulnerable; developing relationships and rapport across social groups and status hierarchies; critical respect for different cultures; communicating professional knowledge in an accessible way/ courtesy and patience	2 Affiliation (solidarity)
Perseverance in difficult circumstances; recognising the need for professional boundaries; fostering hope; having a sense of career security	3 Resilience
Community empowerment approach/promoting human rights; contributing to policy formulation and implementation; identifying spaces for change/leading and managing social change to reduce injustice; working in professional and inter-professional teams; participating in public reasoning/listening to all voices in the 'conversation'; building and sustaining strategic relationships and networks with organizations and government	4 Social and collective struggle
Empathy/narrative imagination; compassion; personal growth; self-care; integrating rationality and emotions; being emotionally reflexive about power and privilege	5 Emotions (emotional reflexivity after July 2012)
Acting ethically; being responsible and accountable to communities and colleagues; being honest; striving to provide high-quality service	6 Integrity
Expressing and asserting own professional priorities; contributing to policy; having confidence in the worthwhileness of one's professional work; having confidence to act for change	7 Assurance and confidence
Having a firm, critical grounding in disciplinary, academic knowledge; valuing indigenous and community knowledges; having a multidisciplinary/multiperspectival, stance; being enquiring, critical, evaluative, imaginative, creative and flexible; integrating theory and practice; problem-solvers; open minded	8 Knowledge and skills

in professional practice. However, technical competence alone, while necessary, is not sufficient for public-good professionalism. By virtue of their professional education at university, we envision graduates who not only acquire the capabilities to function as public-good professionals, but also acquire the values which dispose them to choose to function in this way. Informed vision and affiliation can be seen as, in Nussbaum's term, 'architectonic', that is, in terms of the production of a public-good professional they are the foundations for and suffuse all the other capabilities.

We also double-checked the capabilities against the South African Constitution, which commits the country to values of equality and freedom and the inherent dignity of each person, and commits the state to respect, promote and fulfill people's rights through the Bill of Rights. The Constitution commits South Africa to 'heal the divisions of the past and establish a society based on democratic values, social justice and fundamental human rights', (Preamble, South African Constitution 1996) (South African Government, 1996). Not only were there no incompatibilities here with our initial idea, but the progressive nature of the Constitution strongly supports the direction we advocate for professionals and professional education.

In Chapter 6, we extrapolate from our data how the public-good professional capabilities in Table 5.4 are seen from the perspectives of different groups and different professions.

Researching educational arrangements and social conditions

The research had assumed that professional capabilities can be formed through education in universities. Thus, at the same time as we were working with our data to identify and select professional capabilities, we looked for the educational processes in curriculum and pedagogy that supported public-good professionalism in each department. (We worked initially across two large whiteboards moving back and forwards from data and categories of capabilities and education.) Working in this way within and across data from each profession we iteratively developed dimensions of educational arrangements and university conditions which point to what it is departments and universities can do to produce public-good professionals. Curriculum arrangements and pedagogies are what Sen would call 'process freedoms' (2009: 28). As Sen (ibid.) explains, while capabilities indicate individual advantages – the actual opportunities each person has – it is critical that the processes by which the opportunities are acquired are fair. Sen suggests that a person having capabilities is not enough, we need to know about:

> The fairness or equity of the processes involved, or about the freedom of citizens to invoke and utilize procedures that are equitable [. . .] fair process and fair deal goes beyond overall advantages of persons into other – mainly procedural concerns – and these concerns cannot be adequately addressed though concentrating on capabilities only.
>
> (ibid.: 28)

Thus, educational arrangements are important for two reasons: for their attention to fair processes; and to locate professional capabilities in terms of broader social arrangements. Both are necessary to develop autonomous, committed and critical professional agents.

In the same way as professional capabilities are vague and thick, we offer 'wide' dimensions of educational arrangements which then inflect differently from site to site. How they appeared in our study is detailed in Chapter 7. The three dimensions of educational arrangements that emerged as likely to support the development of public-good professional doings and beings in schools and departments were: transformative curriculum (for example, incorporates key questions of social and political significance); appropriate pedagogies (for example, engendering respectful interactions and valuing diversity); and attention to departmental cultures (for example, encouraging projects responsive to poverty). We provide further examples from our data in Table 5.5.

We found university conditions that support public-good professional education in departments from the South African literature (e.g. Higgins, 2007; Potgieter, 2013), interviews with university leaders, and in interviews and discussions with lecturers, students, and NGOs, were: transformative institutional culture and environment; critical, deliberative and responsible; and socially engaged. First, we found support for an institutional culture and environment which values diversity and respect for all, more specifically, one which acknowledges an institutional history of injustice in formulating strategies of transformation; has expectations of high-quality teaching, learning and research: has developed a fair access policy; has an inclusive language policy; and values democratic governance and open debate about transformation. In addition, the institutional culture should work to build a just future, offering visionary leadership and a mission to foster public-good aspirations in students. The second significant dimension is that of a university which is critical, deliberative and responsible, for example prioritizing critical knowledge-making and dissemination; transformative curriculum policies and debates; and spaces for robust public reasoning about ideas. The third dimension was a socially engaged university, including: producing research which engages with national and global social and human development challenges; a student diversity profile in line with social demographics, and worked towards for staff; a commitment to improving schooling; community dialogues and partnerships; public accountability in terms of mission and goals to all who contribute to higher education; attention to economic opportunities for graduates; and engagement with the African continent. The three dimensions are normative though they might be differently inflected in different contexts.

Together these interlocking elements of educational arrangements (department and university) professional capabilities and meta-functionings make up the normative elements of the Index. Each element supports and reinforces the others, and is iterative rather than linear. In order to function as a public-good professional, an individual needs to have developed their personal powers and freedoms (capabilities), which in turn are fostered through opportunities and processes of professional education. Educational arrangements form functionings and strengthen the underlying professional capability.

Table 5.5 Educational arrangements to form public-good professionals in the university

Transformative curriculum	Appropriate pedagogies	Inclusive departmental culture
Interdisciplinary; socially responsive; coherent; research-led	Cultivates critical, open, independent minds and stances (e.g. opportunities to do research)	Engenders an awareness of the difference professional work can make to communities
Incorporates key questions of social and political significance, including opportunities to learn how the poor can be empowered	Exposes students to a range of competing ideas and perspectives	Supports developing professional judgement, ethical behaviour, and evaluation of personal strengths and weaknesses
Increases and deepens knowledge base of professional field	Engenders respectful interactions and values diversity	Instils the importance of accountability to service users
Service learning/experience in poor communities	Fosters both analysis and imagination	Continuous improvement of teaching, learning and assessment (e.g. good student throughput)
Opportunities for practice-based experience and contacts with practicing professionals	Produces confident communicators and advocates for social justice	An ethos of service to others
Includes content about contexts of professional practice, locally and globally; historical, political, socio-economic	Takes account of and supports variation in academic preparedness	Staff sympathetic to mission and teaching goals
Opportunities to learn different languages and discourses	Creates safe spaces for students; builds students' confidence	Welcoming to students and engendering a sense of belonging in the programme
Includes leadership and management	Integrates theory and practice	Academic staff provide diverse role models
Includes professional ethics	Organises peer learning, teamwork and collaboration across diverse groups	Involving parents of prospective students
	Ensures equitable uses of languages of instruction	Lecturers involved in professional standard-setting
	Prioritises discussion and dialogue	Encouraging research agendas and projects responsive to poverty
	Employs case studies and experiential learning	Culture of respect for all
	Insistence on reliability, punctuality, attendance etc.	Communicating high expectations
	Lecturers act as role models	
	Provides opportunities to learn clear and confident written and oral communication	
	Supports students to deal with interiorised guilt and anger	

Socio-historical conditions, constraints and enablements

In order to convey the real-life location of the Index, there is a further key element which reflects context and history. In this element there is an operational principle at stake: that social, political, economic and historical contexts need analysis in order both to avoid the lapse of public-good professionalism into utopianism and unrealizable ventures, and to produce a rigorous understanding of actual and possible realizations of public-good professionalism. Indeed, Deneulin (2006) criticizes the capability approach for not paying sufficient attention to history and argues for 'thickening the capability approach with socio-historical narratives' (ibid.: 118) in order to shed light on what – in our case – stands in the way from history of realizing public-good professionalism. Deneulin explains:

> Because the exercise of human freedom and choice cannot be separated from *history* and *community*, a freedom-centred theory of development, like the capability approach, needs to be thickened by giving attention to these collective and historical processes which underpin all human choices and affect the conditions in which human well-being can be promoted.
>
> (Deneulin, 2006: 209, author's emphasis)

We need, she argues, to understand better the relationship of individual agency with what she calls 'socio-historical agency' (ibid.), without falling prey to determinism. In the case of South Africa a social transformation agenda is part of the context, it is exemplified in the National Planning Commission's 2030 vision (National Planning Commission, 2011) and the acceptance of the NPC Plan at the December 2012 Mangaung conference of the ANC. At the same time, we cannot avoid the severe constraints discussed in Chapter 3 and talked about by our respondents (see Chapter 8). We had, therefore, to consider the reality for public-good professionalism and take account of the social arrangements that enabled or constrained the formation of public-good professional capabilities. Further, Nussbaum (2000, 2011) reminds us that while personal powers or internal capabilities are cultivated through education, nonetheless they require additional support if these powers are to develop and become effective. The political climate, policies and structures are especially important, as are professional organizations and work environments, as well as families and voluntary organizations.

Interlocking influences

Bringing together the eight professional-good capabilities, the elements of educational arrangements in university departments and the four meta-functionings results in a set of interlocking influences on the formation of public-good professionals in South Africa, which can be conveyed in tabular form (Table 5.6).

The broad normative elements should be applicable in a wide variety of contexts. At the same time, they will be shaped by the context in terms of what

Table 5.6 Public-Good Professional Capabilities Index: normative and contextual

Meta-functionings	*Professional capabilities*	*Educational arrangements*
(South African) context and history: social, economic and political constraints and enablements		
Able to recognize the full dignity of every human being.	1 Informed vision	*Department:*
	2 Affiliation (solidarity)	Transformative
	3 Resilience	curriculum;
Able to act for social transformation and reduce injustice.	4 Social and collective struggle	Appropriate pedagogies;
		Inclusive departmental
	5 Emotional reflexivity	culture.
Able to make sound, knowledgeable, thoughtful, imaginative professional judgements.	6 Integrity	*University:*
	7 Assurance and confidence	Transformative institutional culture and
		environment;
Able to work/act with others to expand the comprehensive capabilities ('fully human lives') of people living in poverty.	8 Knowledge and skills	Critical, deliberative and responsible;
		Socially engaged.

is possible, in other words by conditions that obtain in everyday non-ideal circumstances. In our case, the circumstances and conditions which constrain and enable public-good professionalism are specific to South Africa, they will be different elsewhere. The proposal is that all the elements of the study – evidence about valuable professional capabilities and functionings, educational arrangements and socio-historic conditions – constitute a framework for educating public good professionals who, in turn, will be equipped to choose to contribute to advancing the comprehensive capabilities for all (Figure 5.1).

It is assumed that who the students are – their backgrounds and personal characteristics – has positive and negative influences on professional education experiences, achievements and career choices. Biographies and choices, however, are not static and will be further shaped by experiences and learning during the processes of professional education – this is the crucial space of possibility explored empirically in Chapters 6 and 7. In addition, resources (university funding, quality of teaching, professionals in the field and so on) and commodities (books, computers, etc.) enable capability formation, and the absence of resources constrains functionings.

We think that the Index is a feasible practical tool for exploring a significant aspect (the education of professionals) of transformation of higher education in the South African and other contexts. The functionings in our data could operate as a grid for participatory curriculum and pedagogical design or for an evaluation of the professional education already in place. For example, the capability of 'informed vision' could be captured by a number of indicators, such as a graduate recognizes social justice issues relevant to their professional field (Nunan *et al.*,

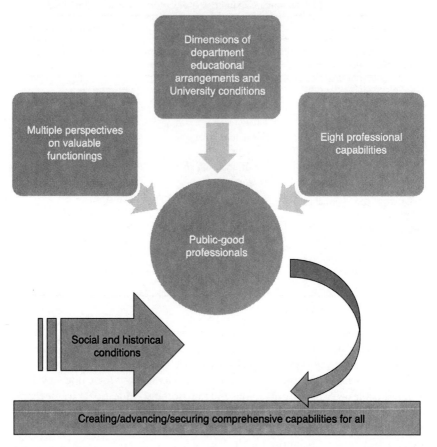

Figure 5.1 Public-good professionals and advancing comprehensive capabilities

2000). Nonetheless, the complexity of professional practices means being careful not to allow the desire for measurement to strip away such complexity. In addition, a process has been modeled: a list of professional capabilities has been generated by combining theoretical ideas with empirical data and dialogue where the latter two elements have served as a form of deliberative consultation.

The next three chapters elaborate on how the elements of the Index were identified and how they played out in each of the five case studies in terms of participants' perspectives on valuable capabilities and functionings, educational arrangements, and social constraints.

Part 3

Applying a Public-Good Professional Capabilities Education Index

6 Participants' conceptions of professional work in South Africa

> The professional ideology of service [. . .] claims devotion to a transcendent value which infuses its specialization with a larger and putatively higher goal.
>
> (Eliot Freidson, 2001: 122)

In the next three chapters we demonstrate how the capabilities approach to professional education might feasibly play out across different fields and universities. The context is a developing country still suffering the legacy of a profoundly troubled and troubling past and in need of professionals to contribute to the goal of social transformation. This chapter employs a capabilities-approach lens to demonstrate how the goals of professional education were thought about; Chapter 7 sets out what we were told about the educational arrangements for achieving these goals; and Chapter 8 discusses the social, political and economic constraints on achieving public-good professionalism for the professional fields that we investigated in South Africa.

Specific aspects of the Public-Good Professional Capabilities Index are illustrated by case studies of five professional fields: engineering, law, theology, social work, and public health. As outlined in Chapters 4 and 5, each case study comprises a detailed account of professional education aims and processes based on the views of lecturers, students, and managers in university departments preparing professionals, and of alumni and representatives of NGOs working in the professional fields, as well as statistical data from each university and professional field. As detailed in Chapter 5, an analysis of our interview transcripts interpreted through the lens of the capabilities approach and theories of ideal-typical professionalism, as well as consultation and dialogue, resulted in identification of eight professional capabilities: informed vision; knowledge and skills; affiliation; social and collective struggle; resilience; emotional reflexivity; integrity; and assurance and confidence. And, as expected, the story of public-good professional capabilities as expressed in the Index is differently inflected in different contexts. In particular, we found that while public-good professional capabilities held, emphasis was varied and functionings differed.

An analysis of the case studies gives substance to our claim that a capabilities approach to public-good professionalism provides a space for evaluating educational goals and processes already in place, as well as allowing a prospective construction of the possibilities of educating for public-good professional capabilities. So while we offer a partial evaluation of the professional education currently on offer in three South African universities, we do not aim to ascertain the impact factor on professional graduates in different communities. Rather, we extrapolate what the impact *might* be and how it *might* be increased were universities to build on what they already do by making use of the Index as a tool to evaluate their own professional education and training, and graduates' subsequent professional contributions.

This chapter is structured in two main parts. First, it takes each professional field in turn and introduces it in terms of its recent history and role in South Africa; it sketches the character and broad approaches of the university departments; and sets out how the participants confirmed and suggested the applicability of the eight public-good professional capabilities in how they thought about what professionals should be and do, and in how they taught and learned and practiced in their specific fields. The reader should be reminded that the undergraduate students interviewed in engineering, law, social work and theology were all in their fourth year of study; and that the public health students were working as public health professionals and taking a part-time, distance course. Given the salience of 'race' in South Africa, we have decided to indicate which group individuals belong to when they are first referred to in each chapter (this information can also be seen in Appendices C 1– C 5). We recount the capability set stories for each case in the same order: informed vision; knowledge and skills; affiliation; social and collective struggle; resilience; emotional reflexivity; integrity; and assurance and confidence. Sometimes, some of the capabilities do not emerge in the participants' accounts, in these cases we move on to the next capability and comment on the lacuna later in the chapter. We have sequenced the case studies to separate engineering and law, which we discuss first, what can broadly be called the 'caring professions' or in Bernstein's (2001) terms 'repairing' professions – theology, social work and public health. The subheadings are intended to convey the essence of the case as we interpreted it.

The second part of the chapter is a thematic discussion drawing out the preoccupations about and emphases on each of the capabilities by showing variations and commonalities across professional fields to illuminate the relevance of the capability approach to the concept of public-good professionalism.

Engineering at Acacia University

Engineering has a central role in socio-economic development. On transition to democracy, South Africa faced a high population growth rate, extensive urban and rural poverty, and rapid urbanization. Many expectations of improvements in the quality of life focused on engineering services, for example, housing, sanitation, power supplies, transportation and sanitation. Engineers take on government contracts to help infrastructures in disadvantaged communities (Watermeyer, 2006) and employ and train people from poor communities in construction skills.

Yet there is a steady outward migration of engineers and an acute shortage of qualified engineers (du Toit and Roodt, 2009).

The engineering case was based in Acacia, a university which had engaged only recently in political and social transformation. (See Appendix C 1 for a table of engineering interviewees.) The Engineering Department at Acacia is large and prestigious, and deals in all the main branches of engineering. In recent years there has been a 50 per cent increase of students, and a significantly higher intake of female and black students. In 2004, the university launched a Community Interaction Policy to restructure academic programmes to include interactions with and service to local, disadvantaged communities. The Department's response was to pilot a module called *Critical Perspectives on Society* which also fulfils outcomes demanded by the Engineering Council of South Africa (specifically, the social impact of engineering and engineering professionalism). The students we interviewed were among those who had volunteered for the pilot, so they were likely to be disproportionately interested in the transformational potential of engineering. Similarly, alumni and lecturers were selected because they expressed an interest in processes of transformation and poverty reduction. As Marius de Beer, the white Head of Process Engineering observed, within the Department as a whole, 'there's no specific focus on poverty reduction'.

Doing the job efficiently, creatively and honestly

The engineers' *informed vision* was discerned in their general commitment to South African development. There were, though, differences in how individual engineers thought about the form of contribution. For a few, the choice was to contribute to poverty reduction directly by building facilities in poor, largely African or coloured, townships. For the majority, the contribution was indirect: by building infrastructure thereby alleviating poverty through the 'trickle-down effect'; and by encouraging disadvantaged children to take up engineering. Despite claims from lecturers at Acacia that it is important to grasp socio-political and economic realities, there appeared to be little awareness among our participants about how to engage in direct work with people living in poverty.

Above all, engineers valued a high level of *knowledge and practical skill*. The knowledge, of course, is highly specialized and not for discussion with non-engineer interviewers. Particularly valued were the cognitive functionings of being logical and innovative, especially for finding cost-effective and workable solutions in a developing country: Pieter, a white engineering student, commented 'We need engineers that find new ways to do stuff easier and better, and cheaper and more reliably [. . .] you really need guys who can think a lot.' Thomas Ryer, the white Dean, was more analytic, observing that if engineers could be produced who are 'initiators, integrators, and innovators', then engineering can be cast as a 'catalyst in poverty relief'.

Engineering students demonstrated *affiliation* towards people living in poverty in the sense of accepting an obligation to help, that is, they accepted the

Department's decision for a community module in the curriculum. Yet there was a hint from them that poor communities are composed of passive others to whom 'good' needs doing, rather than being composed of equals with whom to consult and collaborate. Working alumni engineers (selected for interview because they work with communities) value affiliation: the alumna Jeanne Marais thought 'You've got to look at everybody as if you were in their shoes.' They spoke of the 'negativity' that can accompany large-scale poverty, and saw a role encouraging colleagues and employees. For example Chantal Brown, a black African alumna, observed that in her work:

> Often you gets lots of people that are de-motivated [. . .] especially as an engineer, you walk around, you work with blue collar workers [. . .] I can encourage people [. . .] I can motivate people to do their best and just speak hope in peoples' lives because [they] can become very despondent.

All participants acknowledged the importance of relationship-building, of understanding different cultures and being able to communicate with people from diverse backgrounds, including knowing basic African languages to communicate with workers on projects: Marian Lamprecht, a white lecturer who leads the *Critical Perspectives on Society* course, identified a need for something beyond knowledge and skills: 'Engineering is very much a formula, A + B = C, and the moment you start dealing with people with different backgrounds, then you have to have a human understanding of their way of thinking.' Nevertheless, such communications skills were often valued as an aspect of efficiency and good management (getting the job done), rather than for solidarity with people living in poverty.

Engineers put great store on being *resilient* because the profession is competitive; more so if an engineer wants to focus on poverty-reduction projects. Christo van Heerden is a young white lecturer who, unusually, works on community projects, and he emphasized the need for resilience: 'You've got to have a lot of hair on your teeth[1] [. . .] There's lots of issues, there are lots of problems getting jobs, finding tenders, BEE [. . .] so you've got to have a really strong will.'

Integrity was taken particularly seriously. Alumni who had been practising for some years were insistent about not being fraudulent, and about being truthful with workers and clients. They also stressed being responsible and accountable; conscientiously constructing products and buildings; and following safety procedures: they pointed out the harm engineers might do by not doing their job properly. In fact, the need for integrity was so emphasized by the groups we spoke to that we suspected a problem within the profession as a whole in South Africa. Christo van Heerden, who reported that he makes a considerable effort to involve himself in community projects, had an opinion on this: 'A lot of engineers, they don't like responsibility, they just do something, but they take a step back.' The Dean, Thomas Ryer, elaborated the reasons for engineers to have a 'very good value system', again efficiency is foregrounded:

You're always in a management position as an engineer, people look up to you. So if you're going to break the rules, you don't come on site, you're not punctual for meetings, you're slack, then that's going to come across to your workers, it's going to affect them. You're going to get people pitching up late [and] stealing, because it comes from management level.

The students who, it must be remembered were studying at Acacia, an historically white, elite university and whose future profession enjoys high status in society as a whole, conveyed a palpable sense of *confidence and assurance* that they will be problem-solving agents of change who can make a difference to society. For example, Dawie, a white student, spoke of the problems of rural communities living near mines: 'We just need to know there is a problem and we can actually do something about it.' While there was confidence about achieving practical solutions to infrastructure problems, it was not the norm to think of giving serious time and effort to community projects either in the Department or in the profession at large.

Law at Fynbos University

By its very definition, law entails a concern with justice for individuals. Yet the legal system has had an ambiguous role in South Africa's recent social justice trajectory. Under apartheid, the law was one of the key instruments for enforcing separation and different levels of civic freedoms, and economic and social resources; moreover, lawyers, prosecutors and judges were central to the implementation of apartheid policies. However, some lawyers actively defied the apartheid regime, arguing that violations of human rights and the destruction of community life were occurring in pass laws, forced removals, and denationalization through the imposition of 'homeland' independence (Dugard, 1978; Abel, 1995). Our understanding of poverty, or capability deprivation, incorporates access to social justice, rights and freedoms, as well as levels of resources, so lawyers play a key role in reducing poverty and expanding capabilities in South Africa. A number of organizations in South Africa, such as Lawyers for Human Rights (1979), the Black Lawyers Association, the National Association of Democratic Lawyers (NADEL), and the Legal Resources Centre, were set up under apartheid and were important in the Truth and Reconciliation Commission. Today, these organizations continue to work in the sphere of human rights.

The history of the Law Department at Fynbos is intertwined with the path of historically black universities under apartheid. Prior to 1991, because of the highly circumscribed opportunities for black lawyers, the main purpose of the Law Department was to produce graduates who would return to serve their respective communities. While serving one's own community was not in itself disadvantageous to individuals, at the time such public service reinforced existing racial divisions and limited career opportunities for black lawyers. After the transition to democracy in 1994, the Department embraced a much broader understanding of the role of the lawyer. In particular, a focus on the role of lawyers has been encouraged by the fact that many senior ANC officials who served in the cabinet trained at the Fynbos Law Department. The Deputy Dean described how the Law Department began to see that we 'can influence policy, people who draft legislation'. Today, the Department is a significant part of the university overall. In 2009, approximately 1,600 students were enrolled in a course at the Law Department (almost 10 per cent of Fynbos's total 15,000 students). It offers the Bachelor of Law degree (LLB), which can be taken by four- or five-year routes, and several master's programmes. There is a part-time route for students continuing in employment. The LLB offers entry into many legal-related professions: attorney; advocate; prosecutor; magistrate; judge; corporate legal adviser; legal consultant; law lecturer and legal researcher. All of these careers have public-good potential.

The mainstream university understanding of transformation is to achieve a proportionate number of students from different racial groups. In this understanding, the Law Department at Fynbos is relatively representative. The proportion of female, coloured and African students is high (none of our student participants was white), and students are more likely than not to have come from disadvantaged backgrounds and are some of the poorest in the country (HSRC, 2007). As law in South Africa has traditionally been a predominantly privileged, white profession, Fynbos's Law Department has played an important role in opening up this profession to disadvantaged groups. (See Appendix C2 for a table of law interviewees.) Although among the lecturers there were differences about the extent to which the Department should encourage what they termed a 'pro-poor' career path, or rather facilitate individual choice which often leads to graduates choosing high-earning paths. Generally, they thought that students should not feel pressurized into choosing an overtly public-interest path, particularly because many students had chosen law to escape a deprived background; so the Deputy Dean, Leonard Smith, observed that, for some, returning to their communities was 'a kind of a giving back'. Yet a female coloured law lecturer Khatidja Bashir observed:

> We cannot put the expectations of 'You must go and work at the Legal Aid Board now and just give back.' If you understand that student – if they become a lawyer they don't just have one person to feed, they've got a family to feed, the mother, the father, the siblings, everybody's hopes and dreams are in that student which means that we must let them succeed within the private field and we must provide them with that skill.

From this perspective, private legal practice enables people from disadvantaged communities to rise to new positions of power and experience, and for the Law Department, giving students the knowledge and skills to make such a choice is an important part of the process of social transformation. Khatidja continued to note that currently, only a small proportion of students committed themselves to pro-poor work, 'it's a small handful of students, it's not a lot'. Nevertheless, the ethos of the Law Department at Fynbos retained the progressive stance that characterized it in apartheid times. It is one of the leading research Departments in the country on local government law, socio-economic rights, and women, children and domestic violence; and it was involved in drafting a Child Justice Bill for the government. Several senior members of staff expressed concerned about the links between law and transformation: Leonard Smith, the Deputy Dean's personal concern is, 'How do you make people own justice, the poor people own justice, so they can believe in the justice system? It is something that enables and capacitates because they can see how it transforms their lives.' While there was not an explicit pro-poor orientation in the Department, Leonard Smith was of the opinion that all staff members shared a concern for instilling values and integrity. William Brown, the coloured Head of Department, too, noted that there is a 'broad commitment to democracy and to human rights'. The Department further presented itself as a place where professionals of a high quality are produced; in doing so it consciously distanced itself from the negative stereotype of historically black universities as suffering from bad facilities and low-quality training.

Knowing the law and prioritizing the client

Some law participants recognized that awareness of the realities of life for the majority of South Africa's population, and understanding the specific social and economic situations of clients enables lawyers to provide access to justice and socio-economic rights. At the same time, there was little confidence that lawyers possessed or acted on such awareness and understanding: the lecturer Khatidja Bashir claimed that what is needed is 'a mindset change of how we provide legal services'. In general, despite South Africa's sharpened need for lawyers oriented to human rights, as anywhere else in the world, the individual lawyers who choose 'public-interest law' from conviction comprise a minority who accept that they will earn less money than in other legal areas of works. The group of students[2] we spoke to was within this minority and held an *informed vision*. Many were from poorer communities themselves and so knew about disadvantage and most felt an obligation to 'put back' into the communities. Be that as it may, for lawyers knowledge of the law is paramount. All groups emphasized the importance of a thorough *knowledge* of the substance and content of the law to being an effective public-good lawyer. Like engineers, the knowledge is dense and specialized; and, like engineers, lawyers should be problem-solvers. Valuable *practical skills* include opening a file, managing a practice, and doing pro bono work.

The law lecturers we spoke to also emphasized that a 'good' lawyer treats people with respect, as dignified human beings, and is not prejudiced by illiteracy and disadvantage. *Affiliation* is particularly important for a lawyer working with vulnerable people, who might have been abused and who can feel baffled, intimidated and alienated by legal processes. Affiliation functions as being able to communicate about the law to clients. One of the white law students, Lynne, commented: 'What is important is that you don't indulge in this legal jargon with indigent clients, stick to the basic language and that's how you respect them as well [. . .] you don't make them feel like "I'm superior and you're inferior"'.

For Lynne, then, communicating the law – in the case of our study in the Legal Aid Clinic in Fynbos University – is communicating knowledge that can empower people. All our law groups thought too many lawyers see clients as a way of making money and drew attention to a tradition of 'dehumanizing' people (Ebrahim, a coloured law student, was distressed that in court people are called 'accused number one', 'accused number two'). So it is important to empathize with clients and to support people's ability to choose their own options. Nazia, a coloured Muslim student, told us 'I try to sit with my client and to first make her feel that she's human again.'

Lawyers spoke less about *social and collective struggle* than about how they might as individual lawyers assist individual clients. Nevertheless, there are a few lawyers who regard their work as part of the process of nation-building. Zolani Ncube is a black African alumnus, brought up in rural Transkei, who worked for a private firm and saw himself working with other lawyers oriented towards social justice to 'uplift' communities. Such lawyers are represented in the range of national legal organizations mentioned above. Nonetheless, being part of social and collective struggle was not, in the accounts we heard, greatly in evidence, and Leonard Smith, the Deputy Dean, did not think that it was essential for being a public-good lawyer. On the contrary, he continued, it was something of an 'over-hang' from the transition period; 'no-one is really doing that [now]'.

Law alumni combined *resilience* with *emotional reflexivity* when talking about working closely with difficult cases often with people suffering extreme poverty and hardship. Students too spoke of the need for resilience when dealing with clients who have been through traumatic experiences, especially when they cannot offer help. For Sandra, a coloured student, 'you get so emotionally attached to your client, but you have to stop and break yourself off from that situation'. And Tozi, a black African student, explained:

> Some [clients] come here without having dealt with that emotional side, so you have to be the social worker, the psychologist and also be a legal person at the same time [. . .] it's very emotional, it gets draining because you see how divided South Africa is.

There were a number of key elements of good professionalism identified by lawyers. It was observed that *resilience* is necessary to remaining committed to legal and social principles for 'the long haul', that is, for a career of several decades. *Integrity* is also essential in law. All groups spoke of the importance of having strong principles and ethical standards of behaviour and acting honestly regardless of what branch of law. Arguably, lawyers also need to have the *confidence and assurance* that their work is worthwhile. Mainly this is to make a difference to individuals and communities, for a few it is also to make an impact on public policy. For example, Thandi Dlamini, a black African alumna who works for a woman's legal aid centre, stated that she preferred to choose cases which will change an existing law, for example, challenging the principle of primogeniture to enable girls and illegitimate children the right to inheritance, for such cases will have a more lasting impact. For Leonard Smith, the Deputy Dean, professional confidence and leadership qualities will empower clients 'to establish businesses, to get into contracts, actually to work for themselves'.

Theology at Acacia University

Religion is influential in South Africa, with 80 per cent of the population professing religious affiliation. Christianity has a large following in South Africa, with 76 per cent of the population identifying themselves as Christians in 1996 (Statistics South Africa, 1999). Our research focused on ministers educated at Acacia to serve in either the historically white Dutch Reformed Church (DRC) or the related black church the Uniting Reformed Church of South Africa (URCSA). The DRC was established in South Africa after the country was colonized by the Dutch in the seventeenth century. In the early twentieth century the DRC was geared towards promoting the social and economic interests of Afrikaaners after their defeat and subjugation by the British in the Boer War (Pakenham, 1979). During apartheid, according to DRC theologians' interpretation of the Bible, it provided evidence for racial inequality and white superiority over blacks. In the late 1930s the DRC promoted the ideology of Afrikaner nationalism and racial segregation, based on a concept of white superiority. When the Afrikaner Nationalist government came to power in 1948, most white Afrikaans theologians and intellectuals subscribed to apartheid ideology (Durand, 1985).

From 1960, however, tensions in the DRC began to emerge with a minority of theologians within the church questioning the DRC's complicity in apartheid structures and particularly its theological position on racial inequality and segregation. By 1982, Alan Boesak, a South African coloured minister in the Dutch Reformed Mission Church (DRMC), was elected president of the World Alliance of Reformed Churches. As president of this alliance, he declared that apartheid was a heresy. Subsequently, this stance was formalized as the official position of the DRMC. In 1994, just prior to the change of government, the DRMC (the 'coloured church') merged with the Dutch Reformed Church of Africa (the 'black church' to become the Uniting Reformed Church of South Africa (URCSA). The URCSA was grounded in the values of the Belhar Declaration, but still composed of black members (Naude, 2003). Since that time there have been ongoing attempts to unify the URCSA and the DRC formally, which have not yet been successful.

Historically, theology at Acacia University provided training exclusively for white, Afrikaner, male ministers in the Dutch Reformed Church. In 1999 a landmark event and catalyst for the transformation of the Department was the merging of the Acacia training facility for DRC ministers with the Fynbos University training facility for ministers in the black Uniting Reformed Church of South Africa (URCSA). From that time the Department became ecumenical. The race, socio-economic class and gender distribution immediately diversified: the student body became multicultural, multilingual and students came from both wealthy and poor backgrounds. By 2007 nearly half of the undergraduate students were black, and about a quarter of the undergraduate students were female. One-third of the staff was black (including coloured and African staff). While this distribution is far from representative of the demography of the South African population as a whole, it is significant for the Department. In 2008 a new white, female Dean was appointed who has been committed to the transformation of the Department. The most dramatic change has been in philosophical, ideological and theological perspectives. There has been a shift in both teaching and research towards a transformative, developmental approach to theology with a strong focus on poverty reduction and issues of human dignity. In 2007 the Theology Department introduced service learning components into some of their courses. (See Appendix C 3 for the table of theology interviewees.)

Jakob Steyn, who is a coloured lecturer and Head of Department, described the Department as playing a social, economic, and political role in South African society. Daniel le Roux, a white lecturer whose research interest is poverty, claimed that a concern with community development was a central unifying focus in the Department: 'Everything we do is geared towards making a difference in society, but doing that from a Christian theological perspective.' The drive to create a Departmental ethos oriented to recognition of diversity, tolerance and respect is strong. For example, the white woman Dean, Jeanne Oliver, spoke of 'embracing', 'celebrating' and 'encouraging' diversity, arguing that it should take the form of:

> Creating spaces where people could account for who they are or what they believe, what they stand for [. . .] We're really taking trouble and time to create these safe spaces and assist people in developing the skills to participate in unthreatened ways. We regard the teaching space, the classroom, very highly as the primary space for developing all these values and skills.

A culture of critical reflection and review of practice in the Department was evident in events where students and staff participate in open discussions, with students often dictating the agenda; in routine evaluation processes; and in an ongoing process of curriculum change.

Synergy between personal and social transformation

Lecturer theologians held a coherent and explicit *informed vision* about the role of theology in South Africa. Ministers should understand the legacies of apartheid and the conditions of poverty of the majority of the population. They should be part of the everyday struggles of people by working with individuals and communities in a 'holistic' way (contrasted to the practice of preaching once a week). Lecturers in theology at Acacia had developed a sophisticated, multi-dimensional understanding of the economic and political process requirements of social transformation. Nevertheless, students and alumni were more inclined to invoke the experience of a 'calling from God' to 'enrich' or 'heal' society, than political motivation for redressing injustices.

Core theological *knowledge* was of the social and historical construction of the theological canon, in order to interpret texts. In contemporary South Africa, the lecturers emphasized, it is important to avoid literal fundamentalist interpretations of both the social world and biblical texts. Ministers should also possess a broad sociocultural political understanding of society, church and religion. For theologians the valued skills are *human skills* which are strongly connected to *affiliation*. The day-to-day work of ministers is to preach, to carry out pastoral duties, and to support programmes in the congregation. Our participants emphasized the overarching role of relationship-building: it is paramount and must be characterized above all by treating people living in poverty with respect and dignity. The connection of affiliation to empowerment was made by André van Wyk, a coloured alumnus who worked at the time of interview as a minister for the black URCSA in a rural area: 'We so often think that we have the answers for these vulnerable people and we don't really give space for them to just talk.' Building bridges *between* people was seen as the key to social integration between communities that in the past and still now would not interact. From the point of view of our participants, ministers, whatever their church, are uniquely positioned to heighten awareness, increase understanding, engender tolerance of diversity and facilitate interaction between people. For example, Linda du Toit, a coloured alumna working in the DRC, described how she would take opportunities to challenge paternalistic attitudes to community development and outreach within her church. As a minister of a traditionally white church she wanted to create a mixed congregation and connect previously divided people. Generally, white students and ministers in middle-class, white communities described their role as motivating their congregants to be active in poorer communities. Whereas coloured and black African alumni, who usually come from poor backgrounds and will work in poor communities, thought that people in the communities with whom they will work might be inspired to see that someone from a poor community can be educated. Mainly, though, the practicing ministers saw themselves as encourage spirituality because God can give people the strength as Andre van Wyk put it, 'to rise above their conditions'.

Related to affiliation was a strong and explicit commitment to *social and collective struggle* which focused on a desire to address the destructive legacy of the traditionally paternalistic, racist and sexist relationship of the white DRC towards the black URCSA. The theologians we spoke to regarded prejudice, ignorance and narrow-mindedness as large social/cultural problems which have led to divisions between different denominations, races, rich and poor, male and female, straight and gay, and able-bodied and disabled. Public theologians and progressive church bodies have played a significant role in the struggle against apartheid and in the transition to a democratic government.[3] So some students, such as Sara who is Afrikaans, thought theologians should take 'theology into the public sphere', she gave the example of the South African Council of Churches which was 'really involved at government level and also public places which have an influence on how policies are made in the country'.

The work of social transformation requires *resilience*. Burnout was a risk for coloured alumni (none we spoke to were black African) travelling long distances to work in under-resourced churches in extremely poor and scattered rural communities. Whereas for students looking forward to working life, resilience was balancing idealism with realism to avoid disillusionment and to persevere: Peter, a white student likely to work for a white church, speculated, 'Yes, we're going to have challenges that you won't be able to solve but that shouldn't throw you off line, just work through it.' In theology resilience was discussed in terms of emotion. Of all the professional fields, only in theology was emotion directly referred to: Jan Hofmeyer, a white lecturer committed to poverty reduction, reflected that making a difference in people's lives requires 'emotional intelligence'. Ministers, he claimed, must 'love' people and to do this they need to examine their commitments, life experiences, virtues and integrity. *Emotional reflexivity* was strongly implicated in ministerial work configured as playing a central role in social transformation. This was because all groups linked difficult personal, individual transformation to the capacity to contribute to social transformation. They emphasized the need for self-knowledge and personal growth linked to spiritual and religious identity. For example, Sara is an Afrikaans student who described herself as being shaped by her natal community's involvement in South Africa's apartheid history (see Chapter 3). She commented that:

> [Even though] we are a different generation and we view this stuff a lot different (sic) than our parents have [. . .] we have to realize that [. . .] we all have that bitter knowledge, whether we were part of apartheid or not. It's something that's passed on and along and I think we have a responsibility to fight it actively.

In the same vein, but from the opposing perspective, Aidan, a coloured student, drew attention to how his future congregations would be made up of people with low esteem because of apartheid. In this context, he needed to know and accept himself: '[I]n accepting myself I give permission to other people [. . .] to be themselves, whatever situation they come from, whatever brokenness [they have experienced].' Being honest about one's own human failings was a strong aspect of *integrity*, again because it puts the minister in the right relation to people: for Ignatius, a theology student, 'People should know that you're human and fallible'; and Linda du Toit, the coloured alumna working in an historically white church, observed 'We need to be real people not pious ministers who think they know all the answers.' Integrity was also associated with taking a responsible and courageous position on social issues. The white Dean of the Theology Department, Jeanne Oliver, wanted alumni to be able to 'articulate and to account for [their] own position [. . .] in respectful ways [even if it goes] against the grain'.

Social work at Silvertree University

In South Africa in recent years most of the focus of the social work profession has been on the multiple social problems rooted in the history of apartheid in South Africa and on challenges associated with extreme poverty and the high incidence of HIV/AIDS. Under apartheid, differential forms of social welfare services provided for different races. The focus was predominantly on the minority white population, while the state expected the needs of black people to be taken care of by families and communities (Earle, 2007). At the transition to democracy the social welfare sector changed to being nationally united and focused on the needs of the majority poor and marginalized black population. Most social work professionals work at the coalface of delivery to the poorest and most vulnerable sectors of society (ibid.).

According to the developmental approach taken up in South Africa, the social welfare system should contribute to developing national human, social and economic capital and aim to create self-reliance in individuals, groups and communities (Earle, 2007). However, in spite of transformative policy intentions, there have been negative effects of policy implementation. Although the overall social welfare budget increased, the rapid expansion of spending on social security services such as pension and child support grants significantly reduced the funding allocated to welfare services. Furthermore, the old welfare approach was associated with the casework method, which involved working with individual clients and came to be considered both inefficient and disempowering by the new national Department of social development. Nevertheless, the need for casework has grown, for example, with the statutory requirements associated with HIV/AIDS and the requirements of the Children's Act (2005). The expanded need for statutory casework has come without additional funding being made available (Earle, 2007; Lombard, 2008).

The Department of Social Work at Silvertree University is located in the Humanities Department (see Appendix C 4 for a table of social work interviews) and its white Head of Department, Miriam Grey, is herself committed to using Sen's capability approach to thinking about how to reduce poverty. The total student population in 2007 was 213 of which 35 per cent were black, Indian and coloured; 35 per cent white; and 30 per cent international. In response to changes in South Africa and in the welfare system, a curriculum revision process had been recently undertaken. This revision was directed at educating social workers who are prepared for the realities of social work practice, and able to act as professional change agents in various contexts. The idea is to educate students to move beyond a main focus on the micro level of individuals, couples or family to intervening at community and societal level. In spite of the transformation process at Silvertree predating 1994, the racial profile of students in the Department is not representative of the South African population as a whole. Members of the Department have strong links with organizations, agencies and communities within the field, and recognize the importance of sustaining these relationships and maintaining their credibility with these groupings.

There was a sense that the Department sat uneasily in the University. Members felt under-valued and under-resourced by the rest of the University; and Miriam Grey, the Head of Department, pointed out that the caring, people-centred values that the Department promoted and aimed for were in conflict with the values of the dominant competitive, individualistic society and which, in her view, were also prevalent in the University.

Empowerment and human rights

In social work, there was a strong *informed vision* underpinning an active role in societal transformation: the lecturers educated social workers as change agents working to reduce poverty and inequality, and to promote social justice. Miriam Grey wanted all graduate from the course to see the rights of people 'living in informal settlements, in squatter communities' as being 'as important as the rights of people who live in [wealthy areas like] Constantia or in Stellenbosch'. Some social work professionals should contribute to transformation of the profession at a macro level, taking up leadership positions. All groups subscribed to the principle of client 'self-determination' which defines social work in South Africa:[4] it represents a break with the past by shifting the emphasis from helping people to cope towards empowering them to change their own circumstances.

The social work *knowledge* base focuses explicitly on being a transformative change agent. Students are expected to understand the roots of poverty and inequality within the context of South African political, social and economic history, and global trends. Amanda Hoffman, a white social work lecturer commented that:

> [Unless social workers] understand root causes of problems [they will be] part of the problem [. . .] they're going to be working on symptoms and perpetuating the inequities of the past [. . .] They're going to be putting on band aid strips as opposed to understanding where the leverage needs to come in order to make shifts in power and in access to resources and access to opportunities.

Students should understand civil, political, social and economic rights as enshrined in the Constitution and Bill of Rights because as the Head of Department Miriam Grey put it, 'the realization of those rights is part of their work'.

Practical skills focused on ways of empowering communities. Alumni were particularly adamant about this. Thandi Matshisa was a black African alumna and was typical in declaring that people must be assisted to 'change themselves' in groups: 'The role of social workers is to strengthen resources and social structures within communities rather than imposing solutions.' (An important example is supporting people in communities who are already playing an HIV counselling role.) Anne Hardy, a white alumna who had worked in a faith-based organization since 1984 when she had graduated from Silvertree, linked empowerment to respectfulness, pointing out that communities can be supported by being respected and by being shown how to build on their own 'inner resources'. Social workers must make sound and creative professional judgements to devise appropriate strategies, so they need the skills of facilitators, managers, advocates and educators.

At the very heart of social work is the capability of *affiliation*. It is expressed in the functionings of empowering and respect characterized by motivating, encouraging, facilitating and mediating: as one Indian student, Sharon, put it, 'So it's not just going out there and getting this project to work, it's [. . .] to really empathize and understand where they're coming from first before you implement the project.' Empowerment and respect means building relationships, as the alumna Anne Hardy points out:

> Relationships before projects [. . .] You earn the right to be among folk by relating to them first, they can either want you or they don't want you [. . .] even if it takes a year before you are effectively in there, even though their needs are tremendous, it takes time to build a relationship and trust.

In South Africa, *social and collective struggle* is integral to social work: the lecturer Amanda Hoffman, described the central purpose of social work as 'redress[ing] the wrongs of the past'. For Anne Hardy, quoted above, redress takes the form of 'giving a voice' to poor communities by 'encourag[ing] advocacy and systems and structures'. Nevertheless, even though it was emphasized by lecturers, collaborating with other components of the social welfare system was little mentioned by students or most alumni. A representative of the professional body, Liezel Nermaak, who was white, thought that poverty reduction 'is really something that must be planned strategically, and there must be a collective approach [. . .] across all the government Departments and professionals in this field', indicating that this capability could be strengthened.

Resilience is critical because economic and social problems appear overwhelming. Again, Anne Hardy gave an insight into the difficulty:

> You've got to be prepared to be committed and to persevere. It's so easy to give up, and there are reasons to give up [. . .] But if you stick long enough and you're committed enough there's a real sense of integrity and transparency and openness to the realness of the situation. I think that's what a social worker needs. And not to be deluded about the situation and not to romanticize it, but to know that humans can change, countries can change, but you've got to be there for the long haul.

Thandi Matshisa worked for an NGO and emphasized that avoiding burnout meant not getting 'over-involved', that is, acknowledging, 'you're just a small drop in a big ocean', and so maintaining boundaries is right, even though it is difficult: 'You're constantly taking your clients' stories home with you. You can't help it sometimes.'

Social work should encompass a good deal of *emotional reflexivity*, for example, students knew they would need to encourage and motivate, while simultaneously pursuing the principles of self-determination. One white social work student, Carla, commented:

> [When] going into impoverished communities [. . .] you can't go in thinking that you're the expert [. . .] people are going to be looking to you for answers because they feel hopeless, but at the same time if you go in there as a mediator between people and draw out those ideas and the needs from them, that immediately takes away that feeling of hopelessness and revives the community.

Yet, while there was clearly emotional work to do, there was little evidence of reflection beyond the observation that it was important not to get 'too involved'.

Integrity means 'going against the grain'. Lyn, a white student, was of the opinion that social workers should be willing to 'get a bit of flak [. . .] because of their value system be willing to fight'. Taking a different perspective, the lecturer Amanda Hoffman described integrity as 'a make or break thing', a social work should be: 'an honest reliable person who doesn't generate false hope, who's honest in terms of what they bring, what their own shortcomings are [. . .] who is never deceptive and never dishonest with money and who can be counted on'.

Arguably, in South Africa social workers have low status, disproportionate to their education, level of skills and important role in society. Yet there was strong expression of *assurance and confidence* in the form of professional pride, for Amanda: 'The social work profession is a fantastic profession. I think that social workers have a huge opportunity to be transformatory, to make a significant contribution to transformation in any society where they're working, particularly in South Africa.'

Public health at Fynbos University

There has been a struggle to transform the South African health system at a national level so that the majority of the population will have the capability to live long and healthy lives. The field of public health also operates in a global context. The postgraduate programme in the Public Health Department at Fynbos University, which was the focus of the study, has a high number of students from other African countries, and the vision of the Department is closely aligned to a global movement to promote a primary health care approach in underdeveloped and developing countries. (See Appendix C.5 for a table of public health interviewees.)

Kautzky and Tollman (2008) outline the process of systematic damage to the health system in South Africa through the enforcement of the apartheid system between 1948 and 1994. It is not widely known that prior to this, in the 1940s, there had been significant efforts by progressive doctors in various locations in

South Africa towards developing a more equitable health sector. These initiatives were crushed after the National Party came into power in 1948 (ibid.). From the 1970s, large-scale implementation of policy entrenching racial segregation and inequity inflicted tremendous damage on the health sector. One of the elements of this policy was the creation of ethnically based rural homelands for Africans. Each homeland had to administer its own public service systems, including health systems. Many of these segregated health systems were not able to provide adequate medical and public health care. They were poorly organized, inefficient and often ineffectively managed (ibid.).

Throughout South Africa (not only in the homelands) ethnically based departments of health were established with separate health services for each racial group. Health services for African, coloured and Indian communities suffered from lack of funding and deficiencies in health personnel, medical facilities and equipment (ibid.). Combined with similar policies in all sectors of South African society, working-class and poor rural black communities and individuals experienced a growth in poverty and severe degeneration of conditions needed for leading healthy lives. Inequities in the health sector during this period were further exacerbated by the deregulation of the health sector and the privatization of health care. There was an expansion of hospital-based curative services with the effect of further depletion of material and human resources for facilities serving poor, black communities in both urban and rural areas (ibid.).

After the end of apartheid in 1994, significant shifts in health policy were introduced. Policy goals signalled an intention to transform the system to a high-quality, equitable, comprehensive community-based system, based on principles of primary health care. It would provide universal access to health care with the emphasis on disease prevention and health promotion (DOH, 1997). The Primary Health Care (PHC) approach was developed in the 1970s as part of an international drive responding to a worldwide crisis in health care. This approach was endorsed as a means to achieving universally available health care at an international conference in 1978. The PHC approach is underpinned by a strong socio-political orientation, which is directed at enhancing social justice. It aims to provide universal access to health care with the emphasis on disease prevention and health promotion. It is informed by the seventh objective of the World Health Organization (WHO) 'to address the underlying social and economic determinants of health through policies and programs that enhance health equity and integrate pro-poor, gender-responsive, and human-rights-based approaches' (http://www. euro.who.int/_data/assets/pdf_file/0016/141226/Brochure_promotes_ health_pdf). Furthermore the PHC approach recognizes the role of other sectors apart from the health-care sector in promoting health. These include sectors such as agriculture, industry, education and housing. Thus, there needs to be coordination of the programmes of these sectors. It requires and promotes 'maximum community and individual self-reliance and participation' in primary health care (WHO, 1978).

In spite of progressive health policy and large-scale structural changes in the health sector, the health of the majority of the population has declined post-1994.

This is shown by some of the key indicators of health. Maternal and infant mortality rose between 1990 and 2006, and life expectancy decreased significantly (Beresford, 2008). The poor performance of the health system is also evident in health-service indicators such as vaccination coverage and tuberculosis cure rates. There have been numerous interrelated reasons for this. As discussed in Chapter 3, during a period of unprecedented growth of the South African economy, poverty and inequality have increased. Furthermore, malnutrition, lack of housing, and access to basic services such as clean water and sewerage facilities have contributed to ill-health of communities. Undoubtedly, the HIV/AIDS pandemic has had devastating effects on the health of the population (Beresford, 2008). According to the Joint United Nations Programme on HIV/AIDS, in 2005 more than 5.5 million adults were infected with HIV/AIDS which constituted 18.8 per cent of the adult population of South Africa (*Mail and Guardian*, 2008). Recent statistics show that in the years from 1997 to 2008 the rate of death has doubled in South Africa, which is attributed to the extraordinarily high rate of AIDS-related deaths (ibid.).

As a middle-income country undergoing significant economic growth, South Africa's health sector has not been significantly compromised by an absolute lack of finances or basic resources as has been the case in some other African countries. The central reason which has contributed to the poor performance of the health sector has been cited as the shortage of staff and lack of capacity among health professionals, particularly in rural and poor urban areas (ibid.). Restructuring of the health system has required health practitioners to engage in new roles and expand their capabilities and functionings to perform these roles. With decentralization of health services to the district level a new layer of managers and middle managers was created. Thus there has been a great need for training in primary health care and public health strategies, in epidemiology, in health promotion and in key health programmes such as nutrition and HIV/AIDS. Furthermore, there has been an urgent need for expansion of management and leadership capabilities at all levels of the system (Department's Annual Report, 2008).

The Department of Public Health at Fynbos University was established in 1993 when there was a surge of policy formulation in all sectors of South African society to prepare for the imminent transition to democratic government. The vision informing the establishment of the Department was that of contributing to the optimal health of people in developing countries, particularly Africa. The population of these countries should live in 'healthy and sustainable environments with access to appropriate, high quality, comprehensive and equitable health systems, based on a human rights approach' (Department's Annual Report, 2006). This vision was based on the concept of comprehensive and integrated primary health care, as defined in the Alma Ata Declaration, the first international declaration about the importance of primary health care for health globally in 1978, and then taken up by the Wolrd Health Organisation (WHO). The postgraduate programme, which was the focus of our study, was established to contribute to policy making in the health sector, to 'strengthen education and research in Public Health and Primary Health Care [. . .] and to build capacity in the health services' (Programme Handbook, 2009).

Formerly, public health was confined to the medical schools, where only medical doctors were given postgraduate training in community health. The need for public health to be established as a formal disciplinary field in universities was recognized by the Medical Research Council in the 1990s, and the then vice-chancellor of Fynbos University played an active role in setting up the Department. The central role of the Department is to contribute to the transformation of the public health system in South Africa, and elsewhere in Africa through the education of practitioners. This educational role has evolved into the Department's postgraduate programme which is aimed at a variety of professionals in different sectors of the system and at different levels, including medical doctors, nurses, allied health professionals such as pharmacists, physiotherapists and dieticians, environmental health officers and educators in the public health field.

The educational work of the Department is based on a coherent vision of health within a social justice framework in underdeveloped and developing countries. Jane Simons, the white postgraduate Programme Coordinator described the vision of the Department in the following terms: 'The transformation of what was a primarily centralized top-down authoritarian, medicalized world view of health with human rights missing to an equitable multi-sectoral approach to health, strongly leaning on the side of health promotion.' From reports and interviews with the Head of Department and lecturers, it is apparent that its vision of public health is commonly shared and Jane Simons claimed that 'people are very proud to be part of that ethos'. The staff then aimed to build the capacity of health professionals to transform health systems to function effectively and in the interests of the majority of the people in South Africa and in other African contexts. To this end there has been ongoing review of the curriculum, the materials and means of delivery of the programme by way of internal reflection, curriculum and materials development and external reviews.

Pursuing policy and forging links that address the complex determinants of health and health care

Public health's *informed vision* is enshrined in international and national policies. All groups envisaged a transformed health system informed by an understanding of the health care systems which centralizes 'the political economy of health – how historical, economic, political, social structures affect health and health services and disease pattern' (Michael Andrews, Head of Department). The Department of Public Health at Fynbos aims to create across the continent of Africa: '[H]ealthy and sustainable environments with access to appropriate, high quality, comprehensive and equitable health systems, based on a human rights approach' (Annual Report, 2006: 1). Furthermore, in a context of extreme poverty, poor education, and a depleted health and welfare system, clinical service should not be decontextualized and 'medicalized' whereby illness is treated piecemeal when presented. Rather, holistic and systematic solutions to health promotion and disease prevention in communities must be established.

The *knowledge* that health professionals need to function effectively and contribute to transformation is about health and health care in relation to multiple and interrelated social determinants such as nutrition, clean water, proper sanitation, housing, social support networks the health of communities; the structures of health systems in developing and under-developed countries; and the relationships between sectors of the system, and between public health structures, NGOs and the private sector. Health professionals should know about how health goals can be achieved through policies which promote integration of sectors. They should also develop several clusters of skills: *clinical skills* that should be practised by treating patients holistically rather than treating specific symptoms. For example, Maureen, a student and practising dentist, pointed out that when patients come with tooth trouble dentists can pick up on other problems, such as HIV, TB and diabetes. *Intellectual skills* were highly valued. Health professionals should be problem-solving, and inquiring and critical when evaluating scholarly and policy texts, when interpreting data, and when contributing to debate and decisions about interventions and programmes. So health professionals need to integrate theory and practice, and be creative and flexible in order to think holistically and systemically about community health. And finally, educated health professionals need to become strong managers and leaders oriented towards transformation, managing effectively programmes, employees, finances and data; and disseminating research findings. Most importantly, those in leadership positions should have a sense of their own agency in order to address structural issues.

Health work requires *affiliation:* good relationships and rapport with clients were seen as paramount. Affiliation requires *human skills:* respect, empathy, caring, listening, sympathy, honesty. The Programme Coordinator Jane Simons indicated that she teaches to develop attitudes of inclusiveness, of community orientation, and of recognition of why people are under-resourced and poor and of how they have been affected by a colonial and apartheid past. All public health groups proposed that a community-centred, empowering and consultative approach is essential to the success of interventions that promote healthy lives. One of the principles of a primary health care approach is 'maximum community and individual self-reliance and participation' in health care (WHO, 1978). So health professionals need to assist people living in poverty to improve or change their own health-care practices and to contribute to change within their communities. Their task is to motivate people to identify their own problems, and consult about solutions by listening to their expression of needs, and ideas, instead of ignoring the organizational and leadership structures in communities and imposing solutions, often derived from foreign donors. In order to work in this way an ethos of respect and treating people with dignity was seen as necessary. Buyiswa, an African student from a poor community, thought that disadvantaged communities 'value respect highly in their hierarchy. And, you know, because they're poor they don't want to be treated anyhow – so that huge respect that you give them, that dignity, space and confidentiality [is essential].'

South African health policy promotes articulation between different sectors of the health system, and partnerships and co-ordination between government and NGOs. Health professionals play a crucial role in implementing health policy and the capability for *social and collective struggle* was much in evidence in the functionings of: implementing a community-empowerment approach to practice; contributing to policy formulation and implementation, leading and managing social change; working in intra- and interprofessional teams; training and educating others; building and sustaining strategic relationships and networks among different components of the sector and with organizations and government departments; and advocating social justice. In this respect, many of the informants, particularly alumni and students, emphasized the need to form partnerships between sectors of the Department of Health as well other government Departments in order to achieve health goals. The case of Laura Bailey, a coloured graduate of the master's programme in public health at Fynbos is illustrative. She was a manager of a programme in an NGO which was assisting with the implementation of the Prevention of Mother to Child Transmission of HIV (PMTCT) programme introduced in 2001 by the Department of Health with the central aim of decreasing the number of HIV-infected babies born to HIV-positive mothers. A comprehensive package of interventions was implemented, including voluntary counselling and testing, advice about infant feeding practices and appropriate administration of anti-retroviral drugs (DOH, 2008). Laura managed interventions on nutrition and infant feeding and her work included advocacy; programme design; integration of policy at a provincial level; working with programme managers at a district level to implement an integrated programme; and training. None of these functions is possible without making links and all our participants identified a need for co-ordination between different levels and components of the national health system. Most of the accounts from public health were descriptions of interventions and programmes being undertaken and planned, the detail of which seemed to preclude what it is like working on the ground. But Maureen, a coloured professional taking the course, hints at *resilience, emotional reflexivity* and *integrity* when she suggested saying to clients: '"These are unfortunately the restrictions we have; I'm here, I'm here alone, I can only see so many people. I can only do so much; I'm also human" they understand.'

Strength variations in conceptions of public-good professional capabilities

As we have explained in Chapters 4 and 5, the capabilities that we identified arose from theoretical considerations and from the complete set of data collected from different interest groups in five professional fields. This does not mean that the valuing of each capability was as strongly expressed by all professions or all individuals, and in some fields expressions of some of the capabilities were faint or implied. In the short sections below under the subheadings of each capability we attempt to convey this variation in a comparative account. By way of reminder, the eight capabilities are: informed vision, knowledge and skills, affiliation, social and collective struggle, resilience, emotional reflexivity, integrity and assurance and confidence.

Informed vision

For each profession, rhetorically at least, there are two main elements to an *informed vision* or a sense of high ground for thinking about what it is possible to achieve in terms of human development and poverty reduction: first, understanding how historical context and socio-economic, political and cultural structures influence the lives of the people whom the profession serves; and second, understanding how the profession itself is shaped by similar forces. It is this dual understanding that allows professionals to grasp opportunities and face constraints in order to make a difference to the lives of communities and individuals living in conditions of poverty; and to contribute to social transformation.

We can see that both understandings are very strong and even similar in theology, social work and public health, and that there is strong congruence between the enunciations of individual professionals, professional bodies and national policy. The context of the common vision is apartheid. The vision of these three professions aims both to explain the effects of apartheid on poor people; and to suggest ways of combating the effects. Our law participants were unusual in the profession for they came from poorer backgrounds than is usual, and their vision was based on human rights and inspired by a sense of obligation to the communities that they came from. Engineering participants held a weak version (or single dimension) version of a social transformation vision, seeing it almost entirely in terms of building infrastructure for the country as a whole, although of course this is important, as Larson (2013) points out, as a profession engineering improves the lives of collectivities.

Knowledge and skills

Two sets of knowledge emerged in connection with this capability. First, an *informed vision* predicates both generic knowledge and understanding of the political and socio-economic context of poverty and inequality in South Africa and globally; and understanding of the historic and current location of the particular profession within these conditions. This knowledge appeared more strongly in theology, social work and public health than in engineering and law because in the former three the vision of the profession's role in social transformation is stronger and, therefore, more closely connected to this particular knowledge base.

Second, is the specialized knowledge of the professional field. It might be argued that the specialized knowledge bases of the fields of theology and social work are more nebulous and less dense than those of engineering and law, which prized specialized knowledge more highly. Perhaps this is because lack of specialized knowledge would be more immediately observable in engineering and law in the form of unstable buildings or lost cases. Certainly, in theology and, to a lesser extent, in social work the value of specialized knowledge of the field seemed (in talk with us) subsumed by personal skills, dispositions and qualities associated with working with people to empower them. Public health stood apart from the rest of the professional fields in that those taking the course were already clinical experts in management and policy positions who needed a firm grasp of both contextual and specialized knowledge in terms of highly complex social, economic, political and cultural determinants of health and health care.

Skills are highly valued by all the groups in all the professional fields, and they cluster differently for the different fields. *Human skills* were highly valued by theologians and social workers, for example, listening, communicating, empathizing, persuading, facilitating, motivating and so on. For engineers and lawyers of paramount importance are *cognitive skills* (problem-solving and being logical). Public health emphasized the need for a combination of a wider set of skills: *clinical skills, intellectual skills* (critical thinking, research skills) and *people* and *project management* skills. We should clarify here that using good professional skills conscientiously (within the structures which define good professional practice) is essential to professional practice for the public good. Our argument is that being highly technically skilled is necessary, but not sufficient for a fully-rounded public-good professional. Moreover, it is likely that being oriented toward the public good motivates being highly skilled, for, as we argued in Chapter 2, the full rewards of professional work for public service are often found in consciously working for others.

Affiliation

As Nussbaum (2000) proposes, the capability of affiliation is 'architectonic', that is, it suffuses all human capabilities. Minimally, all participants in all professional fields emphasized the central importance for successful professional work of relationship-building with people from different backgrounds. Here, though, we draw attention to two functionings that were particularly important to professionals working in post-apartheid South Africa: respecting clients and empowering communities of people living in poverty.

Under apartheid, black and coloured people were treated with far less respect than white people and often brutally, as less than human. The professionals we spoke to were acutely aware that social transformation in South Africa cannot be achieved without equal respect to all individuals becoming a reality in everyday lives. Most of our participants named respect explicitly and claimed that it was central to their relationships with people living in poverty. The lawyers we spoke to saw clients who had been severely cast down in their lives and they identified how, in the context of (even now) dehumanizing legal processes and traditions, part of their job was to make their clients feel respected and human. For the theologians, the need to function respectfully and to be sensitive to people's dignity was urgent because they need to bring two churches together, one of which had been complicit in apartheid. Similarly, for social work and public health, respect for people was the *sine qua non* of building relationships with the recipients of their services.

'Empowering' people living in conditions of poverty to help themselves was a major aspect of a vision of social transformation for theology, social work and public health and is supported by professional and national policy. Empowerment was seen as necessary to counteract feelings of helplessness and hopelessness in poor communities. All participants in theology spoke at length about facilitating the development of poor people for self-reliance rather than creating and perpetuating dependencies. This approach was set against the traditional approach of the church to collect money or food to give handouts to the poor, which works to divide people. For both social work and public health 'self-determination' of clients and communities is the backbone principle of their work understood and discussed by all participants.

The weakest expression of affiliation was in engineering (keeping in mind that participants were selected for a strong interest in community work); there was no evidence of having thought clearly about respect or empowerment (and we will show below that how participants think about this lacuna can adversely affect professional practice). Yet we could discern 'narrative imagination' (Nussbaum, 2000), that is, attempts to understand what it feels like to be a person living in conditions of poverty.

Social and collective struggle

As a professional capability, relevant to the South African context, the capability of social and collective struggle can be defined as a strong, explicit and collective approach – with other relevant organizations and networks, as well as intra-profession – towards empowering communities and promoting human rights. It is a capability that appeared in interviews with theology (though not with an explicit human rights stance), social work and public health.

In theology the struggle mainly takes the unique form of trying first to capture hearts and minds (either on an individual or on a community basis) and second to bring people together. On the one hand, they tried to move white people away from prejudice towards some kind of reparation for past indignities to black people by encouraging them to engage with people who live in poverty; and, on the other, aimed to inspire poor black people to help themselves shed the psychological and material legacies of apartheid. While ministers were expected to provide spiritual guidance to congregations or faith communities; the stronger message among those we talked to was that they should also facilitate broader social change within their faith communities. The latter is achieved indirectly by aiding the formation of communities with a shared vision by motivating or inspiring leadership; by preaching; and by acting as a role model.

Conversely, and unexpectedly for us, the capability of social and collective struggle was less vividly in evidence in social work when goals were being discussed, rather the emphasis in what we heard was firmly on the nature of the role and work of individual social workers in assisting poor communities to become self-determining. Yet, as will be seen, the education of social workers *does* emphasize a policy-making role. Public health professionals by their own accounts are constantly engaged in, or would like to be engaged in, complex collective efforts to translate policy statements into practices in communities. A further aspect of social and collective struggle mentioned by some law, theology, social work and public health participants (most strongly in the latter) was that some members of the profession should be involved at national level in debates about the policy direction of their professions specifically and more generally about the direction of social transformation.

We could find nothing in our engineering data set that corresponded to social and collective struggle. Rather, action towards empowering people living in poverty was conceptualized at a micro level: either as individuals learning to be ethical at work or through making a marginal contribution to small-scale community projects. It is difficult to explain the lacunae, but it is possible to see how the lecturer Christo van Heerden's difficulties in attempting to get community projects off the ground would be greatly eased by a more collective approach within and outside the profession. Similarly, in law, with the exception of lawyers who ally themselves with human rights causes and groups, a sense of collective and social struggle is missing – it is as if individual lawyers behaving well can put the country to rights (and, of course, it does make a positive difference).

Resilience

In any national context there are options for and constraints on public-good professionalism. Steering a path between cynicism or disillusionment and naive idealism is always difficult. Like democracy itself, public-good professionalism is always precarious, it is

> never a given, but always a quest that must be renewed and reshaped over time. It demands considerable individual self-awareness and self-command. Yet, it also depends for its realization upon the availability of actual social possibilities
>
> (Sullivan, 2005: 220)

Chapter 8 deals with participants' responses to the considerable barriers to public-good professionalism in the context of the long haul to recovery from apartheid. We found that it is difficult for professionals not to feel overwhelmed by the multiple constraints: entrenched poverty, increased inequality, the incompetence and sometimes corruption of professionals in their fields. Statistics tell us that a response is to retreat to the private sector and the provision of private services. So the strong emphasis on resilience that we heard is to be expected. Across the professions with different emphases, public-good professional work was characterized as requiring resilience to bear the suffering that is witnessed; to overcome day-to-day obstacles; to retain some ideals; to remain motivated; to get work done; to avoid long-term burnout; and to sustain a twenty-year or more career in difficult circumstances.

Emotional reflexivity

Emotional reflexivity and emotion emerged weakly in our data, but insistently from the research working group at Fynbos. We identified emotional reflexivity as a need arising from the strong expressions relating to affiliation and to resilience. As a capability it was little discussed explicitly, as we have framed it. Uniquely, theology informants reported being constantly emotionally (though it was often referred to as 'spiritually') reflexive as they took on the inner task of personal transformation to grow their capacity for the outer work of social transformation. In social work there appeared to be less emotional reflexivity than what is called the 'emotional labor' (Hochschild, 2012) of operating the human skills of encouraging, motivating and so on to 'uplift' communities and deal with very difficult circumstances. Individual students and practising lawyers spoke of the problem of getting emotionally attached to clients, as did lawyers, yet there was nothing to show that any deeper thought had been given to how to respond. The only mention of what might be called emotional reflexivity in engineering was indirect. Theuns le Roux, an alumnus of Acacia and working engineer, spoke of encouraging workers by being 'patient' rather than 'shouting' and 'going mad' when things go wrong. In public health emotional reflexivity appeared to be subsumed under the sheer complexities of project and people management.

Integrity

Most explicit in law and engineering, integrity was defined as functioning in a principled way according to the profession; as behaving ethically; and as being honest (in the sense of not embezzling and so on). Lawyers pointed out that they cannot be seen as anything less than paragons of integrity. As we commented, in the engineering case, integrity was so stressed we came to think of it as 'protesting too much' – though nothing of the sort was made explicit, we were given the impression of a profession that had, at least in the past, too many practitioners 'making a fast buck' and not setting a good example to site workers.

In the other professions, the definition of integrity expanded to include being honest about what it was possible to do and not do – the issue of not making promises that could not be kept was a strong theme for social work and public health; being honest about oneself (theology); and being courageous enough to stand up in public for what is right (mentioned by at least one respondent in all the professions).

Assurance and confidence

Assurance in one's profession and confidence about the worthwhile nature of its role in a transforming South Africa played out differently in different professions. Somewhat paradoxically, given the lacunae we have identified in terms of public-good professional capabilities, engineers expressed most confidence about their professional role, specifically in developing the country's infrastructure (rather than directly by development in poor communities). Most of the lawyers we spoke to emphasized that individual lawyer confidence is necessary to winning cases, including cases that might change existing law. Social work participants were particularly eager to express assurance and pride in the profession; and it could be argued that it is particularly salient for public-good social workers if they are to fulfil the developmental and transformative role required of them. The profession needs to be accorded a high status for expanded agency and power to contribute to change. Neither in theology nor in public health did participants discuss their professions in terms of assurance and pride. Yet both appeared confident about their vision and the means they were proposing to achieve it. Theologians implied that God was their guide; while public health participants were guided by an established set of policy principles for health promotion in developing countries.

Professional field similarities and variations in public-good capabilities

In this chapter we have interpreted what we were told by a range of interest groups in five different professions about what kind of professionals South Africa needs in order to pursue its project of social transformation. This interpretation is framed by a list of eight public-good professional capabilities which we drew up by combining literature about the capabilities approach and ideal-type professionals with the analysis the interview data sets. What we are trying to do here is to show how a principled capability set can reveal possibilities that are not merely idealistic and allow an exploration in the space between realism and utopianism.

In the first part of the chapter, we gave a synoptic account of each profession in terms of the public-good professional capability set. The subheading for each intends to convey some the essence of each, which distinguishes it from other professions. Yet we should draw attention to what unites the professions: at a macro level all see themselves as part of South Africa's great and ambitious project of social transformation; and, at a micro level, all realize the crucial importance of transforming human relationships – whether with individuals or communities – to foreground equality, respect and dignity. From our perspective, such unity is a cause for celebration for it constitutes a decisive break with the degradations of the apartheid past. Furthermore, many of the efforts towards social transformation described take intelligence, serious hard work and courage. Nonetheless there were variations which might be worth considering. We found a sharp distinction between engineering and law on the one hand, and theology, social work and public health, on the other. We attempted above to characterize this variation by synecdoche conveying central values:

- Engineers value efficiency, creative problem-solving and honesty in dealings with clients and workers.
- Lawyers value knowing the law and placing the client first.

- Ministers value God's guidance in transforming themselves to transform the communities they work in.
- Social workers value being change agents who empower clients to grasp their rights.
- Public health professionals value understanding and addressing in policies and collaborative practices the complex determinants of health and health care.

The distinction can also be identified in a weak/strong dichotomy in terms of the specific capabilities informed vision and social and collective struggle; and, in terms of knowledge about the socio-economic, historical and political context of the professions and its work, and, of the empowerment dimension of the capability of affiliation. In the 'repairing'[5] professions these capabilities were strongly expressed; while in the 'shaping' profession of 'engineering' and the 'regulating' profession, they were weakly expressed.

At the level of conceptualization of the goals of public-good professional work, theology and social work seem to us unexpectedly close in that they both articulated strong and coherent visions of social transformation which incorporate close work with communities that empowers groups and individuals to solve their own problems. They differ in that theology is driven by a belief in God and a strong psychological need to mend the social divisions sanctioned, in the past, by the official white church. Social work, on the other hand, has been handed a policy mandate to develop communities by promoting self-determination and as a profession is motivated by a human rights agenda. Finally, public health, which we investigated through the lens of postgraduate, rather than undergraduate, education, was strongly driven by national and international policy which is underpinned by a sophisticated analysis about the complex determinants of health and health care.

As weak expressions of these capabilities and functionings, engineering participants prioritized completing work efficiently and honestly and, relative to other professional fields in our study, reflected a limited and indirect understanding of public-good professionalism: contributions to poverty reduction tend to rest on unproblematized understandings of the indirect benefits of aggregate economic growth or of improving the human capital skills of individuals living in poverty. Our law participants' weak expressions were differently inflected: they gave us the impression that (in their experience) there were few lawyers focused on broader, human rights issues, and, given their work in the clinic at Fynbos, this group were focused on knowing the law and prioritizing the client's needs.

It is possible now to draw up a table (Table 6.1) based as a heuristic referring to weak and strong manifestations of each public-good capability in each professional field.

The table represents tentative judgements on our part, which (like the identification of capabilities themselves) are open to challenge and debate. The judgements themselves are both theoretically and empirically derived. The empirical derivations rest on interpretations of what we were told, including

Table 6.1 Weak and strong manifestations of public-good capabilities

Capability	Engineering	Law	Theology	Social work	Public health
Informed vision	3	3	5	5	5
Knowledge and/or skills	5	5	5	5	5
Affiliation	3	4	5	5	5
Social and collective struggle	0	2	5	4	5
Resilience	5	5	5	5	5
Emotion reflexivity	0	2	5	3	3
Integrity	5	5	5	5	3
Assurance and confidence	5	4	5	5	3

0 = weak, 5 = strong.

interpretations of what was not explicit. Furthermore, the table elides the articulation of aims by our participants and statements about actual practices. Notwithstanding its impressionistic nature, it illustrates how questions might be raised in relation to a capability set in the absence of 'hard' measures. For example, assuming it is desirable to have all eight capabilities working strongly and coherently together, how can it be achieved? Or, why is it that emotional reflexivity appeared weakly in most professional fields?

It must be kept in mind when we evaluate conceptions of professional public-good capabilities in the professional fields that the picture painted here about professional public-good capabilities might or might not be similar to other sites where the same profession is taught or practised, that is, we are not pretending to making definitive comments about the state of the professions as a whole, in South Africa or elsewhere. Moreover, the reader should be reminded that each set of participants was in some way atypically interested in the pubic good. The engineering course and lecturers in Acacia were engaged in initiatives for community engagement, similarly for law at Fynbos; theology at Acacia employs academics who publish about the churches' role in social transformation; social work at Silvertree is directed by an expert in capabilities; and the Department of Public Health at Fynbos is a flagship Department in the area. So we do not aim to make general claims for what actually goes on everywhere, rather we aim to convey what possibilities and lacuna might look like in real-life settings. The real-life story about public-good professionalism which the eight capabilities tell unfolds as we consider how professional goals emerge as professional capabilities as thought about, taught, learned and practiced in specific settings.

While the concept of public-good professionalism was theoretically informed, the eight specific professional capabilities arose empirically from talking to the participants, who identified valuable functionings from which we extrapolated capabilities (see also Chapters 4 and 5). This chapter explores these conceptions as they were present or absent in talk and in pedagogical action, for example, in the goals and content of educational programmes. Yet, as noted in the previous chapter, whatever agreement emerges, it must be kept in mind that the spirit of the capability approach demands that the specification of professional capabilities should be collaborative, visible, defensible and revisable (Alkire, 2002). The capabilities are not universally complete or exact; they have been developed in specific contexts in post-apartheid, transformation-seeking South Africa. The purpose is public dialogue with others who may be interested in this approach to promoting public-good professionalism.

In South Africa professionals are seen as an essential element of the goal of social transformation, akin to how professionals were seen in relation to 'reconstruction' in the UK after the 1939–45 war (Clarke and Newman, 1997). What we have found in our investigations is by necessity a selective snapshot of the professional fields as they operate now and as they might in the future, if desired goals are achieved. Despite inevitable variation, we found a remarkable convergence of goals. South Africa's current context is one in which there are many clients who are living in extreme poverty and who have in the still recent past experienced serious humiliations and deprivations: in all accounts resounds the need for professionals to involve themselves in redress. The capabilities suggested by the professionals and student- professionals we talked to represent a different way of relating to and working with people who are living in conditions of social and economic deprivation. In this chapter we have hoped to convince readers that the co-construction of a public-good professional capability set is a process that has value for debate about setting goals and for providing both an evaluative space and a normative framework.

In most cases, as might be expected, the strongest expressions about public-good professional goals came from lecturers charged with the responsibility of educating the next generation of engineers, lawyers, ministers, social workers and public health professionals. It is fitting then at this point to turn to what they had to say about educational arrangements.

7 Pedagogical environments for the production of public-good professionals

> Education can have a crucial role in creating tomorrow's optimism in the context of today's pessimism.
>
> (Basil Bernstein, 2000: xix)

In the previous chapter we established the commonalities and variations of our five professional fields in terms of the conceptualization of public-good professionalism expressed as eight professional capabilities of the Index. In this chapter we take up the elements entitled 'educational arrangements' which encompass at the departmental level 'transformative curriculum', 'appropriate pedagogies' and, 'inclusive departmental culture'; and, at the university level: 'transformative culture and environment', 'being critical, deliberative and responsible' and 'being socially engaged'. The approach here is to take each department in turn to indicate what we were told in interview about how educational arrangements were deployed to support what we are calling public-good professional capability formation.

We can judge whether goals and processes as reported are more or less congruent. We can also report on and interpret what students claimed they gained from programmes of study. However, it should be kept in mind that the 'educational arrangements' that appear in the Index are normative, that is they convey ideal conditions for the production of public-good professionals. Moreover, we did not expect to find a close a fit between educational goals (which we have expressed as capabilities), educational arrangements, and the outcomes of teaching programmes. This is because constraints operate at all levels: from the level of the individual students to the national level, which we shall expand on in the next chapter. Crucially, within a national context of transformation, the departments themselves were in a dynamic process of transformation which was itself subject to ongoing factors beyond the agency of staff and students. We aim to show how the capability set provides an evaluative framework *and* prospective applications in terms of what educational arrangements might expand public-good professional capabilities, taking into account both enabling and constraining factors.

It is important again to remind the reader that we explored the pool of 'best-case' conceptions about what it means to be a public-good professional and this means both that we explored specific parts of curriculum designed for public-good professionalism and that we spoke to people with an interest in public-good professionalism. In the sections below, for each case an outline of educational arrangements in terms of curriculum and pedagogy in which messages are sent about professional ways of being is followed by a summary that distils educational arrangements in terms of advance towards and constraints upon university-based education for public-good professional capabilities. Our conclusion attempts to sketch commonality and variation in terms of public-good professionalism.

Training engineers at Acacia University

In the Engineering Department, we found a strong emphasis on producing graduates who are the country's best engineers: knowledgeable, analytic and practically skilled. Otherwise, we found much of the public-service curriculum residing in the fourth-year *Critical Perspectives on Society* module, introduced in the previous chapter, which was, in subsequent academic years, to be 'rolled out' to all the students in the department. Lectures on philosophy and political science provide a theoretical component aimed at developing students' understanding of the wider political context and the causes of poverty. The practical component involved students in tutoring secondary school students in mathematics and physical science at two secondary schools in disadvantaged communities close to Acacia. The module is high-profile within the department, and the white Head of Department, Marius de Beer, and white Dean, Thomas Ryer, thought that it represented a shared vision of future graduates who are aware of the realities of South Africa and the needs of poor and disadvantaged communities. Nevertheless, the main educational goal of the department is to 'put out' enough technically proficient engineers to strengthen the country's infrastructure as a basis for economic growth, because, at present, there are not enough engineers to undertake the task. So it was rare for an awareness of the realities of South African society (or, indeed, as we have seen in the previous chapter many of the other professional capabilities of the Index) to permeate any part of the course other than *Critical Perspectives on Society*, and, when it did, it depended on the individual lecturer.

The *Critical Perspectives on Society* students reported that they had acquired an increased understanding of South African politics and awareness of the realities of disadvantaged communities. For all the white students, entering such communities was a new and shocking experience. Pieter, a white student who had taken part described his reaction:

> You drive along the freeway and you see all the shacks. I've never been inside – and then we went in. You see the poverty and it is really bad how the people live [. . .] I think really something should be done.

Nevertheless, they appreciated being 'force [ed] out of comfort zones' (from an evaluation of the course); and black and coloured students, as Jaya, an Indian student, put it, were pleased to see their white classmates' 'eyes opened'. Though, coloured students, too, can express disbelief, Fabian, who is coloured, observed:

> Even we [coloured students] don't always understand the gap between rich and poor. But when you actually go from [names town where the university is situated] [. . .] the nice areas where the streets are so clean and then you go to an area like that where the houses are built of tin, old motor parts and stuff [. . .] how can we be in – not even the same country – just be in the same town and have those extremes?

South African elite society avoids seeing the extreme poverty that exists (as the white engineering lecturer Christo van Heerdon put it 'they won't expose themselves'). So it should be appreciated that this educational experience was engendering discomfort, frustration and feelings of rebellion about the status quo: students in an elite university were being oriented to 'do something about it'. Yet students were also repelled and could not analyse or suggest solutions, for example, Fabian described how he felt in the township:

> [We] could see sewage, and the school smelled of stale urine in some places, I mean, in the school. I can't understand that, I think something should really be done about that. I don't know what, but something [. . .] I wouldn't want to be there at night because it's really scary and dangerous.

So here was a sense that an informed vision had not emerged: the world of poverty that the students went into was a curious 'other' rather than a catalyst for re-framing their world views.

The main goal of Marian Lamprecht, the white lead lecturer for *Critical Perspectives on Society*, was to invoke in students a sense of affiliation with the children they taught. She wanted the students to understand, for example, that 'these kids might not be attentive because they hadn't been eating for the whole day, or they hadn't slept properly'. Some students did realize that people living in poverty are, as Pieter expressed it, 'the same as us just in different circumstances' and that, in Fabian's words, they 'have their big dreams, the same as the kid who comes from the cleaner town'. Affiliation was expressed also in the students' satisfaction at having helped children. Pedagogical attempts to inculcate integrity occurred in modules such as 'project management' and 'environmental engineering' in the form of business ethics and environmental awareness; and, again most explicitly in *Critical Perspectives on Society*. Such attempts encouraged students to think about how as future engineers they will consider the needs of communities and act honestly, responsibly and respectfully. More implicitly, the work in the township prompted students to reflect about their responsibilities towards people living in poverty; and the first-hand, practical experience might have had a deep and lasting effect in terms of pro-poor value formation:

> [I]t is a good reminder of how privileged we are [. . .] it is thus important for us to have an understanding about the less fortunate communities around us, and that we take them into consideration when we do the work that is expected of us (from an evaluation of the course).

While there was disagreement among the participants about the extent to which values can be taught, the students reported that they learned 'a lot about qualities and values', as the black African student Mandla put it, and were exposed to new ideas. On the whole, though, students were not explicitly encouraged to consider the value of being oriented to poverty reduction. Exceptionally, the young lecturers Christo van Heerden and Jonathan Landsman, who is black African, told us about their eagerness to integrate an interest in community into their mainstream teaching 'upliftment' by using community projects as cases to discuss. They felt, though, that they were going against the grain.

Summary

The central importance of acquiring engineering *knowledge and skills* and of producing innovative problem solvers permeates the courses. It was the conviction that the students were being educated as the country's best engineers, along with the high status that engineers enjoy in society that bestowed on students a sense of *assurance and confidence* about what they can contribute to society. For the department, the embrace of the *Critical Perspectives on Society* programme and its move eventually to enrol all students demonstrates a bold vision of producing engineers more inclined to work for poverty reduction. In this module the capabilities of *informed vision, affiliation* and *integrity* are clearly in focus.

What we see in engineering is still far away from the strongly formulated version of public-good professionalism embodied in the Index, particularly if we keep in mind that our participants are the most poverty-aware in the context of engineering at Acacia. Students were being made aware of the realities of poverty and about the South African political system past and present. But the limits were evident: affiliation was hard to achieve and appeared to be rare; and, in terms of the capability of *social and collective struggle*, students did not talk about the value of engineers working collectively to alleviate poverty, particularly in a radical and transformative sense. Nor were students specifically prepared for the *resilience* needed to face the trials and hardships of poverty alleviation work, which, as our two committed lecturers made clear, demands more than the usual professional resilience.

Despite evident limits, for us, what is going on in the engineering department at Acacia amounts to progress towards transforming engineering professional education in the direction of public-good professionalism. At the departmental management level, interest in values associated with affiliation was heard in the Head of Department, Marius Beer's determination to create a departmental culture based on respect and on understanding and acceptance of racial difference. Teaching methods are a way of building this culture: there was a strategy to organize mixed gender and race study groups. Moreover, there had been a shift to a new 'parallel language medium of instruction' policy which allows students to attend lectures in either English or Afrikans. The historic language of instruction was Afrikans – and is still the primary language of teaching and social interaction – which disadvantages Xhosa and English-speaking black students. As the Dean pointed out, to serve the public good in South Africa, students need to know several languages to communicate well and appropriately.

Furthermore, it is not only in South Africa that social values in engineering might seem underplayed. A report on engineering education in the US concludes that 'students have few opportunities to explore the implications of being a professional in society' (Sheppard *et al.*, 2008: 6) especially ethical issues. And an adaptation of Sen's idea of 'comparative justice' allows 'cautious optimism': whether the steps being taken are evaluated as small or large depends on perspective. The Dean, Thomas Ryer, claims a significant achievement in the shift in the department 'to where we are today'. He detects the same shift within colleagues in engineering faculties across the country: 'It's engineering in [a social and political] context, it's not anymore engineering just for the sake of technical issues.'

Legal education at Fynbos University

The first aim of the law curriculum at Fynbos is to instil graduates with a thorough disciplinary knowledge of South African law. Within this, despite the lack of evidence for informed vision in the profession as a whole, Fynbos law students are provided with an understanding of how the profession is shaped by the current and historical socio-economic and political context. Courses in the LLB include critical knowledge of the historical development of certain strands of law, and knowledge of human rights law, including gender law; HIV/AIDS and the law; international human rights law; and the South African Bill of Rights.

The elective *Legal Process* module, which was the focus of the study, was a particularly powerful vehicle for advancing the public-good professional capabilities of the students. At the heart of the elective is practical experience at the Fynbos Legal Aid Clinic. The department pays for two legal clinicians so that students can learn through supervised practice, and it allows students to obtain course credits. The clinical experience does not aim to guide students towards community-level work, but rather to give them knowledge and skills for a variety of branches of law and to create lawyers who will be able to practice confidently and competently. Shamiel Jessop, a coloured Afrikaans-speaking lecturer, explained how 'the focus is now more on trying to train the students to think for themselves and not only to study from the textbook'.

Practical experience greatly enhances the acquisition of knowledge and skills by integrating theory and practice. For example, Zubeida a Muslim, coloured female law student, was of the opinion that:

> The *Legal Process* is excellent because it gives you practical experience and also forces you to see what type of incidents the people on the ground face [. . .] we have many cases of eviction and it tells you what it entails, the eviction, and how you go about it, how you can come to get maintenance [from an ex-husband] [. . .] which you learn about in theory, but you don't really know what it is until you get here.

In addition, working with poor clients raised awareness of poverty and diversity and encouraged the functionings of affiliation. For example, Themba Vilikazi, who was a black African alumnus now working as a legal advisor for the State, thought that the *Legal Process* elective at Fynbos

> [T]aught you to care about other people's situations and it taught you that there are people that are suffering outside in different ways, whether you're a refugee, whether you're a woman, it doesn't matter, but you learn a lot from it and that's how you find yourself.

Lecturers on the elective and in the curriculum as a whole strove to encourage the students to develop empathy, respecting client wishes and understanding the position of the client. The module also engendered resilience among the students. Themba Vilikazi went on to say:

> At first it was difficult to work with divorce matters because people were emotional and at the beginning I ended taking problems and making them mine, but my supervisors taught me that I had to separate the two, and that I had to be objective. I learned slowly, but surely, that I was able to do that.

A similar degree of emotional reflexivity in terms of keeping an emotional distance came from others (while still manifesting compassion), for example, Yusuf, a coloured student explained the difficulty:

> I find that's the hardest part for me, what do you tell the client, once you go home you have to do this or that [. . .] we are not psychologists, even though we play the part of a psychologist, we are not, we can't solve this person's problem [. . .] So we try to make them as comfortable as possible [. . .] and it is very difficult.

Khatidja Bashir is coloured and Director of the Clinic and of the *Legal Process* elective. She is keen that the clinical model should be adopted for all students through all four years of their degree, so that no matter what career direction each student chooses, they have been given some form of social consciousness, which she believes cannot be taught through lecturing: 'social consciousness, you can't teach in class, it's impossible'.

More broadly than the *Legal Process* module, awareness and understanding of diversity arises from experiences within the classroom, as well as the Legal Aid Clinic. Lecturers spoke of how they draw on diversity of the student body in their teaching to raise awareness of different socio-economic backgrounds: for example, the lecturer Shamiel Jessop talked about how teaching depends on getting to know the students: 'We look at backgrounds, where they're from [. . .] so you can draw from that experience and that also assists not only students but myself as well as the person standing in front.'

Jennifer is a coloured student, whose account concurred:

Some of [the students] are from other parts of South Africa, like Eastern Cape, and even Zimbabwe, so that also helps you to be able to understand Africa, not just be limited to Western Cape. So also being able to interact with so many different people and cultures, it helps a lot [to be receptive to diversity is] not exactly a good way to look at it 'cos then you're closing yourself up to what you could do.

In student focus groups there was general agreement that the department aimed to instil values and integrity among its students, Alice, a coloured law student, explained:

I think that [. . .] the law department wants us to [. . .] [be] trustworthy, people are coming to you with their problems and they want you to have the right etiquette [. . .] if you're coming out of the clinic they don't want you to be the lawyers that are into fraud and all these bad things. I think Fynbos wants lawyers to be trustworthy with respect and caring.

Some students saw these values as a crucial part of Fynbos's identity, of which they were proud and wanted to show the world. The Department strives to instill discipline, punctuality, reliability, and communication skills. Leonard Smith, the coloured Deputy Dean, observed that these efforts are of particular significance for many of the students will have come from deprived backgrounds in which they might have become accustomed to 'cutting corners' as a basic survival mechanism; or they might not have been taught such principles because their schools were badly run.

Leonard Smith claimed that teaching is directed towards inculcating the values of service, whoever the client:

The fact that you are serving an illiterate or innumerate or underprivileged or undereducated community does not mean that you have to be less professional [. . .] we try and inspire or let these values rub off in the way we interact with the students in class, just to drive home the fact that being a lawyer means service and service to the other means being professional.

In general, participants felt it centrally important that a law course should enable students to discover their authentic, valued goals, and enable them to pursue them in their professional life. This was underpinned by professional ethics of hard work and trustworthiness, which are hard won. As Themba Vilikazi, state legal advisor and alumni of Fynbos, explained: 'To be honest, it's not an easy thing, it's hard work, those assignments [. . .] [but] those things that we take for granted at the time, they build you for the future'. And the student Sandra was emphatic about being ethical throughout a career: 'The principle which has been brought across to me is that in whatever field you go into, maintain principle, maintain what is right and what is the truth basically and be honest in whatever you do.'

Summary

Similarly to engineering, *knowledge and skills* are at the heart of legal education at Fynbos, without these nothing else follows, in particular *assurance and confidence* about practising as a lawyer. Based on the students we spoke to who have chosen to take the *Legal Process* module an encouraging narrative emerges about the possibilities for public-good professional education. Notwithstanding that *informed vision* resides mainly with the lectures, rather than students, the students demonstrated *affiliation*, seeing themselves as expanding the capabilities of people living in poverty in terms of respect and recognition for their dignity and humanity. While studying law was perceived as a route to exercising control and change in students' own lives; they also appeared to have a sense of obligations to others within some understanding of the realities of South African society. This orientation found strong support in the department and the university as a whole. It was also in the context of the *Legal Process* module by way of actual practice that students saw the need for *resilience* and a weakly expressed *emotional reflexivity*. Yet there was no evidence that students believe that feasible and efficacious means of improving the lot of people living in poverty exist or might be created through *social and collective* action – their focus is almost exclusively on being advocates for poor people. In the department as a whole strong messages about professional ways of behaving were being sent to students, in particular about various aspects of *integrity*.

There were significant educational constraints. The four-year curriculum was crowded leaving little opportunity as in the past for wider exposure to subjects like criminology, language courses, political science, and economics. Student numbers were very high and the level of student preparedness problematic after their poor levels of schooling, while pressures from home facing students from disadvantaged backgrounds (e.g. having to send some of their bursary money home) was also a hindrance to learning. Finally, among the members of staff at the department, none are African so the department itself lacks full diversity.

Teaching theology at Acacia University

Training to be a church minister at Acacia is lengthy. The Bachelor of Theology (BTh) is a four-year degree offered to students who intend to be ministers, as well as others who have an interest in theology or community work. After this, in order to qualify as a minister, students need to take a one-year Master's in Divinity and a one-year Licentiate in Theology, which consists mainly of practical 'on-site' training under supervision in local congregations, in association with reading and writing components. The main focus of our research was on the Practical Theology course within the BTh degree, which aims to teach practical aspects of the work of a minister, including degree subjects such as preaching, pastoral care and congregation studies.

The alumni interviewed had all started their course too early for the changes described above to take effect. Therefore, they provided an insight into the problems of the previous curriculum which was based on an American model predicated on idealized conditions and which emphasized the role of the 'minister in a congregation' rather than a pastoral role. The alumni agreed that they had not been trained to be pastors in the poverty-stricken communities in which they all now worked.[1] At the time of interview, much of the discussion of the curriculum focused on the balance between theory and practice and on efforts to include a far stronger practical component. However, according to coloured alumnus André van Wyk, even now opportunities offered by the poor black townships surrounding Acacia are being missed:

> [The Department should make use of these opportunities] to equip us better for when you go into ministry [. . .] Things like community projects, care of HIV/AIDS people, vegetable gardens, assisting people on the farms with basic rights, with basic knowledge, employment projects [. . .] At the end of the day that will empower us with certain skills and how to utilize that in the community that we are going to serve.

The cohort of fourth-year students we spoke to confirmed that they had been exposed to little practical experience in their formal curriculum, though some had gained such experience by way of involvement in church groups, which they had joined on their own initiative.

Nevertheless, the department was clearly responsive to feedback and in 2008 a six-month service learning course was introduced into the Practical Theology Curriculum (our interviewees had yet to take this course), which, according to Jan Hofmeyer, who is a white lecturer and the lecturer responsible, aims to give the students 'a practical theological framework in which they can start to interpret culture, the needs of people within different communities and look at the different ways in which faith communities operate'.

At the heart of any theology curriculum is interpretations of the scriptures. The lecturer Jan Hofmeyer was clear about the role of theological texts, 'the scriptures, in this case of the Christian tradition and Christian theology, paint imaginative alternatives'. The approach of looking for alternative perspectives and traditions was taken with church history too. For example, students were being encouraged to listen to the voices of women and the marginalized in scripture or in history, which tend to be silenced in traditional theological interpretations. Jan Hofmeyer continued to say that students also study various theologies such as liberation or feminist theologies which pose 'imaginative alternatives to the traditional theologies'. He believed that it was imagination that enabled people to envision a new reality, and to make the slow and difficult transition from existing conditions to a reality closer to the ideal.

Daniel le Roux, a white theology lecturer, thought that the immediate diversification of students resulting from the merger (of the theology departments at Fynbos and Acacia) had been both difficult and enriching because it helped the white students understand poverty and inequality: it was not possible to 'talk in an abstract way about poverty' because students from very poor, rural areas tell 'real-life stories' about poverty. A concrete illustration of affiliation concerned the ordination ceremonies which used to be separate for the URCSA and DRC students. A few years ago it was students themselves who insisted on a joint ceremony, which has since become standard practice.

There was a common view among the fourth-year students that they were exposed to a range of perspectives in their courses and that their lecturers encouraged them to be critical, open-minded and independent thinkers. Peter, a white theology student, provided a vivid example:

> You've been taught things for twenty years and now suddenly a lecturer walks into a class and says 'You know what, Daniel was never in the lions' den, it's a folk myth, it's a tale they told in Exodus to get people's morale up' and you sit there and think 'I based my religion on that'.

In similar vein Nico, a white student, described having his assumptions challenged:

> You come here with a lot of views and perspectives on what you want to do, conceptions of what theology is about and what the ministry's about and then you get here and you start to realize that what you actually thought it is beforehand, is not exactly what it is.

Students were encouraged to develop complex and nuanced understandings of religious issues and social problems. As Aidan, a coloured theology student, put it:

> There are a lot of grey areas. In those grey areas there's room for creativity to come forth. When something is cut and dry, black and white, there's no real struggle, 'cause it's clear, but in the grey area there's a struggle, there has to be a self-examination on your own viewpoints and other people's viewpoints and what the church teaches and how to make sense of all of that and so I think it opens up your mind definitely to different perspectives.

In this respect, the new service-learning courses emphasized linking theory and practice through what is recognizably a 'reflective practitioner' model (Schön, 1983). The lecturer Jan Hofmeyr described the academic expectations. Students were required to:

> Link what [they] did immediately during that week in practice [. . .] be it through a mentor or having a conversation with a person on an individual basis [. . .] there's a conversation the whole time so that when they come back and they give feedback, they've also got to write down what they experience there and bring it back to class – you've got a theory–practice interaction the whole time. So you put the theory on the table and then they go and experience it and come back and reflect whether the theory is sound or whether they experience different things from what the theory is teaching.

The purpose of visiting, for example, informal settlements (squatter communities), Jan went on, was for students to be exposed to and begin to understand 'what it means to live in circumstances like that'. The students undertook structured interviews with residents and community leaders, asking questions like, 'What's life like in an informal settlement? In what ways can faith communities help you?' Jan aimed to get students to think both theoretically and strategically about how they might change circumstances for these people as future ministers who might take a leadership role in similar communities.

All groups emphasized the value of the discussion and debates which formed a significant part of practical theology and the department as a whole. They referred to discussions about poverty and inequality in society, and the role of ministers in the church and community. They also spoke about how relational aspects of dialogue facilitate growth and individual transformation. The lecturer Daniel le Roux emphasized the importance of bringing into the open and confronting 'sensitive issues' even if it caused conflict:

> Actually we want that, we want people not to sidestep the issues but to talk. We've got a whole module on conflict management where sometimes the debates get heated. The person lecturing will open up sensitive issues concerning poverty, race, gender [. . .] sexual orientation, you can name it, because we want to stimulate dialogue, we want to bring this out into the open.

However, this approach was not universal. Students also had lecturers who, they felt, closed down debate: a white student, Inez, for example, drew attention to how social divisions played out in classrooms and was ignored:

> I wish that the lecturers could help us to be made aware of the challenges and issues that we face right now within our class, within the people that we have sitting right in front of us. I often feel that it's all about how you will become a minister, but that you should instead be made aware of [how to relate to

other people] right now in this context [. . .] I mean sometimes you notice that there is a line of white people on one side and coloured people on another side. And the separations that we experience in the macro world, we see here, but we're not [made] aware of them.

Some students noted that there were also long-established lecturers who maintained the conservative views which had characterized the department in the past: Peter commented that 'You sit in their classes and you still get this faint aftertaste of apartheid in your mouth.'

Nevertheless, by and large we heard from students that lecturers were role models for students. For example, Adele, a white student, was inspired by

The way that they treat us [. . .] as people with intelligence who can think for themselves and can ask and answer questions. [It] gives you a sense of identity and [. . .] inspires me to go and give that to somebody else as well, when I go and work in a community.

Notwithstanding his earlier comment, Peter observed of one lecturer: 'You sit here and feel so welcome in these surroundings and despite age, race, colour, gender, he treats everybody equally.' For the Department, it was important for all students to have black lecturers as role models. In 2008 the department still had a significant majority of white lecturers (69 per cent), while 23 per cent of the lecturers were coloured and 8 per cent were African. It was symbolically highly significant for the university that the Vice Chancellor was black, and the Theology Department was particularly proud because he had previously worked in the Department.

Summary

Taken as a whole, the education of the students is rhetorically strongly focused on producing a generation of theologians who will be leaders and take an active part in social transformation, so an *informed vision* is emphasized and in this case the values of Christianity take a large part (in this sense, *integrity* is taken for granted). Simultaneously, though, students are expected to be highly committed to the public good and poverty reduction and are being educated to be critical and knowledgeable about the South African context. *Affiliation* is the key capability. Students are expected to develop understanding of and compassion for people living in poverty and to have people and management skills. The personal transformation of students and hence *emotional reflexivity* is central, and this task is inflected differently, depending on background, colour and which church the student will work for in the future. The unity across barriers of race, class and denomination that students experience in the department is seen as developing values that they will take into their working lives. The *knowledge and skills* base and the *assurance and confidence* that might flow from acquiring them is somewhat nebulous and concerns, in the main, management of people, including being prepared to be involved in *social and collective struggle*. The alumni indicated that *resilience* has had to be learned on the job and that they had not been well prepared. In future, the establishment of more practical elements might address this problem.

Despite the strong focus on personal transformation there was a sense that more could be done to facilitate students' reflection on the way that apartheid has influenced their own assumptions and ways of interacting. As Inez does above, some students spoke about a focus of students on problems in the world outside the classroom, while they lack awareness of these same problems manifesting themselves in the micro contexts which they inhabit in the department. However, the transformation of the department is an ongoing process and as the Head of Department Jakob Steyn, who is coloured, noted: 'Every day we still have to struggle together [and] nothing can be taken for granted.'

Social work education at Silvertree University

To practice as professional social workers, students undertake a four-year Bachelor of Social Work degree programme which complies with the requirements of the South African Council for Social Service Professionals (SACSSP). The core course consists of a combination of social work, psychology and sociology with specialized streams dealing with clinical practice in social work, social development, social policy and management, and probation and correctional practice. These are intended to make the curriculum more relevant and responsive to the needs of South African society, and to enhance the capabilities of students to contribute to processes of transformation in their fields of practice and in the welfare system.

Elizabeth Goodwin, a white lecturer, envisioned graduates in a wide range of settings. They would:

> Work in any sector, whether it's a clinical setting [such as] a psychiatric hospital or whether it's in a neighbourhood working at a development organization, or whether it's in the policy division of the department of social work, or whether it's working in the profit-making sector like for Volkswagen.

So curriculum and pedagogy are geared to produce social workers who are effective change agents, and as Dorothy Williams, an Indian lecturer put it, can 'bring about transformation at whatever level they find themselves [. . .] whether they set up in the corporate sector or whether they're in a very humble NGO'.

Yet one of the main challenges which lecturers in the department wanted to address related to affiliation. It was the lack of exposure of their middle-class, 'sheltered' undergraduate students to the realities of poverty in South Africa. The legacy of apartheid urban and rural geographies means that many white and now a new black middle-class have little contact with people living in conditions of severe deprivation and poverty. A white lecturer, Amanda Hoffman, pointed out that older postgraduate students were aware of the apartheid history of South Africa, as they had lived 'through a whole lot of the major events of the transformation of the country'. However, Amanda claims that on the whole:

> You're dealing with kids who [say] 'The what uprising?' 'The who?' and that is a whole challenge because our graduates have to go out with a very good understanding of why things are the way that they are, where our country's come from and what is impacting on the current that's come from the past. You can't understand the present if you don't understand the past.

Both lecturers and students articulated the need for students to understand how such problems manifest in individuals and families in communities and in broader society. The first-year course introduced content about the political, economic and social contexts which affected social work practice in South Africa. For example, *Community Connections* aimed to 'develop students' understanding of the interactions between different social systems in the context of selected contemporary social issues' (course handbook). In the second and third years the students did modules on the political economy of the social services. Here the Department aimed to deepen and broaden students' understandings of macro contexts of professional practice. Miriam Grey, the Head of Department, who is white, told us that there were also modules on 'contemporary social problems, HIV/AIDS, sexuality and the importance of the Constitution and understanding professional ethics in a changed environment'. Within the course, critical theory is emphasized. Dorothy Williams, a lecturer, told us that a critical, reflective professional approach was 'informed by a whole range of people like Gramsci and Habermas, particularly Paulo Freire's education for critical consciousness, and barefoot economist, Max-Neef'.

While the degree programme expressed a commitment to developing an informed vision, the value of the practical component was strongly emphasized: experiencing realities; gaining confidence and resilience; and integrating theory and practice. There are placements in NGOs or communities from the second year where students assess problems and resources in partnership with members of a poor community. During a third-year placement, students facilitated development projects, with the objective of considering the sustainability of the project by 'connecting with other key organizations and task groups which is vitally important, so that's a theory plus practice component which gets integrated at that point' (a comment by a lecturer during a research working group meeting). During their fourth year, students spent most of their time working in placement organizations and produced a research project.

The benefits of the placements are mediated by supervisors (some of whom were reported by students to be better than others at helping them) to cope with their responses to harsh realities. Dorothy Williams emphasized the importance of supporting students to work through their experiences 'theoretically, intellectually, but also emotionally'. And Elizabeth Goodwin claimed that the department strove to help students to:

Build the resilience to survive the course as a student because I believe that we really can't protect the students from reality, that it would be better for them to hit some of these awful things while they have a total system supporting them than once they get out in practice where often they [may not] even get decent supervision.

Certainly, experiences on placements invoked the need for support with 'emotional reflexivity'. For example, Sharon, an Indian student who had recently been on placement, reported that: 'I went away with feeling a whole lot of different feelings that were evoked and not knowing what to do with this.'

It is where theory and practice meet that the students are seen to develop reflexivity and Miriam Grey, the Head of Department, emphasized its importance in professional work:

We don't expect our graduates to think that after a four-year generic degree they have arrived, there has to be this constant reflection in practice [. . .] And if there's anything that we would want to emphasize in our training and education it is that this has to be a lifelong cycle for our graduates that in the professional work setting, they need to reflect not just what they're doing but their ability to do it and learn from what has happened.

Lecturers argued that studying psychological theory helped the students to understand the psychological dimensions of clients' issues and problems and to engage with these clients in an effective way. Furthermore, it developed self-insight and resilience, Dorothy Williams described the process:

Our students come in here as very green eighteen-year-olds [. . .] and very often it comes from their own backgrounds, they come in as wounded healers as it were, [. . .] and they come on a journey [. . .] the first year is actually more of a self-discovery of who I am and [they have a lot of exposure to] the psychology of self in terms of defence mechanisms and group dynamics and family therapy and [. . .] they have access to the staff members in terms of what's happening to them and very often they come out of a human sexuality class and then actually say 'I've been abused'. We encourage them to go for counselling.

Throughout the undergraduate curriculum there is an emphasis on relationships with civil society organizations, with government organizations at different levels as well as with the private sector. The Head of Department, Miriam Grey, highlighted the role of social work in transformation: 'So social work is actually determined by the level of interaction that takes place between government and civil society and they become the bridge between government action or inaction and community-based structures.' In addition, the department aimed to enhance the knowledge and skills necessary for higher-level policy formulation, managing departments and institutions, and managing social change.

Lecturers were attentive to pedagogic processes. Dorothy Williams described the Department's pedagogical efforts to balance didactic teaching with 'the experiential stuff and it's about translating and not reproducing that same pattern of discrimination and inequality in the way we design the curriculum and the way we carry out the work'. There had been some increase of black students from extremely disadvantaged backgrounds after 1994, and Dorothy commented that this had:

> Impacted on the whole pedagogical approach to the students [leading to thinking of] alternative ways [. . .] of bridging that gap between high school and the university and that was exciting for us, was a new learning curve in that we brought in educational specialists to help.

Addressing these challenges demanded commitment and investment of time from staff and according to the lecturer Elizabeth Goodwin, the Department was known as having one of the best completion rates at the university.

There has also been a task to engage students in dealing with diversity. For example, by entering into a contract with them to practise respect in the classroom as a way of bringing values and the professional code of conduct into their classroom interactions; or by openly discussing critical incidents experienced in placements or daily life. More generally, students were being encouraged to engage with different viewpoints. Lecturers also acted as role models. Elizabeth Goodwin reflected on how:

> At the beginning when I taught, my black students would sit in pockets and cliques and the white students would sit separately. Over the years I've seen that change and it's changed because they've also seen how we as staff behave with each other and I think a lot of modelling happens at that point when they actually meet the staff, see them in staff meetings 'cos we have students and staff meeting together and the way we engage with them in the classroom. There are problems, I wouldn't say there aren't, because I think it goes along with prejudice and prejudice reduction stuff happens over time.

Throughout the programme students were taught to speak in public, to formulate and voice their own views on issues, and to communicate with a diverse range of people. In the fourth year, students were required to present the findings of their research projects to the whole department and to members of some of the placement agencies. Students gained greatly in confidence: for example, Mary, an African social work student thought, 'It develops you into a public person, to speak for other people, to speak in front of people [. . .] I used to be very timid speaking in front of people.' A white student, Carla, described how she has overcome lack of confidence:

> Before coming to university I've always had this thing [. . .] I can't really challenge what they're saying because they know what they're talking about.

Whereas since being in the department I've challenged a lot of things [...] And now I feel [...] I could probably go talk to the State President and not have a problem with it, but then I could also go and talk to somebody who has never gone to school and be able to be at their level as well. So [...] in that way I've really developed as a person through my studies.

Heavy emphasis was placed on inquiry learning. A small third-year research project was seen as preparation for the larger fourth-year project which is carried out in collaboration with government departments. The aim was that students learn the skills and value of applied research and heighten their awareness of relationships, partnerships and coordination between different government departments in facilitating transformation.

Summary

The Head of Department, Miriam Grey, espoused a human development approach reflected in the Social Work Department's integrated and coherent approach to educating social workers as change agents oriented to the public good, in particular to poverty reduction. All eight capabilities were strongly in evidence in what we heard and read about curriculum and pedagogy. An *informed vision* permeated the curriculum, while *knowledge and skills* were taught through judiciously relating theory and practice. Extensive placements supported by supervision developed the capabilities of *affiliation, resilience and emotional reflexivity*. Empathy, caring, and above all, having respect for diverse people were seen as the basic qualities that the education and training of social workers should inculcate. And these qualities were contrasted to a competitive, individualistic and materialistic approach prevalent in the broader society. Miriam Grey proposed that the Department wanted to show students alternatives:

> There is another way of doing things that is not rooted in this individualistic society and that is not as competitive; and that's really hard for graduates to take on board. Because everywhere else they engage with competition and individualism as a driving force.

Strong messages about expectation to engage in *social and collective struggle* were sent, along with some opportunities given to develop skills of managing people, making networks and public speaking that are necessary to function. Students and alumni evidently develop *confidence and assurance* from the demands and quality of their education and there seemed to be a special effort at engendering pride in the profession in the context of lack of clear and strong professional identity. All groups of participants strongly projected innovative, flexible and adaptable social workers who can integrate the roles of clinical social work; development or community work; and for some, policy development.

Educating public health professionals at Fynbos University

The central goals of the postgraduate programme which was the focus of our study were to increase and deepen health professionals' knowledge and understanding of the health system in the South African and other African contexts as well as in relation to global factors; and to build the capacity of health professionals to perceive and apply this knowledge and understanding to their own contexts and practices. The programme was offered through a combination of distance learning and optional contact sessions which allowed the capacity of health professionals across Africa to be built without taking them out of an under-resourced health system, though there were difficulties of access to resources for students living in remote areas. It consisted of two postgraduate courses of study: a postgraduate diploma in public health which could lead on to a Master's in Public Health (MPH) which consisted of coursework and a dissertation. The MPH was the main focus of our study. The open learning nature of the programme allowed students to choose whether to complete the MPH within two or three years. The MPH consists of six coursework modules and a dissertation. The modules are Health, Development and Primary Health Care (core module); Measuring Health and Disease (core module); Understanding Public Health (core module); Health Systems Research; Elective module 1; Elective module 2 (2009 Student Handbook). In the second year, the students also start working on their dissertation which they would aim to complete in the third year (2009 Student Handbook).

There appeared to be a close relationship between the goals of the programme and the content of the curriculum. Taken together, the modules dealt with public health within South African historical, political and socio-economic contexts as well as global trends in health care. We heard from the Head of Department Michael Andrews, who is white, that the modules include: 'A notion of equity and the historical perspective on health improvement and an understanding of how globalization is impacting on health and so on. And then what kinds of health policies are appropriate in response to this situation.' The modules combined to enable health professionals to bring a critical and analytical insight into public health decision making by providing tools and skills for the assessment and interpretation of health problems.

A central plank of the department's vision was for health practitioners to understand health and health care in relation to multiple and interrelated social determinants. For example, Thumi, a black African health professional who had been working in a small hospital in the Eastern Cape (an impoverished region in South Africa) told us how before her studies in public health, she would scold a woman who came in with a malnourished child, as if the malnutrition was a product of the mother's negligence, and treated it purely as a medical problem. As a result of her involvement in the postgraduate programme, she had learned to see malnutrition within a broader context. She started to understand all the informants of that malnutrition and was able to respond differently and more productively.

Implementing new policies and transformation of the health system require strong capacity for management. In the old system, management skills were lacking in health professionals who were responsible for implementing changes. For example, alumna Nomvuyo Langa, a black African manager of a nutrition programme in the DOH, reported to us that her programme needed to work in conjunction with partners within the DOH, such as environmental health, mother and child and women's health. Furthermore, there was a need to work with other government departments such as the departments of agriculture, social development and water affairs. The programme had assisted her to see the importance of making these connections.

In general, the capacity to make such connections was emphasized. Public health needs linkages between different government departments in order to address health issues in relation to multiple determinants of health. Partnerships needed to be formed, sustained and used productively between health facilities and NGOs. Furthermore, there is a need for public–private partnerships to achieve health-care goals. In order to achieve these linkages and partnerships health professionals needed to be knowledgeable about the health-care system. Students repeated to us that they needed to be able to co-ordinate and facilitate. A number of informants emphasized the need for advocacy skills to promote a multi-sectoral approach and to influence decision makers. Public health workers should be able to identify critical stakeholders and create platforms for lobbying. Moreover, they needed to be able to mobilize resources, and set up networking between different groupings.

The value of doing research was strongly supported by many of the students and alumni and the dissertation was an important vehicle for learning to think critically, for engaging in problem-solving, and for developing an inquiring approach to knowledge and a reflective approach to practice. Lecturers thought that student professionals needed to know basic research principles in order to be able to read and understand literature reporting on research and to apply knowledge based on research findings in their work. Community participation is a fundamental dimension of a primary health-care approach, and so it follows that action research and participatory research are encouraged in the programme.

Pedagogically, the programme was based on adult education principles. Jane Simons, the Programme Coordinator, claimed that students were treated as colleagues and practitioners with a strong emphasis on 'equalizing the relationship between educator and student'. The distance learning materials were written in an informal voice, getting students to formulate opinions which the lecturers showed respect for. She described the approach as a 'facilitated, constructivist approach' particularly in the contact sessions, which involved a lot of group work and interaction. Alumni supported the claim by reporting to us that doing the programme had encouraged them to build equal, respectful and reciprocal relationships with poor people. This view corresponded with Jane's description of the course materials as 'infused with a community-orientated, consultative, caring approach to communities'. Alumni told us that that the lecturers had not imposed their views on them when they were students, but rather had encouraged them to be independent thinkers: for example, Laura Bailey, a coloured alumna who worked for an NGO, reported that'they were not dictators, they were trying to get us to be independent and to think and encouraged us and did support us'.

An important pedagogical principle was to encourage critical thinking. Members of the department argued that an effect of apartheid was that 'many health workers in South Africa, although clinically competent, are unable to problem solve, interpret policy or manage and evaluate their own work' (Annual Report 2006). While the national health policy promotes comprehensive primary health care, many of the policy makers, managers, and implementers of programmes are not sufficiently critical of systems, structures, processes and practices which work against the transformation of the health care system either because they were carried over from the old system or because new interventions contradict the principles of the stated policy (ibid.).

There was a strong emphasis on application to practice. Michael Andrews, the Head of Department, explained that the learning became 'concrete or applied to the extent that we do get students to engage with how they would apply these sorts of concepts and approaches in their own work settings'. The fact that students were practising professionals provided rich opportunities for practice-based learning which needed a creative pedagogical approach. Liziwe Mabi, a black African alumna, praised the programme for its experiential character, for example, 'community-based education on problem-orientated type of educational methodology and other approaches towards teaching, built around cases or scenarios'. Distance learning required materials being designed in an interactive format, and the integration of experiential learning into the design of tasks and assignments, through relating them to students' work practice.

To mitigate the lack of contact, marking of assignments was seen as a form of dialogue with students. The policy on marking was that lecturers should give extensive feedback on students' assignments within three weeks of submission, though some lecturers did not comply. Attention had been paid to making assessment congruent with the goals of the programme. As the coloured lecturer Paul Daniels observed:

> We want students to be able to apply what they've learnt in their own setting. That would be a key output for us, which is also why we don't have exams [. . .] and why we teach in a problem-based way.

Students concurred, explaining how assignments were designed in such a way that they required practical application. Tsidi, who was black African from another African country, described how the programme is useful:

> [Assignments are] structured in a way that you have to go to somewhere as if you are working there to get the information [. . .] For instance, with the monitoring and evaluation module we were given an opportunity to look at a programme or an intervention that is running, and you do monitoring and evaluation on that programme. It gives you a practical theme and you also

learn through that because you develop your own monitoring and evaluation systems to do it. And then in the second assignment you evaluate the programme. You do the actual evaluation.

Students were provided with opportunities to improve their work as it proceeded by sending drafts of assignments for feedback from their lecturers on parts that they were struggling with or about issues that they needed to clarify.

One of the serious challenges that needed to be addressed was the poor educational backgrounds of many of the students as well as the fact that for most students English was a second or third language. Difficulties with academic writing were tackled by the university writing centre and postgraduate support programme, strongly encouraging students to send drafts of their assignments for formative feedback, and encouraging communication with lecturers by phone or email. And lecturers dedicated large amounts of time to coaching educationally disadvantaged students in research writing as part of the research project supervision process.

The programme appeared to be achieving its goals. Students and alumni indicated that they had broadened and sharpened their understanding of and vision for public health so that they could contextualize their practice in relation to a more complex understanding of the health system, and primary health care. They had learned to implement theory and policy in practice; and in particular, their ability to involve and facilitate capability expansion of other health professionals and poor people had been enhanced. The contribution of research experience to health professionals' confidence and authority in the field was seen as significant in terms of building confidence and the capacity to contribute. For example, Lila, a black African student who was a laboratory scientist in another African country told us how she has developed critical thinking:

> There are times when we have meetings where you report on your findings and there are decisions to be made by supervisors. Before, all I did was to agree on whatever they say, well, they are experts I'll have to agree. But now I have to look at whatever they say critically, and because I have results in front of me I am able to argue out things which I was never able to do before.

Students and alumni had also learned about managing health information, monitoring and evaluation and how to apply the results to improving programmes.

Summary

The department of public health and its postgraduate programme are tightly aligned to a specific *informed vision*, espoused by the WHO, about the improvement of health in developing countries. The postgraduate programme is designed to support students to acquire the *knowledge and skills* that will make the vision appear to enhance the capacity to contribute to improving public health systems. There is a strong emphasis on encouraging students to understand the 'bigger picture' of health promotion and the complexities of contributing to improvement, which was seen to reside largely in developing critical and analytical thinking; high-level management and coordination skills; and research skills. The emphasis on collaboration and co-ordination of health promotion efforts can be translated as *social and collective struggle*. All of these capabilities were seen to contribute to the *confidence and assurance* of health professionals to be change agents in their working contexts. In the context of teaching practicing professionals, *affiliation* with people living in poverty (and, therefore, living with high levels of ill-health and sickness) appeared taken for granted, similarly *integrity* and *resilience*. *Emotional reflexivity*, however, did not emerge.

Constraints arose from the nature of distance learning itself. Some students felt a need for more opportunities for face-to-face learning, and some would have liked the additional option of studying full-time on campus. Daniel, an African student from another African country, would have liked to have come for six-week blocks and work on group practice-oriented projects. He complained that 'outside in the field where we work, we are just alone there. It is actually very difficult sometimes to comprehend things'. He valued the opportunity to learn in a group, sharing ideas with fellow students and lecturers. It was the case that students who attended the contact sessions valued the opportunity for interaction with professionals in different fields and these interactions also enhanced students' capability for working in multidisciplinary teams. One of the constraints on students' participation in the postgraduate programme was a lack of time and resources to attend the contact sessions. While health professionals in government departments of health were able to access funding to study, there was very little financial aid for others, such as those working in NGOs.

Nevertheless, most of the students valued the lecturers' openness to other forms of contact: for example Moira, a coloured South African student, was grateful that, 'Even though sometimes you do feel very alone and you don't understand, you can always pick up the phone and call somebody, send an email and they will respond to you.' Moreover, students undoubtedly gained from innovative use of information technology, even though there were limitations because Fynbos University was under-resourced and one of the effects of this was inadequate information technology facilities, website and connectivity. And there were further constraints for students located in isolated and under-resourced rural areas where there was a lack of technological and human resources to draw on. For example, one student, a doctor, had received from the programme a DVD which she needed to learn and work with, but no-one within the hospital she worked in knew how to use it. There was one computer in the hospital and the doctor had tried to load it, but nobody had been able to load the software that she had to use to do the analysis. This student was described by Jane Simons, the Programme Director, as highly committed to the programme but unable to continue because of lack of resources in her workplace and community. Jane also spoke about the lack of access to libraries in the rural areas and the failure of mentoring schemes because too few knowledgeable people in those areas were available to provide mentoring.

Summary of educational arrangements for the five professional fields

All the Departments were thoughtful about teaching, all had undergone review and change since 1994 and for most this was an ongoing process, and most capabilities were evident in curriculum and pedagogy in some form or another. Yet the commonalities and variations played out rather differently than in the conceptualizations of public-good professionalism discussed in the previous chapter. The commonalities in pedagogy and curriculum clustered around messages that the past must be redressed. There were five major strands (inevitably more strongly expressed in some departments than others) that relate to five of the capabilities: first, in all the departments, even if only in one course or module, students were expected to understand that they were entering a professional field in specific socio-historic circumstances in a country where a lot of people are living in conditions of great poverty (*informed vision*); second, in all departments there were attempts to inculcate respectfulness (clearly seen as a part of a necessary break with the past), often through relationships in the classroom (*affiliation*); third, *knowledge and skills* were seen as vital to make some form of contribution to a society that needs a great deal from its professionals, whatever the field, and, in particular, all professionals need to be and were expected to be creative, problem-solving, critical thinkers; fourth, professionals must display *integrity*; and fifth, students were gaining *confidence and assurance* as they were being educated, though it was differently inflected for engineers and lawyers who enjoy high status in society; theologians who are accepted into communities as ministers; for social workers who knew that their profession has not been held in high regard in the past and even now; and for health professionals who were already working in the field and can reap an immediate benefit from their studies.

We can see, therefore, that the other three capabilities disappeared almost altogether in some fields. *Social and collective struggle* made almost no appearance in engineering or in law. In theology there was a strong focus on bringing black and white people and churches together, although in the South African context of deep religious divisions based on race, this could be understood as a form of social and collective struggle. As a functioning in social work and public health it appeared as 'networking', 'forging links' or collaboration'. In public health appreciating and acting on the necessity of services and systems working together to promote the health of people living in poverty was a central value.

Both theology and social work education stressed *emotional reflexivity*. However, they took quite different forms, which relate to pedagogy. In theology emotional reflexivity related to making personal transformations that were expected to occur in the context of the university and department through discussion, prayer and thought. In social work it related to the extensive placements students are given during which they come face-to-face with the harrowing realities of extreme poverty. The relatively light emphasis on practical, concrete experiences in communities in theology might also explain the absence of discussion about *resilience* (except from the alumni), which was in contrast with social work for which it was a central capability. Public health appeared to assume resilience on the part of their working health professional students. And there were hints of the need for both emotional reflexivity and resilience in engineering and law insofar as students and alumni saw themselves as working directly on poverty reduction.

Overall, in terms of curriculum and pedagogy, we could connect the explicit vision of theology, social work and public health to a strongly articulated transformative, critical curriculum and pedagogies aimed both at students' acquisition of knowledge and skills, and at encouraging an attitude of aware and responsible action in society. Nevertheless, the balance between actual concrete practice and experience, curriculum content, and opportunities for discussion and reflection is crucially important for the development of the full range of capabilities. Despite the similarity of the visions of theology and social work, the former appeared underdeveloped pedagogically because too much emphasis was placed on transformation in theory – this was set to change with the 'community service' elements being strengthened. In engineering and law specific parts of the curriculum and a general ethos from some lecturers (shared in the case of law) lent themselves to the development of public-good professionalism – and the issue is one of extending innovative courses to more students.

Ideal-type professional literature, as we discussed in Chapter 2, sees the mission of university-based professional departments to educate for professional judgment (Sullivan, 2005). The role of the department is to engender commitment to the profession as a life project and to a shared professional identity (Freidson, 2004). Of course, these roles are not necessarily for the public good. Whatever the effects, for all novice professionals, the discursive practices of the department in which they study represent the professional world to which they aspire. And, from the perspective of ideal-type professionalism, the expectations that should be internalized concern concern, competence, trustworthiness, honesty and service – and we certainly witnessed these expectations being pursued in our five departments. Yet we are going further and defining public-good professionalism in the South African context as involving the professional capabilities to assist the capability expansion for the poor, and to carry out agency obligations to disadvantaged others.

Now that we have examined the educational practices and trajectories in terms of producing professionals oriented to the public good, in the next chapter we turn to our participants' awareness of the constraints on functioning as a public-good professional.

8 Universities and social conditions

Constraints on public-good professionalism in South Africa

An account of the continuities of the present with past injustices is important, moreover for understanding how the present conditions are structural, how those structures have evolved, and where intervention to change may be most effective.

(Iris Marion Young, 2011: 181–82)

In *The Idea of Justice* Amartya Sen (2009: 18–19) takes a comparative approach to judgements about justice; that is, he is less interested in pursuing ideas of 'perfect justice' than in actual 'social realizations' of justice. Similarly, we take a comparative approach to the production of public-good professionals by way of university education, that is, in the debate of realism versus idealism we do not look for perfection, but rather for tendencies towards and away from an ideal-type public-good professionalism. We recognize that strongly formulated suggestions for transformative social change are always in danger of being pejoratively labelled 'Utopian'. Moreover, we also recognize that some may question whether public-good professionalism need be advocated at all: after all, the interests of people living in poverty might be served as well as is possible by engineers who design excellent bridges, roads and buildings; by lawyers who have a full grasp of the law; social workers who have a thorough grasp of psychology and sociology, and project management; and so on. Knowledge and skills are foundational, they are at the heart of professional work and are essential to claims to professionalism (MacDonald, 1995). Yet, the history of professionalism tells us that being technically highly skilled is not sufficient: professional work has always involved ethical dilemmas and the need for integrity which cannot be taken for granted (see Freidson, 2004; Larson, 2013; Sullivan, 2005). As discussed in Chapter 2, the claim to deserve professional autonomy and prestige on the grounds that being called to a vocation implies trustworthiness is highly contested, clients complain and States take steps to regulate professions. Of course, the occupational structure (hierarchies and cultures within profession) and professional associations are key to ethical standards within a profession. However, for all professions, education and training is pivotal. It is discussed and reconfigured over time as a response to socio-historic circumstances and the concerns of publics and States

(Sullivan, 2005); and educators themselves are influential within professions (Larson, 2013). Here we have focused on professional education as a crucial part of what directs professionals towards specific beings and doings: we have argued that the capabilities approach is a powerfully useful tool for discussing and thinking about the goals and contours of professional education because it allows a focus equally on the well-being of clients who live in poverty and on professionals themselves, who we envisage as reaping rewards from public-good work (additionally to the material rewards of professionals, which in themselves do not detract from working for the public good). Sen (2009) guides us by proposing that we evaluate the proximity of local socio-economic arrangements to feasible conditions of justice. In parallel, we can usefully think of public-good professional education comparatively.

Sen describes as 'public reasoning' the discussions that arise from such comparative evaluations; those involved make their own evaluations. All our case studies show that the education of public-service professionals is characterized by considerable gaps, tensions and boundaries between the ideal (what is right, what is desired by many and towards which justice points) and the real (what actually happens and what is feasible). In Chapters 6 and 7 we focused on which capabilities/functionings appear to be valued/evident more than others in specific educational sites, in this chapter we address the socio-historic contextual element of the Index.

We found that systemic, material and cultural constraints are intimately tied. The differences between professional fields as revealed through our interviews appear to become more marked as the data has moved from conceptualization of public good, through curriculum and pedagogy to constraints on public-good professionalism. All fields in South Africa face considerable constraints in terms of relating to poor communities professionals serve, yet, while there are some common themes, they play out quite differently in different fields.

Constraints on public-good engineering

A reality at the level of the Engineering Department was the sheer hard work and slow speed of making changes in educational arrangements which promote a direct version of public-good professionalism. The lecturers Christo van Heerden, who was white, and Jonathan Landsman, who was black African, were among the youngest lecturers in the Department and were keen to embed pro-poor content in the engineering curriculum, but found it difficult to fit in; they also found it difficult to find time to undertake research and do community work, which, they reported, is least valued by the university. Finding time and motivation is especially hard in the face of interest and opposition from other (older) members of staff: Christo commented, 'You say to yourself "Well, I'm kind of fighting a losing battle".'

At the level of the profession, Jonathan Landsman claimed 'I don't know of anybody that has studied engineering who is not working to make a good living for themselves.' Similarly, Christo van Heerden regretted the lack of 'will' among engineers to contribute to the 'upliftment' of their country rather than to their own individual prosperity, often by leaving the country. Student responses confirmed the trend. For example, Jaya, an Indian student, agreed that he was after the 'the best package, the best benefits' for himself at work; and, for Fabian, a coloured student, money was the prime motivator, followed by 'self-actualization'. Jeanne Marais was a white alumna and practicing engineer who disowned a direct contribution to 'political transformation' but made the point, 'At the end of the day, we are the ones doing the work, making sure that services and housing do get out at a desired cost.' There are disciplinary paradigms at work, engineering is identified as practical and problem-solving – that in itself is the contribution. Building a better individual life does not preclude also working, at least some of the time, with others in mind.

Infrastructural growth in South Africa has required an increasing number of engineers. Between 1996 and 2005 there has been a 7 per cent average annual growth in the numbers being employed in engineering positions, and a corresponding increase in numbers studying engineering (Roodt and du Toit, 2009: 38). Yet South Africa is still suffering from an acute shortage of qualified engineers, described as one of the worst capacity and scarce-skills crises in years, with local municipalities hardest hit (Lawless 2005, cited in Du Toit and Roodt, 2009: 3). Du Toit and Roodt (2009) note that South Africa currently has 473 trained engineers per million citizens, whereas Japan, which co-hosted the 2002 World Cup with Korea, had 3,306 per million citizens (ibid.: 130).

Only half of those trained to be engineers continue to be employed in engineering, with the rest moving to other industries for managerial or consultancy positions, often attracted by the higher salaries on offer, and frustrated by the lack of on-the-job training and opportunities to learn from others with more experience (ibid.: 15–16, 19). Those who remain in the field of engineering may work in the public or private sector: in 2005, 32.4 per cent of engineers and technologists worked for the public sector, and 67.6 per cent worked for the private sector (ibid.: 14).

Some of the shortage is due to outward migration of qualified engineers, either to escape high levels of crime and violence in the country, or to move to more favourable employment and salary prospects overseas (Du Toit and Roodt, 2009: 30). As South African engineering degrees are recognized internationally, South African engineers are highly mobile globally, making outward migration relatively straightforward, and attractive to those in search of higher salaries and keen to escape high crime rates at home.

For those who remain in the country and practice as engineers, it was reported that there is a chronic lack of skilled labour on sites. So foreign workers are employed while South Africans, hampered by exceptionally poor schooling, remain untrained and unemployed and continue to live in poverty; and the poor quality of engineering work contributes to poor living conditions: Theuns le Roux, a white alumni and practising engineer, told us that 'buildings fall down'.

Working engineers felt tied down by how engineering work is commissioned, the regulations and the funding available. A Catch-22 pertains, Theuns le Roux claimed: 'Maybe we want to put in a water system for a township, but if the municipality doesn't have the financial support for that, we can't do that [. . .] We rely on the economy and other investors to give us projects.' Jeanne Marais, another practicing engineer who had graduated from Acacia, described times when she had been successful at 'pushing' government or municipalities. Engineers are often at one remove from the communities they are working for, Jeanne Marais commented that 'We are handed the criteria [from a client] so we don't have that much involvement with the community.' And the lecturer Christo van Heerden revealed the messiness of realpolitik by speaking of his recent attempt to build a bridge in the local township: the project had been 'hijacked as a political thing' with the local municipality wanting to claim credit and gain political leverage. Similarly, the NGO[1] representative we interviewed, Fiona Perkins who is white, identified a lack of co-ordination in the government's support of regions: 'There's a myriad of different institutions, corporations, committees, councils, each doing their own little bit of intervention programme, there's no synergy and synchronization.'

In summary, from the perspective of our respondents it appeared that prejudices in society continue and this leads to a lack of skilled labour, necessary for good-quality engineering work, and difficulties in building trust and respect both in the university and at work. Our participants (who had involved themselves in our project because they wanted to push a social agenda) thought that most engineers saw engineering as a profession for bettering oneself; and if the lecturers we spoke to are typical, engineers work long hours which is likely to leave little time and energy for the extra effort which public-good work entails.

Constraints on public-good law

Thinking like a lawyer means smoothing out the rich complexity of real-life problems in favour of abstract legal argument (see Sullivan *et al.*, 2007). Yet the Head of Department, William Brown, who is coloured, described how law as a profession does not foster close contact between the practising professionals and their poorer clients. Indeed, he felt that within the profession, compassion was often regarded as something which might hinder the proper course of justice and therefore was not encouraged. Moreover, law, he proposed, is fundamentally adversarial, 'We fight basically, we teach students to fight', with the emphasis on winning, rather than fostering the notion of service, and social and community rights. The question is whether being a good advocate, while absolutely necessary, is enough when serving the interests of people living in poverty. For example, the law is couched in non-accessible language, and focused on individual justice rather than a notion of helping people collectively, so that, William Brown claims, the law historically 'has never been for everybody, it's always been almost an instrument available to those who rule [. . .] Law ultimately is about power whether we like it or not.'

Just as we have sketched above, Sullivan and colleagues' (2007: 6) study on educating lawyers for the Carnegie Foundation reveals how law schools in the US support students learning 'to think like lawyers' by abstracting the processes and procedures of law from 'the rich complexity of actual situations let alone the job of thinking through the social consequences or ethical aspects', inadvertently giving the students the impression that moral issues, including those of social justice, are of secondary importance:

> Students are told to set aside their desire for justice. They are warned not to let their moral concerns or compassion for the people in the cases they discuss cloud their legal analyses [. . .] students have no way of learning when and how their moral concerns may be relevant to their work as lawyers.

With medicine, law is the most powerful of traditional professions. Larson (2013) describes the profession of law as the 'epitome of social stratification' and explains how historically the profession failed to secure the solidarity of its members and resolved the problem by segregating into different, and hierarchical, areas of practice (for example, there are solo practitioners dealing with immigration on the one hand, and large firms of corporate lawyers on the other). She also argues that loyalty to clients comprises a temptation to collude with the unethical practices of clients that can violate public interests. So the stereotypes of lawyers as conservative, elitist and cynical that can be found all over the world, have some basis in the culture and nature of the work. Nonetheless, the students and the lecturers we spoke to, as we show below, suggested a mild version of the stereotypes and gestured towards engaging 'the moral imagination of students as they move toward professional practice' (Sullivan *et al.*, 2007: 6).

Keeping in mind that our law respondents had a particular interest in serving the public good, a strong theme was that the material motivation of lawyers was a key barrier to a public-good career path. A black African alumnus Dumisani Bangeni, who worked for a private law firm, observed that things had changed and for 'black lawyers who want money it's not about helping out and giving back. And not only lawyers, that's a general trend, most black professionals [. . .] it's more about bucks – it's unfortunate.' Making a similar point, the lecturer and Head of Department William Brown noted that:

> I think the majority of law students are not here to serve [. . .] It's one of the big ironies of South African history that a lot of, most of our students come from fairly impoverished backgrounds and they don't see legal education, even higher education in general, as a general kind of poverty-combating mechanism.

Similarly, Robert Michaels, who was coloured and worked for a legal professional body, observed 'the younger crop [. . .] I find them apathetic and really just interested in their career as opposed to being driven by other things such as social justice and human rights'.

Students mentioned the trend too, for example, Jennifer, a coloured law student, noted:

> About 60 per cent of black students enter law for the mere factor of the money that they're able to get out of it. So not many people will look at 'How can I help my community?' They more look at 'How can I help myself?'

Recent moves to cap legal fees in South Africa in order to make legal services more widely accessible have not been welcomed by the legal profession (Umar, 2012). Yet a coloured student Sandra envisaged the sacrifices that some families make for their children to become lawyers:

> We send you to university, we spent thousands of rands, are you going to do that so that you can become a community lawyer or attorney? [. . .] I don't blame my friends who come from disadvantaged communities [. . .] who want to make money.

Almost everyone expects and is interested in being paid for work and we would expect in all professions to find a continuum of how interested in money individuals are, the question is the extent to which, taking a critical mass, professionals in a particular professional field are motivated by money in ways which undermine the public-good possibilities in their work (there are also other influences, like the ideology of apartheid in South Africa, which might lead professionals away from the public good). In the study, some law students indicated that they sought a middle path: a stable and lucrative enough career path that also had public-good elements. Ashiek, a coloured student, commented:

> I want to be able to play golf and stuff, but I also want to have the ability to be able to help in the community as well and giving other people an opportunity to be able to better their life as well, so I want to be that person as well.

Alice, also coloured, similarly remarked:

> I'm not going to lie either, I'm not going to be able to go out every weekend and serve the community, I won't be able to. So maybe even contributions [. . .] doing pro bono work [. . .] I just want to do something, because in South Africa, there's too many things going too wrong.

There were also suggestions of other constrains such as the continuation of prejudices and restricted access to the law. In Dumisani Bangeni's view, prejudice against African lawyers persisted, that is African lawyers were more likely to be offered menial work before they had 'proved themselves'. Both lecturers and students felt that Fynbos University's history as a previously disadvantaged university also meant that graduates were not respected as much or considered as good as those from other more prestigious universities, and so they had a harder time finding employment.

A further constraint concerned the real difficulties of carrying out work for disadvantaged individuals and groups. In South Africa, there can be many barriers to people realizing their legal rights, given the high levels of poverty in the country. For example, the high financial cost of legal proceedings constitutes a significant barrier to realizing equal access to justice. Without legal aid, advice is unaffordable to the majority in South Africa: an average black household would need a week's income to afford an hour's consultation with an attorney (Open Society Foundation for South Africa, 2005). In these cases, legal aid clinics play a particularly important role in enabling people to take a case to court. Moreover, insufficient knowledge of the law and their rights frequently hinders people in gaining access to the legal system. Thus a white NGO worker, Felicity Green, stated that one of the most important capabilities for the population is to understand the law because: 'People [. . .] don't understand their rights at an absolute basic level – not understanding their rights it means they can't access those rights.'

Constraints on public-good theology

The lecturers in the Theology Department were unusually and explicitly optimistic about South Africa's progress towards democracy and a more equal society. They wanted students to be aware of poverty and social issues, because they wanted ministers educated at Acacia to contribute to transformation in South Africa and they believed that 'conscious' Christians should be responsible for society in all its aspects. A good deal of hope was invested in the students as future ministers facilitating transformation of the churches, which was seen as a long-term goal. However, like the lawyers they faced prejudices and inequalities in society, which were often in sharp contrast to their educational experiences at university.

Despite the optimism of lecturers, students pointed out the contrast between life within the department and life outside. Many of the students came from geographical areas and communities where there were still strong racial divisions and discrimination. Aletta, who is white, observed: 'In my town I think there are two houses where coloured people live, the rest of the town is white.' Similarly, Jacques who is also white talked about the lives of farm workers in the rural area he came from: there had been no change in their poor social and economic circumstances; and they lacked education: 'Nothing's changed, the people working on the farms have never left the farms. They can't read and they're treating me like a hero just because I'm white, so we're not past it [apartheid] at all.' A third white student, Marieke, described her experience at Acacia University as living:

> [I]n a bubble because that [racial] division isn't really there [. . .] If you stay at a residence, it's white, black, coloured mixed together and all of a sudden it's not that big an issue. You share a room and you're friends and you go to

church together, it's really not something weird, but then you go home and you're in a totally white church and four coloured people walk in and it's like 'What just happened?'

Moreover, Marieke thought that the 'racism in our heart, in people's hearts' was not the main problem. Rather the historical and current economic system was 'one of the biggest factors dividing people', which did not pertain in the sheltered context of the university. Yet Peter, also white, argued that while students accepted racial differences in relation to their classmates and students in the residences, they still saw people outside that locus as 'other'. In his view:

People still make a big fuss about race, but you can be black if you fit into my framework of, you study along with me, so we've got the same mindset, studying at the same university, so we're rather up there in the same social circle thing and that's still fine, then you're still in my category.

Other discriminatory practices were referred to, for example that of gender. The Dutch Reformed Church (DRC) used to consist of white, male ministers only. Then in the early 1990s it allowed women to be ordained. The Department at Acacia had been training women before that time, although they could not be ordained to practise as ministers. Marie, a white student who was a member of the DRC, remarked that in theory women were accepted as ministers, 'but in practice if you go to more rural areas, then the people are still very conservative, they will definitely frown on that'. Linda du Toit a coloured alumna who had a short-term contract with the DRC, she spoke about how difficult it was for her to get a permanent post as a minister. Marie confirmed Linda's experience, saying that 'when women do get full-time positions, it's usually not as a full minister, it would be like a youth work post or specializing in pastoral counselling'. The Department tried to make the students sensitive to gender issues with an optional module on gender studies. Yet Marie reported that some male students made jokes that subtly undermined women. 'It's always in jest but [. . .] underneath I think most people still have a problem with it.'

Students' comments reflected their conscious views about race, class and gender issues, but we also noticed unconscious forms of othering and silencing taking place. This was evident in one of the focus group meetings where a Peter, a white student, discussed the difficulties of understanding poverty when students had not experienced it themselves. He used the pronoun 'we' implying that all students present had the same difficulty, yet sitting silently next to Peter was coloured student, Lukas, who came from a poor rural background, where he had worked as a minister for many years and would have experienced poverty first hand.

In summary, the lecturer theologians were highly committed to poverty reduction and to redressing the wrongs of the apartheid past. Nevertheless, the education they were providing did not seem connected enough to the current realities of a divide in the Christian churches, which mirrored that in society, between, on the one hand, white, prosperous, conservative elitism and, on the other, black poverty and powerlessness. The alumni ministers we spoke to worked in quite different contexts and have different missions. Some ministers in the Uniting Reforming Church worked in poor, rural, black or coloured communities where they assisted people, especially the young, to be equipped with basic life skills and knowledge about how to deal with social problems affecting them. The alumni ministers working in these conditions worried about burnout. For ministers located in wealthy churches which used to be mainly white in the past (DRC churches were exclusively white during apartheid) the task is consciousness-raising about poverty and the need for integration.

Constraints on public-good social work

In sharp contrast to theology, we gathered an enormous amount of data about the difficulties that face the social work profession in achieving the ideals of public-good professionalism. In spite of transformative policy intentions, there had been negative effects of policy implementation on the social welfare system and the working conditions of social workers in South Africa. Aspects of the system had been put under strain through changes in funding allocation. Although the overall social welfare budget had increased, the rapid expansion of spending on social security services such as pension and child support grants significantly reduced the funding allocated to welfare services overall. One of the aspects of budget reallocation was a substantial reduction of funding to the NGO sector. Historically, the provision of social welfare services was shared between government and NGOs with government providing financial support to organizations through subsidization of social worker posts (Earle, 2007). The reduction of government funding to NGOs coincided with a diminishing of donor funding to NGOs in South Africa since 1994, when simultaneously, the demands on the NGO sector have increased dramatically (Earle, 2007).

At the same time, policy shifts deemed the casework approach to social work both inefficient and disempowering by the new government Department of Social Development (DSD). As a means of affecting transformation within the sector, the ANC government changed the subsidization model from supporting social worker posts directly to supporting selected programmes with outcomes in line with the new social development policy. These programmes utilized group and community work methods so that subsidization of equally necessary remedial and statutory casework virtually disappeared. Yet the need for casework had grown, for example, with the statutory requirements associated with HIV/AIDS and the requirements of the Children's Act (2005).

As an unintended consequence of what is essentially a progressive and transformative policy, social workers, particularly those in the NGO sector, were reported by the alumni we spoke to to have become over-burdened and demoralized and that experience is compounded by a number of factors. Not only are social workers under-resourced, their number is inadequate to meet the social welfare needs of desperately poor individuals and communities. Case loads are high and social workers are reported to struggle with the required shift in roles and with developing the capabilities to contribute to transformation, and have experienced conflicting demands and pressures (Earle, 2007; Lombard, 2008). Moreover, they earn low salaries compared to other professionals with an equivalent level of education – in general, in South Africa, as elsewhere, the caring professions and work which has mainly been done by women, have had low status and remuneration. Our respondents pointed out that these factors impact on motivation and result in a high rate of burnout.

Sheila, an older white student who had worked for an NGO, described her experiences of how the lack of capacity of the social welfare system affected communities. She spoke of the huge case load of individual social workers, saying the social workers in the NGO she worked for:

> [J]ust don't have time, they just do not have time, because they work with such a huge geographical area and farmland etc., and they just do not have the time for individual cases. The other week, a little girl died, and she's been [on the case load of the NGO] for the last three years and she died of unnatural causes, we know that, but nothing's done. It's very frustrating, the social workers there have a very difficult job because they have such a big case load, I mean two hundred, I'm not sure, two hundred cases or more, how can you do justice to any of those cases?

Yusuf, a coloured student who had also had several years' experience, highlighted the position of the social worker with little to offer beyond the 'empowerment' approaches:

> I think social workers are actually being set up for failure [. . .] I think there's reach (sic) a level where communities have become depleted of resources and the resources are so few that it actually becomes a point of conflict, you know, because they are battling for it. So, on the one hand, sending a social worker in to deal with poverty and not giving that social worker the necessary back-up is actually setting the social worker up to failure. But if you come in there and you're going to say you're going to network people, you're going to build social capital, for me that's a lot of words coming out of my experience with government. They've got all these brilliant strategies and it's a lot of words, it's not always about money they say, it's about building resources, capacity and network [but] at the end of the day you need to put some power behind, some muscle needs to go behind it.

Carla, a white student, echoed Yusuf's discouragement in more concrete terms:

> A lot of the time what is happening is social workers are being sent into what are seen as impoverished communities. They're being sent in there almost to

like calm the storm for a while, you know, it's like 'OK go in there, settle them down', but a lot of the time social workers don't have that power to make decisions. They can't say to somebody 'OK, you will have running water within a month.' They can't say that because the amount of red tape they need to go through, it's going to take them more than a month to get that done [. . .] So many promises are being made, but nothing is being delivered.

There are political constraints on the agency of social workers. One of the elements which students discussed was being able to manage and locate oneself within different political perspectives and agendas which impact on their professional practice. Carla was backed up by others in the focus group when she noted that:

If you're working for government and they send you to go and work in a particular community and you then start lobbying for that community against government, you know, [others laugh] there's always going to be that conflict and those barriers that you need to stay within.

Low pay was an issue for students. Joy was a black African student who was of the opinion that incentives and salaries of social workers needed to be improved 'so that they can also be motivated because I'm surely not going to go and motivate someone who is poor when I cannot take care of myself or my family you know'. And Charmaine Jacobs, a coloured alumni and school social worker, pointed out to us that she had constantly to reconcile the lack of financial reward with the fact that the work was meaningful. She felt passionate about clinical work and working with children, but was not sure she could continue on the pay she received. As Charmaine suggests, the difficulties in working conditions contrasted vividly with the ideals – based on human development – promoted in the degree courses for social workers at Silvertree University. The contrast is instructive for thinking about what is possible for the approach of respect and empowerment at the heart of the educational efforts at Silvertree.

As indicated in the section above, alumni and students conveyed the sense of powerlessness experienced by social workers who want to make an impact on poverty. This powerlessness is in good part explained by the conditions of work outlined in the section above. It is also, more subtly, about negotiating a new way of thinking about individuals and communities living in poverty that is multilayered and compounded at each layer. For example, alumni social workers complained about the dependency and sense of entitlement they had experienced in communities, of the 'learned helplessness' of poor people who, if they do not receive 'handouts', fall into disillusionment and despair. They found people in communities resistant to social work interventions. Sheila, the student who had been an NGO worker, was sceptical about the empowerment model of intervention in a context of intense material deprivation, arguing that it could be a vehicle for change only if it was accompanied by resources and the meeting of basic material needs. She elaborated:

> It's OK to go in there with an empowering approach like a Freirian approach, 'Don't just domesticate the people, but actually liberate them.' But then there's not much you can do! Then you have to say 'OK, this is your situation', but how can you help them to improve their situation? Because it takes more than just you, it takes government, it takes housing, it takes policies. I know it's quite negative, [laughing] the way I'm speaking at the moment. But I mean it's very realistic. Those types of programmes are wonderful if you can have the resources, the backing to actually do something. They can actually get to some sort of conscientization and realization that 'These are the reasons why I'm in this situation so now how can I get from here to there?' And that's the difficulty, it's OK getting them to that realization, but then it's having the resources and the skills and the professionals to be able to get them from a to b, and that's the frustrating part.

A further dimension of reality versus idealism which students brought up was that they were unable to use what they had learned in university once they become part of institutions in the welfare system. Yusuf, a student who had also worked previous to his studies, observed that the education of social workers developed their capabilities to be creative and innovative professionals. However:

> Somewhere along the line, either the government, which employs most of us, or the NGO sector does not provide the environment for us to work on those levels and use those creativity and innovations and the government is very bureaucratic. So they're static and the NGO sector often – their ideas and innovations are stifled by lack of funding and a lack of risk-taking as well, and poor management generally.

Under these conditions, it is not surprising that many social workers do not stay in South Africa. In the context of globalization and international mobility, social workers have highly transferable skills/capabilities. Despite local application, they base their practice on international bodies of theory and knowledge and are in great demand in the international labour market. The movement of professionals is usually from developing to developed countries and many leave South Africa, which feeds into a vicious cycle of a shortage of social workers and lack of capacity in the system. Data on the emigration of social workers from South Africa is patchy, but Earle (2007) estimates between 10 and 30 per cent of each graduating class.

In addition to the factors mentioned above – poor working conditions, high workloads, emotional stress of working with severely poor communities, with a high incidence of HIV/AIDS and low salaries – Elizabeth Goodwin, a white lecturer, thought that concern about violence also drove trained social workers abroad. Added to the movement out of the country, movement out of the social work profession is common in South Africa. Anne Hardy, a white alumna working for a faith-based organization remarked that she had: 'Seen people come and go [. . .] and seen social workers leave the profession and go into human resources or into [the business sector] and of my graduation class of 1984, there's only about three or four of us still practising.' The students we interviewed were acutely conscious of issues such as the low salaries, difficult working conditions, and the high level of social workers leaving the country; half of those interviewed were planning to go abroad after qualifying.

In 2003 the government started to recognize social work as a 'scarce skill' and developed a strategy for retention of social workers (DSD, 2005). There have been indications that relations between the NGO sector and some provincial government departments are starting to improve (Earle, 2007). Earle reports that the extent of emigration of social workers peaked in about 2002/3 and that there has been a drop in numbers of emigrations since then, which is encouraging. Nevertheless, the stronger sense was that the 'calling' or passion for being a social worker was being crushed by a sense of powerlessness set up by systemic and cultural barriers. In summary, there are too few social workers working in extremes of poverty and social breakdown, and they are under-resourced, low paid, and low status. The education at Silvertree prepares a high-quality social worker who the lecturers hope will have the capabilities to change some of these conditions in their careers.

Constraints on public-good public health

According to the South African Health Barometer 2008, the health of the South African population declined between 1997 and 2005. The increase in poverty, the slow pace of change in basic living conditions and inadequacy of service delivery to poor communities contributed to the worsening health of the poor majority of South Africans. The high rate of HIV/AIDS was the main factor contributing to the country's escalating rate of deaths. In spite of more people needing health services, there had been a decrease in numbers of health professionals compared to the overall population since 1994 (Cullinan, 2009). In 2008 there were 1.1 nurses per 1,000 people in comparison with 2.5 nurses per 100 people in 1994 – a decrease of more than 50 per cent (Cullinan, 2009). These factors have made it extremely difficult for health professionals to affect changes in the public health system.

All groups participating in our research were sharply aware of the factors constraining students and alumni from effectively functioning as change agents in the systems in which they worked. Both structural constraints and resistance to change from professionals in the health system whose views and practices were shaped in the old system were cited. Jane Simons, the white Programme Coordinator, claimed that in the Department there was:

[A] great consciousness of the precariousness of the health system in South Africa, the immovability, the difficulty in transforming however many departments into one, the fact that most people were trained under the old system and therefore will carry much of that with them as they attempt to change it into a more people-centred system, issues of poverty having probably put people in a worse position than they were previously.

Jane thought that while the Department's postgraduate programme was making a contribution to transformation of the South African health system, it was on a very small scale and she attributed this to the low numbers of health professionals in management positions who study on the programme. She remarked that many of the people are working at a clinical level rather than at management level and many of the students who've come onto our course have and 'if only you could get our managers onto this course, then they would understand what we're talking about'. Jane went on to quote one of the students, who had told her:

> You're alone, you come back with this new understanding and you can't get it through because you're alone with that understanding and you're silenced because it just annoys people who were trained under the old guard, however much they hated the old guard, they still trained under the old guard and they can't see beyond that.

Nobuntu Tladi is a black African woman lecturer who found it difficult to accept that even when health professionals who were studying on the programme were in positions to implement change, there were structural constraints which blocked them. These included shortage of staff, staff rotation and lack of resources:

> [T]hey're in the positions where they can implement the changes, but the health system is sort of blocking them in a way. So they can't just introduce [. . .] their own ideas. We have to consider the whole system from the province and district and other implementation [sites].

Part of the problem were gaps between more educated health professionals who had developed a more informed understanding of health policy and the health workers on the ground who were responsible for implementing the policies. The main areas identified were: understanding the multiple determinants of health; critical thinking; management of people and projects; and collaborating for policy implementation. Lack of integration and co-ordination was cited as a severe problem. The term 'vertical' is used to refer to programmes that are run in a separate, compartmentalized way rather than through the integration of services across programmes. Laura Bailey, a coloured aluma whose work involves co-ordinating NGOs and health facilities, identified this as a major problem. She argued that effective health workers need to understand the structures of the health system and the relationships between different sectors. In order to provide adequate health care to poor communities, health workers must effect co-ordination between services. But, she continued, 'health professionals are just doing the day-to-day crisis management. Patients go home but there's no link, or referral, or tie-up between what happens in the health care facility and the community.' She thought that the DOH had not communicated adequately about the need to form linkages, do referrals and support for sustaining programmes. For example, as part of the policy of decentralization to district level, another layer of health practitioners, community health workers, had been established. Laura argued that community health workers were 'a pivotal part of the system', essential for successful implementation, but if these services were not co-ordinated, the clients would be disadvantaged, 'because they go from one service to the other and [don't get] proper linkages, referral and follow-up care, treatment, support'. Similarly, community- and faith-based organizations played an important role in health services provision, but while the government contributed funding to these organizations, they had not formally embraced them as partners in the health sector, and there was not sufficient co-ordination to benefit the clients.

More specifically, Laura Bailey spoke about constraints effecting the cycle of monitoring and evaluation and the translation of results into practice:

> At the next level the data gets sent to them, it's analysed, but they don't communicate it to the people, to the implementers, and the implementers are key if we want to really understand or address the problems. So the kind of health workers will be able to work with data. You know, so many people do these courses but the more they understand it the further away they move from the actual place where this analysis needs to be understood so that we can make a difference. Even the communities need to be involved and understand the issues so that they can be able to come up with some suggestion of what can be tried.

Laura also thought that there is a disconnection between academic research and practice and policy because findings tend to be 'communicated at such a high level, [that] the people that are implementing don't ever benefit from that'. She gave an example:

> I mean, I came across something the other day when I asked the World Health Organization for some papers and I saw articles about studies that were done in Khayelitsha[21] and I said 'But do the people in Khayelitsha know about this?' How do you do it because maybe they are fed back to the very big directors and deputy directors. They just file it and then its business as usual.

Similarly, Moira, a coloured student who was a professional working at the Medical Research Council, thought that the senior researchers in the Council were too removed from the contexts that were being researched. And there are gaps between policies and their implementation, again identified by Laura:

> [A]ll these policies, many facilities have a stack of them sitting in a cupboard somewhere, many of them haven't been read, but [the National

Department of Health] thinks that the policies have been sent down or disseminated. They talk about it at a senior level, explore what the policy entails. But it gets down to the people that really need to understand it, it's just a photocopy of the original and it's in a shelf or a file and nobody knows what's in there.

In addition to problems on the ground a further problem of great concern is that of health professionals leaving government health services. Jane Simons, the Programme Director, argued that HIV/AIDS, which focused heavily on the provision of anti-retrovirals (ARVs), was having a draining effect on the health services because health professionals were drawn to the ARV projects which 'were often in NGOs because salaries are better, [thus] leaving the services even less resourced than they were before'. The 'brain drain' of professionals, particularly doctors and nurses, who leave South Africa to practise abroad, has had a negative impact on the health services (Department's Annual Report, 2008). There was also a movement of staff to the private sector. Doctors in the public sector have been extremely badly paid, compared to other professionals in the public service, and have to work under appalling conditions with long shifts, insufficient staff and a lack of necessary medical equipment. The government's failure to respond to doctors' demands over a number of years resulted in strike action by doctors in mid-2009 (Malan and Ndlovu, 2009).

In summary, the department of public health is tackling a serious lack of knowledge and skills in health professionals in Africa; too often when students return to their work with new knowledge and skills the calibre of other health professionals stands as an obstacle to their efforts; and it is not within the gift of individually educated health professionals to deal with systemic problems.

Summarizing constraints on public-good professionalism

The main focus of the study which is the subject of this book was on professional education university departments and their populations, and the universities have featured as a backdrop. We did not find any *consistent* correlation between university, race, gender, social class and the presence or absence of public-good values. Nevertheless, we could see an obvious lack of social diversity among the engineering groups and here the university was significant: being rather late in taking up a transformation agenda and process, Acacia still recruits more white and Afrikaans-speaking students, generally from better-off and more politically conservative backgrounds. There are other engineering faculties in South Africa (for example at Silvertree) which are far more diverse with regards to country, race and gender. We might speculate, therefore, that when race and class were added to engineering, which in South Africa has tended also to be a conservative male-dominated profession, students were less aware of and committed to public values. What was significant here though were the effects of exposure through the curriculum and practice to a different South African reality and the impact of this on male, mostly white students.

With reference to the set of 'repairing' professions, the public health department curriculum was shaped by its location in Fynbos, a university which had a history of commitments to transformation and to people in poverty, a majority black student intake, and large numbers of poorer students. The department's own early and continuing public-good values (which had also been strong university values), attracts students with very similar orientations towards a 'working with' rather than 'working for' public health practice. The university setting for law at Fynbos was more ambiguous, for example, some black students at Fynbos felt discriminated against because of perceptions that their degree was not as good as that from Silvertree or Acacia. Yet they were supportive of the university's inclusive mission. Students from poorer backgrounds were conscious of racial and social oppression and for the most part wanted to contribute to change through the law. Yet all the law interviewees also commented – more than in the other four professions – on a growing materialism among black and poorer students, not least those who had extended family obligations. Silvertree attracted better-off and a larger number of white students but there was little evidence that this overrode the professional commitment students brought to social work. Here social work effectively constituted the 'best case' scenario for the functionings development of middle-class students and white students. Theology brought its own distinctive vocational orientation the location in Acacia of both black and white students (who had previously studied in two different universities) raised discomforting and important questions about diversity in the classroom and the communities graduates would serve, and how they would do this. Moreover, the vision of the department was closely aligned with the new mission of the university.

Thus the diversity of universities, students and professional fields were all notable in some way, although the mix varied across professions. The mission of each university further complicated the narrative in that Silvertree has a firm social commitment, but this was not experienced positively by social work which did not think it was valued in their own work in the face of more managerial practices on the ground. Fynbos had an historic involvement in change and an inclusive mission of which students were aware. (Nonetheless the impact of materialism in society had its effects at the micro level.) Acacia had a recent but striking commitment to putting something back into society and advancing a mission of hopefulness. This had propelled engineering into revisiting its curriculum to bring about changes which were aligned with this mission. Here the profession and the advantaged white, male students made the operationalization of this mission in education somewhat uneven.

Finally, from the myriad systemic, material and cultural constraints on public-good professionalism outlined from the case studies above, by way of summary we draw attention to the following, which arose in some form in all the professional case studies: (1) disinclination to practice as a public-good professional; (2) lack of knowledge and shortage of skills; and (3) uncoordinated efforts.

In the accounts above two main explanations were given by our respondents for disinclination to function as a public-good professional oriented to poverty reduction. The first was when doing 'pro-poor' work is pro bono and means sacrificing making money doing some other work, which is most prevalent in law and engineering where individuals will be self-employed (we do *not* condemn individuals who want to maximize the financial returns on their long training and hard work, rather we suggest that the profession as a whole and university-based education and training should ensure that students understand the potential for both making money for themselves and their families and contribution to poverty reduction and inequalities). In theory the tension should not be irresolvable, professional fields have always been important sites of social mobility and this is the case in South Africa: there is no doubt that in itself it is important to have black engineers and lawyers. Students have multiple motives for undertaking professional education: most students we spoke to want to 'make a difference', while simultaneously aspiring to social mobility or maintaining their social position (as the middle-classes always do). Second, in relation to disinclination to work as a public-good professional, the motivation for social workers and health professionals to leave public for private work (or to go abroad) is differently inflected. The professions themselves are strongly oriented to promoting public good and to poverty reduction, but the conditions of work, including poor pay, lead to attrition that in turn contributes to poor conditions, and one important condition is lack of knowledge and shortage of skills in the system and poor working conditions and pay leading to demoralization.

The second serious problem that emerged from all fields is lack of knowledge and shortage of skills. University-based professional education is central to raising the quality of professional work generally. It is clear from what we heard that whatever other capabilities are needed for poverty-reduction professionalism, knowledge and a wide range of skills are essential. In capability terms this capability is foundational: a *sine qua non* of being a high-calibre public-good professional. Yet still in South Africa there is a shortage of highly-skilled people in all the professions that we investigated. The third major constraint on public-good professionalism was unco-ordinated efforts. Although most respondents did not think in terms of a 'social and collective struggle' capability, many of the functionings that might be associated with it appeared as crucially important to gearing the system towards the public good. These are building partnerships collaborating and networking with other professions and groups; and working in teams. The participants at the meeting of the research working groups in March 2009 identified it as a critical capability if goals are to be achieved. In all professions the problem of (to use public health terms) too much 'vertical' organization was hampering professional efforts: no amount of knowledgeable and skilled individual effort will orient the whole profession to the public good, social and collective effort is essential.

The case studies demonstrate how historical, political, economic, social and cultural contexts set permeable if not fixed boundaries on what it is possible to achieve in terms of public-good values and practice. It is clear that, interested as we are in the possibilities of education, lack of resources, understaffed services being and inappropriate government attitudes toward the proper role of professionals can demotivate even groups strongly motivated to serve the poor, the needy and the disadvantaged. In the final chapter that comes next we discuss the possibilities for establishing public-good professional education.

In any national context there are options for and constraints on public-good professionalism. South Africa has a specific context, and despite the challenging features noted here and in Chapter 3, nonetheless, we should also note enablements. The Constitution enshrines the ideals of improving the quality of life of all citizens and establishing a society based on democratic values, social justice and fundamental human rights. The South African Bill of Rights anticipates a free, equal and just society, with human dignity as a core value. The 2011 report of the National Planning Commission (2011) outlines a hopeful development vision and agenda for the next 20 years and draws on the language of capabilities to make the case for the necessity of forging a 'capable state'. Moreover, South Africa is a more or less functioning democracy, with the resources to underpin significant economic development provided that the leadership is in place; and there is a redistribution of some material resources, social grants being the best example, to the poor. In the final chapter we summarize our position and propose some productive ways of thinking about embedding social reform.

9 Public-good pathways to poverty reduction

> Freedom is not merely the chance to do as one pleases; neither is it merely
> the opportunity to choose between set alternatives. Freedom is, first of all, the
> chance to formulate the available choices, to argue over them – and then,
> the opportunity to choose.
>
> (C. Wright Mills, 1959: 174)

Universities are shaped by public policy and social conditions, and potentially
influence relationships, practices, knowledge and values in society. Although
our research was located in a specific context, it stimulates reflections about
broader complexities, problems and questions related to social change and
to university-based professional education. In the first part of this concluding
chapter we deliberate on the case study itself, drawing inferences about university-
based professional education. The second part is a discussion about how social
and educational reform might be embedded in policies and practices. Our aim in
the final chapter is to leave space for continuing vigorous debate about public-
good professional capabilities at the levels of politics, profession, institutions
and individuals.

Reflections on the South African research case study

South Africa is a country where poverty and inequalities are endemic and
entrenched. We argue that such conditions cry out for professionalism oriented
towards the public good, even if it is difficult to attain in such conditions. The
project, therefore, set out to investigate the contribution of universities to
the public good through the academic preparation of professionals. From our
perspective, professional education is located at the intersection of universities,
the state and the public, and its purposes and character is shaped by their often
competing interests. The product of the research – the Public-Good Professional
Capabilities Index – articulates our position on normative and relevant meta-
functionings, capabilities and educational arrangements, taking into account how
historical, social and cultural contexts enable or constrain educational attempts to
develop public-good professionalism.

Three universities and five professional education sites revealed variations and commonalities across professions and universities, producing a more robust evaluation of capabilities-based public-good professionalism than would have been possible by looking at one professional field only. Chapters 6, 7 and 8 demonstrate both how – for students from diverse backgrounds – professional education can form or support commitments and possibilities for acting as public-good professionals, and how circumstances extraneous to individuals and education can set up barriers. The Index is intended for a 'second-best world' (Sen, 2009). We have, therefore, been concerned at all times with real lives and real circumstances. At the same time, as explained in Chapter 2, we have tried to capture in the concept of capabilities-based public-good professionalism how professional work might systematically contribute to a democratic, just and equal society. Working in a non-idealized way enables us to address what can be done to advance justice *now* in societies which may be unjust in their distribution and quality of public services. As Schouten (2012) argues (in relation to schooling) professionals need to begin somewhere in a non-ideal world. For example, it would be dispiriting to ask a social worker to equalize life prospects for all of their clients. The demand to engage in redistribution lies beyond their individual powers. Schouten suggests a scenario which we can adapt. Imagine that the social worker is asked to identify children in a school for whom prospects for flourishing were especially poor and to do what they can in their capacity as a social worker to improve their lives. Such a request offers the social worker a realistic place to begin to take a just course of action in non-ideal circumstances. Now they are able to mobilize their capabilities by way of appropriate functionings.

The eight broad and vague professional capabilities had resonance for the professionals we worked with in South Africa. We noted that student professionals need to develop actual functionings. In this respect, there is something qualitatively different about educating a social worker from, say, educating a sociologist. In Bernstein's (2000) terms it is because teaching and learning are focused on a specific 'performance' (rather than the internal quality of knowledge). In the terms of a capabilities approach to educating for public-good professionalism, the focus must be on the functionings that will be formed and mobilized during professional education and training. These functionings will appear differently in different professional fields, nevertheless they will express professional-good capabilities. Moreover, we believe that the Index could be taken up in any professional education site in developing and developed countries (see for example East *et al.*, accepted). However, although the expectation is that the capabilities will transfer across contexts, they are likely to require different nomenclature in different contexts (for example, in one project in the UK the notion of 'struggle' did not translate well [ibid.]).

Undoubtedly, lecturers in professional education departments are making strenuous efforts to educate students with the capabilities to tackle South Africa's many problems, and the students we talked to see themselves as part of social transformation. Nonetheless, our participants were also disillusioned by entrenched poverty, increased inequality, the incompetence and sometimes corruption of professionals in their fields. The legacy of apartheid still poses great material and social difficulties, and in South African society more generally, moral indifference is an obstacle to change and action. Such indifference can be experienced as a protective 'membrane' insulating the better off from the distress of lives lived in poverty. For example, Kalati and Manor's (2005) study found that the elite perceptions of South African society were that it was not particularly unequal; that the prevalence of poverty did not affect its own well-being in terms of health (for it still had access to high-quality private medical services); and that poverty was not connected to the possibility of political upheaval. While crime was a preoccupation with the elite, it was not seen as a consequence of poverty, rather as a breakdown of law and order. The elite also thought that it contributed disproportionately to the needs of the poor by way of taxes distributed by the government. Thus, Kalati and Manor found a still deeply segmented society with social and physical distance between elites and the poor. Yet they found too that people belonging to the elite responded 'powerfully' (ibid.: 177) when informed about how inequitable their society is; and that they could be persuaded that the end of apartheid has not solved the problem of inequality and that people living in poverty are an important resource for society.

That elites can be persuaded in this way brings us directly back to education. In Chapter 2, we identified De Swaan and colleagues' (2000) work as being helpful for its explicit focus on elite social contributions to making changes or to maintaining the status quo. De Swann *et al.* (ibid.) claim that how elites perceive poverty and their own role in bringing about more equality 'can powerfully affect social policy and the lives of the poor' (ibid.: 1). In South Africa, all university-educated professionals might be considered as elite: only 16 per cent of the population have access to higher education and professional groups have radically better social status and earning power than people living in poverty. The stance we take on the education of professional elites is not unique. From our perspective, university-based professional education can foster exactly what De Swann *et al.* (2000) propose for elites: awareness of the interdependence of groups in society; a disposition to take some moral responsibility for the conditions of people living in poverty; and belief in the possibility that their participation in public action can reduce poverty.

The capabilities approach focuses on the individual and we are left with the problem that social justice takes more than the actions of individual, rather it requires social and political institutions to ensure the just distribution of benefits and costs (Nussbaum, 2000). Nagel (2009: 116) expands on the problem: individuals' desire to live on fairer terms with others is insufficient to bring about just order which 'depends on consistent patterns of conduct and persisting institutions that have a pervasive effect on the shape of people's lives'. Separate individuals, he argues, however attached to ideals of justice, have neither motive nor opportunity to conform to just patterns or institutions on their own, 'without the assurance that their conduct will in fact be part of a reliable and effective system' (ibid.). This assurance requires a justice-enabling centralized system or authority or sovereign power, which confers stability on institutions so that other-regarding individuals are not forced back on to aspirations for justice that they cannot practically realize. From our capabilities-approach perspective forms of affiliation might provide this type of stability: affiliation built in departments of professional education; affiliation promoted by professional associations; and affiliation with clients. We discuss each in turn below.

First, then, professional education university departments, whether or not their goals are explicitly oriented towards the public good, educate professionals for performance, for ethical judgement and for a disposition towards society and clients. Such departments institutionalize distinctive cultures through their pedagogical and research practices. The professional department is highly influential: Sullivan (2005: 186) describes the decisive impact of professional education at institutional level on professional identity as a 'deep effect upon attitude and character' and this is because through a range of discursive practices the departments 'structure attention and impose sanctions to reinforce the dispositions appropriate to their ends' (ibid.). Freidson (2004: 84) also emphasizes the role of the professional department in developing 'commitment to the occupation as a life career and to a shared identity, a feeling of community or solidarity among those who have passed through it'. He argues that this commitment is engendered because the students have freely chosen the occupation; and are educated and trained in cohorts undertaking the same courses over a long period; in these conditions 'a distinct social identity and a privileged official identity supports the inclination to make their work a lifetime career' (ibid: 102). So for novice professionals, the discursive practices and values of the department in which they are studying represent the professional world to which they aspire. For practicing professionals returning to take higher degrees, the department can provide a new lens on their everyday work. For both groups, as we saw in our case studies, professional expectations, standards and values are expressed in the overt and hidden curriculum, pedagogy and assessment.

Second, and similarly to professional education departments, professional associations might be thought of as justice-enhancing institutions which can promote consistent patterns. They both protect the interests of members and debate about 'professional ideals' (Sullivan, 2005). Collectively, professionals could have considerable power. As Freidson (2004: 217) proposes, 'the most influential source of evaluation and protest comes from a collegial body which provides authoritative support to individuals and expresses forcefully the collective opinion of the discipline'. Making alliances within one's own profession – and with progressive groups in society – could be a sustaining part of professional work. Though Sullivan (2005: 285) makes the point that the extent to which interactions are productive depends 'upon the extent to which qualities of civic cooperation prevail in the larger social environment'. In South Africa specifically, professionals oriented to the public good will need to raise strong and principled voices in policy-making forums and in the communities where they practice. Courage and resilience will be needed.

The third focus for the capability of affiliation is clients. In South Africa heavy emphasis is put on empowering communities to develop and sustain their own projects, working within the context of such projects could provide opportunities for collective action. We have argued for 'associative responsibility' (Nagel, 2009: 125) whereby professionals develop a sense connectedness to disadvantaged lives and of solidarity with disadvantaged people and their life projects. Everywhere professional elites have a voice and some access to political and collective professional power. The capabilities of affiliation and for social and collective struggle, in particular, could promote cohesion and unity to work for change that strengthens democracy and tackles severe poverty.

Whatever the possibilities for sustaining an orientation to the public good, there are serious constraints – detailed in Chapters 3 and 8 – on pursuing public-good professionalism in South Africa and elsewhere. The knowledge, skills and public service values of professionals *can* make a positive difference to the everyday lives of the people. Moreover the case study data shows that there are some grounds for hope. Agency in professional work involves the meaning the work has for the individual and the formation of an identity in relation to the work (for example, being compliant, resistant or creatively engaged). Cohen (2000: 142) reminds us that 'Personal choices [. . .] are fateful for social justice'. In South Africa there have been a number of recent challenges from public-good lawyers, for example, regarding the failures in the provision of basic education and a Constitutional Court case pending (at the time of writing) arguing for basic education as a human right (see for example *Mail and Guardian*, 2013a, b). So we turn now to a more general discussion about the possibilities for embedding social reform.

Looking forward: transformation pathways

We have both theorized capabilities-based public-good professionalism and operationalized the theory to demonstrate its applicability to professional education departments and the everyday lives of professionals. What has not yet been addressed is the question of how to conceptualize what it would take to embed and sustain public-good professional capabilities and functionings. Having conducted empirical research, we now want to take a clear-eyed look at the future prospects of promoting/creating public-good professionalism, in this case in the context of South Africa. In this endeavour we have found both Davina Cooper (2001) and Onora O'Neill (1996) helpful because they eschew grand plans of wholesale change for starting where we find ourselves.

For O'Neill (1996: 183) advances towards social justice are likely to be piecemeal and a 'remodelling of what is to hand, of repairing or redesigning parts rather than the whole'. Given what we know about what goes on university-based education departments, it is possible to conceptualize the advance of a capabilities-based professional education in this way. The Index as process and product is yet to be systematically taken up, although as we detail in Chapter 7 there are all kinds of promising educational practices which can and are working to remodel professionalism. As O'Neill (ibid.) points out, we need to try out new actions: they might turn out to be imperfect or 'defective' but without them we cannot know 'what new institutions, policies and practices can be forged'. Similarly, a capabilities approach to professional education need not wait, but rather be attempted.

Taking a rather different approach, Cooper (2001) uses the metaphor of 'social pathways' to develop a detailed explication of the problems innovations face in becoming sustainable. The main question she asks is how new practices are adopted and sustained in circumstances when there is gap between beliefs (for example in transformation in South Africa) and actions (for example, a co-ordination of efforts to improve public health). She makes the point that that new routines which are at odds with their social and institutional environment tend to disappear, but suggests that new social pathways might be generated which challenge the reproduction of dominant social relations of inequalities and might persist *de jure* (for example, by policy) and *de facto* (through usage). The character of the social constraints facing public-good professionals in South Africa might be seen at odds with public-good professionalism, yet many of the educational arrangements we saw align with public-good values and practices, and the South African social transformation agenda, at least rhetorically, permeates everything. Some argue that it is still a short time since the end of apartheid and that it is still possible to interact strategically with dominant ideologies to forge pathways which 'produce adjustments in domain norms, practices and procedures' (Cooper, 2001: 123). Moreover, Cooper describes social pathways as being 'walked and woven' (ibid: 128) by individuals and groups of individuals. Usage involves 'multiple tramping of the same soil – leads pathways to deepen and become entrenched, rendering the activities they articulate increasingly naturalized' (ibid.: 129). This repeated treading is how oppositional pathways emerge. For our purposes there can be no social pathway to public-good professionalism without individuals whose personal trajectories have been shaped by their experiences, including their university education, to walk the public-good professional pathway into existence.

So reform comes by way of repetition rather than dramatic one-off challenges. We can imagine, with the example of Unabantu Mali that opened this book in mind, that more nurses and other health professionals repeatedly doing things differently and better in public health clinics would improve public health. Or more lawyers acting over and over again more humanely in the ways described by our participant lawyers would forge a more open legal access pathway for the poor, and so on. Yet such pathways are difficult to tread if the harsh environmental pressures (for example the shocking inequalities detailed in Chapter 3) are relentless and unchanging. Resonating with Sen's (2009) argument for comparative assessments of justice over an ideal form of justice, Cooper suggest that durable pathways forged through repetition 'evolve beyond the idealist Utopian narratives of the impossibly good place' (2001: 124). This is important for the argument we make in this book. Steering a path between cynicism or disillusionment and naive idealism is always difficult. Like democracy itself, public-good professionalism is always precarious, it is 'never a given, but always a quest that must be renewed and reshaped over time. It demands considerable individual self-awareness and self-command. Yet, it also depends for its realization upon the availability of actual social possibilities' (Sullivan, 2005: 220).

Hope resides in the strong and clear visions of public-good professionalism that the students, lecturers, professionals and others we spoke to held; and in the strenuous efforts to equip professionals by way of education. There *is* an ideal at work: in pockets education is producing outstanding professionals whose solidarity, rationality and reflection will make them more likely to act as agents for transformation in a country that faces serious political and social problems. In reality, history, structure and professional agency interact in complex ways. Iris Marion Young (2011) reminds us that we should not resign ourselves to historic injustice. We can take responsibility, as discussed in Chapter 2, to make practices more just. The development and use of the capabilities-based Index reflects the historical and social complexities of professional education; it allows a sophisticated evaluation of goals, policies and practices; and can hold together different professional groups with different interests. The Index is the result of negotiations, arguments and compromises with those dealing with a harsh reality. Yet it expresses the hopes and actions of these people and has the potential to be 'critical, transgressive, transformative' (Fournier, 2002: 192). It is not a blueprint for a perfect public-good professional education for the durability of such an Index will always require re-negotiation. Like the utopian visions Fournier (2002: 192) discusses, the Index:

> undermines dominant understanding of what is possible and opens up new conceptual spaces for imagining and practicing possible futures [. . .] it is about what moves us to hope for and to cultivate, alternative possibilities; and it is about establishing the conditions for the development of alternatives and [it] resist[s] the temptation of closure around another 'best' alternative'.

Guarding against absolutism avoids the impossibilities and illiberalities of classical utopianism (Fournier, 2002).

From this point, a threefold practical strategy might be suggested:

- Good professional governance (regulation and policy) addressed over time through the capability of social and collective struggle, and through the multidimensional list of public-good professional capabilities as each supports the formation and strengthening of the others.
- Building on and securing professional attitudes in the direction of the public good by way of a capabilities-based ethic embedded in professional education; thereby
- Making social pathways in practice and sustaining these over time through practices in universities and in professional work.

It is our hope that university educators in professional fields, professional bodies and NGOs will use or adapt the Index and the processes by which it was generated to develop, evaluate, think and argue about what they are doing individually.

We have offered a combination of the capabilities approach and the concept of public-good professionalism as a way of thinking about and evaluating professional education that can pose challenges and frame curriculum reform efforts directed towards social justice. We further hope to encourage contributions to justice by generating possibilities, springing from professional education, for individual, educational and social change pathways which can endure.

Public-good professionalism as we conceptualize it is always in process towards an ideal of a society in which professionals will value creating capabilities for all (Nussbaum, 2011) under the conditions of a 'second-best' world (Sen, 2009). The hope is that universities contribute to poverty reduction and reducing inequalities by embracing their role in producing public-good professionals who will see themselves as contributing to a better society and a better world. Embedded in the Index is the following assumption: given that all professionals – engineers, lawyers, doctors, nurses, teachers, economists, business leaders, social workers, and so on – are now university educated, that education could be a significant contribution to poverty reduction in South Africa if it combines the acquisition of knowledge and skills *and* the development of other-regarding transformation values. In this view, education is a means to advance justice by providing capability-expanding services to people living in conditions of poverty or having precarious and vulnerable lives. Within the ambit of professional services there are injustices which are 'redressable' (Sen, 2009: vii), without waiting for perfect social structures, or perfectly just institutions to be put in place, or even perfect public-good professionals.

Appendix A
Interview questions

Professional bodies and NGOs

1. Please comment on this list of 13 categories which we think are important for any person's flourishing (well-being). They can be described as things which one would value being and doing. Please go through them and comment on them. In particular we would like to know which you consider especially valuable in the lives of the poor/disadvantaged. Are there others which you would want to add?
2. Taking this into account, what qualities do you think are important in a professional [so that they contribute through their work to social transformation, specifically improving the lives of the poor/disadvantaged]?
3. In your experience, what kinds of professionals are coming out of higher education? Are there gaps in professional education and training?
4. What ought professional education departments in universities to be doing to develop the qualities you think are important?
5. Do you know or have you worked with students or graduates from Department X at University Y? What is your perception of what this university department is doing to develop important qualities, based on your personal knowledge of students and graduates?
6. Is there anything you would like to add about the role of: i) universities; and ii) the professionals they educate in social transformation in South Africa?

Pro vice-chancellor (PVC)

1. How has this university transformed since 1994? How has the student body changed? What have been the effects? How does this university understand and deal with the issue of race and/or social class?
2. How does the university leadership understand social transformation? How do you conceptualize social transformation yourself, in your PVC role?
3. Are there, or have there been, contested views across the university? If there are, how do you implement change?
4. Can you describe specific concrete examples in research, teaching and social involvement of transformation? What about poverty reduction and the MDGs? Is this a concern? In what way?

5. Which would be the most important qualities and values you would want this university to develop/form in its graduates?

6. Is there anything else you would like to add about the role of this university in social transformation? What about the role and future of South African universities more broadly?

Dean

1. How do you conceptualize social transformation yourself, as dean?

2. What are the ways in which this faculty understands social transformation? Is there a singular view, or contested views?

3. Given all this, how has this faculty and its departments transformed since 1994? How has its student body changed? How do you account for these changes?

4. Can you describe specific concrete examples of what has been done in relation to transformation (whether of research, teaching, community engagement, or values]? What about Department X?

5. Is poverty reduction a concern? If it is, how is it addressed?

6. Which would be the most important qualities and values you personally would want this faculty to develop/form in its graduates? Who is doing this well in this faculty? How are they doing it? What would need to change for every student to develop these qualities and values?

7. What ought the role of this faculty to be in the city, the region, and South Africa now, and in the future? What kind of professional does South Africa need now and in the future?

8. Is there anything else you would like to add about social transformation and this university/this faculty?

Hod

1. How has this department transformed since 1994? What has been easy and what has been hard in making these changes? How does it still need to change? [How has the university been transformed? How have these changes enabled or constrained change in the department?]

2. Why does this department do what it does? Which would be the most important qualities and values you as HoD would want to develop/form in your graduates? What kind of professional are you trying to produce – why? Has this changed over the years/your career? Has it become more or less difficult?

3. What kind of contribution do you hope they will be making? Can you describe/talk about one or two current students and two or three graduates who exemplify what you are trying to do here?

4. What kinds of things do you/this department do to bring about/produce these kinds of students and professionals? Could you talk about the curriculum and pedagogy, community engagement and professional ethics you develop

and foster and how you do this? How successful are you in achieving your goals? What about research in the department? What approaches do you take and what research questions do you ask? What about involvement in developing and/or critiquing relevant policy?

5. Is there a common understanding of what social transformation is in the department? How and where has this been/is this discussed; what are the disagreements (if any)? Can you describe a particular occasion in the department when transformation was debated?

6. What, in your view, is the role of a professional in today's South Africa, and in tomorrow's South Africa? Is there the possibility and responsibility to contribute to social change?

7. Is there anything else you would like to add about professional education and training in this department?

Lecturer

1. How has this department transformed since 1994? What has been easy and what has been hard for you in making these changes? How have your students changed? [How has the university been transformed? How have these changes enabled or constrained change in the department?]

2. Why do you do what you do? What kind of professional are you trying to produce – why? Has this changed over the years/your career? Has it become more or less difficult?

3. What are the most important professional goals, qualities and values you are trying to develop among your students?

4. What kind of contribution do you hope they will be making? Can you describe/talk about one or two current students and two or three graduates who exemplify what you are trying to do here?

5. What kinds of things do you do to bring about these kinds of students and professionals? Would you talk about the curriculum and pedagogy, community engagement and professional ethics you develop and foster and how you do this? Can you give concrete examples of teaching and learning or clinical practice and what you are doing and what the students are doing and learning? How successful are you in achieving your goals?

6. What is your own understanding of social transformation? Is there a common understanding of what social transformation is in the Department? How and where has this been/is this discussed; what are the disagreements (if any)? Can you describe a particular occasion in the department when transformation was debated? Is race an issue at all for staff and students?

7. What, in your view, is the role of a professional in today's South Africa, and in tomorrow's South Africa?

8. Is there anything else you would like to add about professional education and training in this department?

Students (focus groups)

1. Why did you choose to be an X? What is it about this profession that especially appealed to you? Do you still feel the same way? So what kind of professional do you hope to be? How typical are you of students in your class?
2. In your view, what kind of professional X does South Africa need now, and in the future?
3. Is this the same or different from what the department wants? And what the University wants?
4. Would you talk about the most important aspects of working with disadvantaged people and communities? What do you think matters to them? What and how do you work with them? What do you think matters to them in the way professionals work with them? What do you do? What do they do?
5. What do you think are the most important goals, qualities and values of a professional in South Africa? In what ways is your professional education and training at this University helping you to develop these goals and qualities? Could you talk about concrete examples of teaching and learning and practical/clinical work where this is happening/has happened for you?
6. Have you changed as person through your professional education? What do you hope for in the future in your career? What would be a good life for you? What do you value in your professional education and for your future career? What choices do you expect to have to make?

G. Alumni

1. Why did you choose to be an X? What especially appealed to you about this profession? Have your views changed at all?
2. In your view, what qualities are most important in a social worker/lawyer/ public health professional/community worker in South Africa now, and in the future?
3. What kind of professional are you? Why is this? How typical are you of your graduating class?
4. How did your university education and training in social work/law etc. equip you for professional life? Were there any areas in which your professional education did not prepare you adequately?
5. Do you think you are you the kind of professional the department wanted you to be?
6. Could you talk about the most important aspects of working with disadvantaged/vulnerable people and communities? What do you think matters to them? How do you work with them? What do you think matters to them in the way professionals work with them?
7. What is the daily impact of your work? What constrains or enables what you want to do? Do you feel you make a difference?
8. What are you hopes for your future professional life? What for you is/would be good life? What do you value in your professional life and why?

Appendix B

B.1 Functionings from social work data

Alumni	Students	Lecturers
Facilitating capability expansions of clients – 'self-determination'	Expanding capability of poor people to bring about change in their lives and communities	Capability to be a transformative professional, informed by knowledge and understanding of South African and global context
Recognising resilience of poor people, recognizing resources of communities	Critical understanding of 'empowering' approach, not romanticize	Expanding capability of poor people to bring about change in their lives and communities
Holistic approach to practice	Understanding individuals, families and communities in a holistic, 'inter-systemic way'	Generalist, flexible, balanced professional, able to respond appropriately to different contexts, drawing on different methods
Vision of a just society	Calling, passion (vision)	Work to reduce poverty, inequality, informed by a social justice perspective
Reliability and accountability	Accountability and obligation, consistency, sustainability, not making 'empty promises'	Ethical, honest, with integrity, not making false promises
Decision-making about appropriate strategies, prioritizing and allocation of funding etc.	Capability to be flexible, innovative, use appropriate strategies	Responsibility, accountability in terms of efficiency
Political sense	Negotiating different interests and agendas, political sense and voicing one's own position	Contributing to policy formation, implementation and critique
Confidence/desire to grow into leadership position	Confidence	Going against the grain

Alumni	Students	Lecturers
Doing research in order to increase knowledge and understanding		Build links with other public good professionals and organizations
Ongoing growth and professional development	Pride in profession	Reflective practitioner, engaged in ongoing professional development
Perseverance		Pride in profession
Establishing professional boundaries/protective boundaries		
Resilience through self-awareness and self-care		
Capability for emotional affiliation, building relationships		Empathy
Learning from the poor		Caring, people-centred in opposition to competitive, individualistic, materialistic, society
Appreciation of diversity and building bridges		Respect in relation to diversity
Ethical values and practice	Respect	Respect

B.2 Educational arrangements from social work data

Alumni	Students	Lecturers
Practical experience built into curriculum	Cultivation of innovative, self-reflective, professional, involved in ongoing professional development	Curriculum that aims to imbue students with 'systemic', contextualized understanding of social development practice
Disjuncture between theory of social work practice and practical experience in 'real world'. Limitations on extent to which university can prepare students	Accountability responsibility Writing reports, meeting deadlines	Communicating particular vision of social development practice
		Engaging with critical theory
Quality of agency supervision	Learning from practical components	Integrating experiential learning and theory
Lecturers engaged in current research	Confidence building, communicative capability through presentations, feedback	Teaching variety of methods and building contextualized judgement about interventions

Alumni	Students	Lecturers
Research projects	Integrating practice and theory	Fourth-year specialism for particular spheres of practice
Evidence of student learning, drawing conclusions and formulating an argument through experience of research project	Discussion of impact of their practical involvement on the communities, and sustainability	Building confidence through presentations to department and stakeholders
Building awareness of and training for knowledge production in a South African context	Positive and negative experiences of departmental supervision i.r.t. practical work	Personal growth aspect building resilience
Cultivating professional excellence	Positive and negative experiences of agency supervision	Supervision within placement, mentoring and guidance
Contextualizing social work practice in SA history	Diversity of lecturers and approaches	Safe space for processing exposure to difficult realities
Application of theory to practice – whole systems model	Balance or lack of balance between theory and practical components of curriculum	Emphasis on developing equal and reciprocal relationships
Resilience building through self knowledge and reflection on self	Difficulty of less support during honours year	Communicative ability for listening and developing empathic relationship Engaging with diversity and prejudice within classroom
		Carefully designed research projects. Develop students' sense of being able to make a difference
		Networking between department, government departments and NGOs etc.
		Knowledge and understanding of social welfare system
		Academic development
		Diversity and expertise of staff in department

B.3 Social constraints from social work data

Alumni	*Students*	*Lecturers*
Inadequacy of institutional resources, finances and staffing	Structural, economic realities that constrain social workers from making a difference. Complete breakdown of social structures	Majority of students middle-class, sheltered and young (haven't lived through or were very young during apartheid)
Poor salaries of social workers	Poor working conditions, low salaries	Reliance on supervision by agency staff, which depends on individual supervisors
Limited capabilities of professionals	Powerlessness to make an impact in the face of multi-layered, compounded poverty	Challenges for recognition and valuing of social development's work within university
Resistance from people in communities to social workers and social work interventions	Resistance of poor people to interventions from social workers	Poor quality of school education of working-class and rural black students
Dependency, sense of entitlement and 'learned helplessness' of poor people	Either wanting handouts or complete disillusionment and despair	Poor quality of many practising social workers
Low status of social workers	Low status of social workers	Desperate shortage of social workers in system, both government and NGOs, but lack of funding
Lack of clear and strong professional identity	Institutional constraints on agency of social workers	Many social workers leave the country
Many social workers leave profession	Vision, 'calling', passion, heart for being a social worker crushed by barriers and own powerlessness	
	Too few social workers both in government and NGO contexts to meet desperate social problems. Lack of resources both staff and financial	
	Contradiction of shortage of social workers, and difficulty for new graduates to get jobs	
	Desire to go overseas	
	Question whether will come back	

Appendix C

C.1 Engineering interviewees (pseudonyms used)

Name	Male	Female	African	Indian	Coloured	White
a) Students 4th year Bachelor of Engineering						
Focus group 1						
Mandla	X		X			
Pieter	X					X
Focus group 2						
Dawie	X					X
Fabian	X				X	
Jaya	X			X		
b) Alumni						
Theuns le Roux	X					X
Jeanne Marais		X				X
Willem Steenkamp	X					X
Chantal Brown		X	X			
c) Lecturers						
Marian Lamprecht		X				X
Christo van Heerden	X					X
Jonathan Landsman	X		X			
d) Other university						
Marius de Beer, head of department of process engineering	X					X
Thomas Ryer, dean	X					X
Hendrik Pretorius, acting dean (interviewed in 2009)	X					X

Name	Male	Female	African	Indian	Coloured	White
e) Others						
Fiona Perkins, NGO representative		X				X
Kobus van Rensburg, professional body	X					X

C.2 Law interviewees (pseudonyms used)

Name	Male	Female	African	Indian	Coloured	White
a) Students 4th year Bachelor of Law						
Focus group 1						
Nazia		X			X	
Lynne		X			X	
Sandra		X			X	
Focus group 2						
Michael	X				X	
Jennifer		X			X	
Focus group 3						
Tozi		X	X			
Bongi		X	X			
Peter (Namibian)	X				X	
Zubeida		X			X	
Focus group 4						
Yusuf	X				X	
Ashiek	X				X	
Alice		X			X	
Ebrahim	X				X	
Daniel	X				X	
b) Alumni						
Themba Vilikazi, state legal advisor	X		X			
Zolani Ncube, from rural Transkei, private law firm	X		X			
Dumisani Bangeni, private law firm	X		X			
Thandi Dlamini, women's legal centre		X	X			

Name	Male	Female	African	Indian	Coloured	White
c) Lecturers						
William Brown, head of department, English	X				X	
Helen Thompson, professor, English		X				X
Rohan Mestrie, lecturer, English	X				X	
Shamiel Jessop, lecturer, Afrikaans	X				X	
Khatidja Bashir, lecturer, English		X			X	
d) Other university						
Charles Lewis, professor and pro vice-chancellor	X					
Leonard Smith, deputy dean of the law faculty	X				X	
e) Others						
Arnold Muller, director of legal education, professional body	X					X
Robert Michaels, professional body	X				X	
Hazel Smith, director, legal NGO		X				X
Johan Wentzel, legal NGO	X					X
Felicity Green, NGO		X				X

C.3 Theology interviewees (pseudonyms used)

Name	Male	Female	African	Indian	Coloured	White
a) Students 4th year Bachelor of Theology						
Focus group 1						
Karl	X					X
Aidan	X				X	
David	X				X	
Nico	X					X
Focus group 2						
Lukas	X				X	

Name	Male	Female	African	Indian	Coloured	White
Peter	X					X
Inez		X				X
Focus group 3						
Jacques	X					X
Adele		X				X
Aletta		X				X
Marieke		X				X
Sara		X				X
Focus group 4						
Ignatius	X					X
Marie		X				X
b) Alumni						
Linda du Toit, contract minister, DRC, graduated 2003		X			X	
Niels Landsman, rural minister, URCSA, graduated 2002	X				X	
André van Wyk, rural minister, URCSA, graduated 2003	X				X	
Saul Fouché, permanent minister, DRC, graduated 1996	X					X
c) Lecturers						
Daniel le Roux	X					X
Jan Hofmeyr	X					X
d) Other university						
Shaun Muller, deputy vice chancellor	X				X	
Jeanne Olivier, dean of faculty		X				X
Marlene Brink, faculty manager		X				X
Jakob Steyn, head of department and lecturer	X				X	
e) Other						
Nataniel Brand, faith-based NGO	X					X

C.4 Social Work interviewees (pseudonyms used)

** The degree was changed to a four year Bachelor of Social Work degree in 2007 to comply with the requirements of the National Qualifications Framework and the national professional council. The students who were interviewed in our study were doing Honours (Bachelors plus one postgraduate year) under the previous system.

Name	Male	Female	African	Indian	Coloured	White
a) Students 4th year Bachelor of Social Science (Honours)						
Focus group 1						
Joy (specializing in social development; from other Southern African country)		X	X			
Sharon (clinical)		X		X		
Karen (clinical)		X				X
Sheila (social development)		X				X
Focus group 2						
Mary (social development; from other Southern African country)		X	X			
Carla (social development)		X				X
Lyn (social development)		X				X
Yusuf (social development)	X				X	
b) Alumni						
Charmaine Jacobs, school social worker, graduated 2006		X			X	
Anne Hardy, faith-based organization, graduated 1984		X				X
Thandi Matshisa, NGO, graduated 2007		X	X			
Lisa Smith, NGO, graduated 2005		X				X
c) Lecturers						
Miriam Grey, head of department		X		X		

Name	Male	Female	African	Indian	Coloured	White
Elizabeth Goodwin		X				X
Dorothy Williams		X		X		
Amanda Hoffman		X				X
d) Others						
Rehaana Desai, NGO		X			X	
Joanne Rose, NGO		X			X	
Liezel Vermaak, professional body		X				X

C.5 Public Health interviewees (pseudonyms used)

Name	Male	Female	African	Indian	Coloured	White
a) Students (Masters In Public Health, distance programme)						
Focus group 1						
Maureen		X			X	
Sipho	X		X			
Michael (from other Southern African country)	X		X			
Lila (from other Southern African country)		X	X			
Focus group 2						
Matthew (from other Southern African country)	X		X			
Malisako (from other Southern African country)	X		X			
Buyiswa		X	X			
Luleka		X	X			
Focus group 3						
Moira		X			X	
Daniel (from other Southern African country)	X		X			
Tsidi (from other Southern African country)		X	X			

Name	Male	Female	African	Indian	Coloured	White
Hafeni (from other Southern African country)		X	X			
Thumi		X	X			
Mpho		X	X			
b) Alumni						
Laura Bailey, NGO		X			X	
Liziwe Mabi, dietician, private sector		X	X			
Nomvuyo Langa, programme manager, DOH		X	X			
Pamela Roberts, occupational therapist, state hospital		X				X
c) Lecturers						
Jane Simons		X				X
Nobuntu Tladi		X	X			
Paul Daniels	X				X	
d) Other university						
Charles Lewis, pro vice-chancellor	X					X
Bongi Maseko, dean of faculty		X	X			
Michael Andrews, head of department	X					X
e) Others						
Felicity Green, NGO		X			X	
Mark Sacks, NGO	X					X

Notes

1 Higher education in a global context

1 Apartheid geography in South Africa which placed black workers in so-called townships at some distance from the city where most worked has persisted, notwithstanding democratic shifts since 1994. Many of these townships have grown considerably over the years to include sprawling informal settlements, still largely invisible to those living in well-off suburbs. People living in poverty are still ill-served by public services, public transport and the like.
2 The Millennium Development Goals are: eradicate poverty and hunger; achieve universal primary education; promote gender equality and empower women; reduce child mortality; improve maternal health; combat HIV/AIDS, malaria and other diseases; ensure environmental sustainability; develop a global partnership for development. It is important to note, as Deneulin and Shahani (2009) explain, that the MDGs do not include concerns for participation and empowerment, or equity and distributional issues, or sustainability over time. They are limited in their philosophy but may nonetheless be strategically significant.
3 The Magna Carta is Online at HTTP: http://www.magna-charta.org/home2.html (accessed 1 December 2011).
4 Online at HTTP: http://www.tufts.edu/talloiresnetwork/?pid=17 (accessed 15 December 2011).
5 Online at HTTP: http://www.unesco.org/education/educprog/wche/declaration_eng.htm (accessed 15 December 2011).

2 Capabilities-based public-good professionalism

1 We use the term 'school' to cover 'department' or 'department' or another academic unit where professional education and training takes place.
2 For example, for social workers there is the inspiring story of Jane Addams who, in the late nineteenth century, set up a settlement for work which became what is recognizable as social work today: '[Her] philanthropy had a civic, political, end: the formation of citizens through the repair and promotion of public life' (Sullivan 2005: 113).

3 Histories, inequalities and context

1 For an overview of South African history see J. Barber (1999) *South Africa in the Twentieth Century* (Oxford: Blackwell Wiley) and N. Clark and W. Worger (2003), *South Africa: The Rise and Fall of Apartheid* (Harlow: Longman).
2 While problematic for their origins in apartheid classification categories, social/population groups are nonetheless still required to monitor change. The four groups

are commonly described as Africans, coloureds, Indians/Asians and whites. The term 'black' is commonly used as a broader category, including blacks, coloureds and Indians.
3 BEE stands for 'Black Economic Empowerment' a programme of the South African government to give economic opportunities to previously disadvantaged groups (African, coloured, Indian and Chinese who were all declared 'black' in 2008). The scheme includes measures such as employment equity, skills development, and preferential procurement.

6 Participants' conceptions of professional work in South Africa

1 'Having a lot of hair on your teeth' is a South African description for having grit or perseverance.
2 It should be pointed out here that the students in the study belong to this group. They were studying a specific elective course which placed them in a legal aid clinic to work for poor and marginalized communities, the very communities from which these, all coloured, students themselves came.
3 The students cited the Dutch Reformed minister and anti-apartheid activist, Beyers Naudé as the earliest practitioner of public theology in South Africa. Theologians such as Desmond Tutu have been involved in processes of transformation and reconciliation. He was the first black (African) archbishop of the Anglican Church in South Africa, was an outspoken anti-apartheid activist and was one of the leading figures in the Truth and Reconciliation Commission.
4 South African Council for the Social Service profession – SACSSP code of conduct.
5 To return to Bernstein's (2001) typology.

7 Pedagogical environments for the production of public-good professionals

1 We did not interview alumni who worked in white communities.

8 Universities and social conditions

1 We interviewed someone from TRAC, an NGO that aims to assist school students with science and maths, ie. to develop more school-leavers who can go into science and technology jobs, especially engineering. Interestingly, we were not able to get hold of an NGO that works directly with engineers despite strenuous efforts.

References

Abbas, A. and McLean, M (2010) Tackling Inequality through Quality: A comparative case study using Bernsteinian concepts, in E. Unterhalter and V. Carpentier (eds), *Global Inequalities in Higher Education*, Palgrave MacMillan.

Abbott, A.D. (1983) *The System of Professions: An Essay on the Division of Expert Labour*, Chicago, IL: University of Chicago Press.

Abel, R. (1995) *Politics by Other Means: Law in the Struggle Against Apartheid, 1980–1994*, New York: Routledge.

Alkire, S. (2002) 'Dimensions of human development', *World Development*, 30(2): 181–200.

—— (2007) 'Concepts and measures of agency', OPHI Working Papers Series. Online. Available HTTP: http://www.ophi.org.uk/wp-content/uploads/OPHI-wp09.pdf (accessed 2 May 2012).

—— (2008) 'Using the capability approach: prospective and evaluative analyses', in F. Comim, M. Qizilbash and S. Alkire (eds) *The Capability Approach: Concepts, Measures and Applications*, Cambridge: Cambridge University Press.

Altbach, P. (2009) 'The complex roles of universities in the period of globalization', in GUNI (eds) *Higher Education at a Time of Transformation*, Basingstoke: Palgrave Macmillan.

Amsler, S. and Bolsmann, S. (2012) 'University ranking as social inclusion', *British Journal of Sociology of Education*, 33(2): 283–301.

Aronowitz, S. and Giroux, H. (2000) 'The corporate university and the politics of education', *The Educational Forum*, 64: 332–9.

Badat, S. (2001) 'Transforming South African higher education: paradoxes, policy choices, interests and constraints', paper presented at Salzburg Seminar on Higher Education in Emerging Economies: Patterns, Policies and Trends into the 21st Century, Salzburg, Austria, 7–11 July 2001.

—— (2004) 'Transforming South African higher education, 1990–2003: goals, policy initiatives and critical challenges and issues', in N. Cloete, P. Pillay, S. Badat and T. Moja (eds) *National Policy and a Regional Response in South African Higher Education*, Oxford: James Currey and David Phillips.

—— (2008a) 'Redressing the colonial/apartheid legacy: social equity, redress and higher education admissions in democratic South Africa', paper presented at Conference on Affirmative Action in Higher Education in India, the United States and South Africa, New Delhi, India, 19–21 March 2008.

—— (2008b) 'Return to critical scholarship', *Mail and Guardian Online*, 15 April 2008. Online. Available HTTP: http://www.mg.co.za/article/2008-04-15-return-to-critical-scholarship (accessed 6 June 2008).

—— (2010) 'Global rankings of universities: a perverse and present burden', in E. Unterhalter and V. Carpentier (eds) *Whose Interests are we Serving? Global Inequalities and Higher Education*, New York: Palgrave.

Badsha, N. and Cloete, N. (2011) *Higher Education: Contribution for the NPC's National Development Plan*. Online. Available at HTTP: http://chet.org.za/publications/papers/higher-education (accessed 5 February 2013).

Barber, B. (1963) 'Some problems in the sociology of professions', *Daedalus*, 92(4): 669–88.

Basu, K. (2006) 'Globalization, poverty and inequality: what is the relationship? What can be done?' *World Development*, 34(8): 1361–73.

Beresford, B. (2008) 'On the way down', *Mail & Guardian*, 21–27 November 2008, 13–16.

Bernstein, B. (2000) *Pedagogy, Symbolic Control, and Identity: Theory, Research, Critique*, Oxford: Rowman and Littlefield.

—— (2001) 'Symbolic control: issues of empirical description of agencies and agents', *International Journal of Social Research Methodology*, 4(1): 21–33.

Bhorat, H. and Kanbur, R. (eds) (2006) *Poverty and Policy in Post-Apartheid South Africa*, Cape Town: HSRC.

Bhorat, H. and Oosthuysen, M. (2006) 'Evolution of the labour market: 1995–2002', in H. Bhorat and T. Karis (eds) *Poverty and Policy in Post-Apartheid South Africa*. Cape Town: HSRC Press.

Bimbassis, H. (2012) 'The government's target of reducing unemployment', *Free State Times*, 30 August 2012, 3.

Bok, D. (2003) *Universities in the Marketplace*, Princeton, NJ and Oxford: Princeton University Press.

Boni, A. and Walker, M. (2013) *Universities and Human Development. A New Imaginary for the University of the XXI Century*, London: Routledge.

Boni, S. and Gasper, D. (2009) 'The university as it might be – contributions of a human development approach to rethinking quality of universities', paper presented at the 6th International Conference of the Human Development and Capability Association, Lima, September 2009.

Booth, A., McLean, M. and Walker, M. (2009) 'Self, society and other: a case study of integrative learning in England', *Studies in Higher Education*, 34(8): 929–39.

Bourdieu, P. (1998) *Practical Reason: On the Theory of Action*. Palo Alto, CA: Stanford University Press.

—— (1990) *In other Words*. trans. R. Nice, Oxford: Polity Press.

Bozalek, V. (2012) 'Interview with Nancy Fraser', *The Social Work Practitioner Researcher*, 24(1): 138–51.

Breier, M. and Wildschut, A. (2006) *Doctors in a Divided Society*, Cape Town: HSRC Press.

Breier, M., Wildschut, A. and Mgqolozana, T. (2009) *Nursing in a New Era*, Cape Town: HSRC Press.

Brighouse, H. (2004) *Justice*, Cambridge: Polity Press.

Brint, S. (1996) *In an Age of Experts*, Princeton, NJ: Princeton University Press.

Brock-Utne, B. (2003) *Formulating Higher Education Policies in Africa – The Pressure from External Forces and the Neoliberal Agenda*. Online. Available HTTP: http://www.netreed.uio.no/articles/high.ed_BBU.pdf (accessed 1 September 2012).

Brown, R. (ed.) (2011) *Higher Education and the Market Place*, New York and London: Routledge.

Bunting, I. (2006a) 'The higher education landscape under apartheid', in N. Cloete, P. Maassen, R. Fehnel and and T. Moja (eds) *Transformation in Higher Education. Global Pressures and Local Realities*, Dordrecht: Springer.

—— (2006b) 'Students', in N. Cloete, P. Maassen, R. Fehnel and and T. Moja (eds) *Transformation in Higher Education. Global Pressures and Local Realities*, Dordrecht: Springer.

Burawoy, M. (1998) 'The extended case method', *Sociological Theory*, 16 (1): 4–33.

Calhoun, C. (2006) 'The university and the public good', *Thesis Eleven*, 84: 7–43.

Castells, M. (2001) 'Universities as dynamic systems of contradictory functions', in J. Muller, N. Cloete and S. Badat (eds) *Challenges of Globalization. South African Debates with Manuel Castells*, Pretoria: Centre for Higher Education Transformation/ Maskew Miller Longman.

—— (2009) Lecture on higher education, University of the Western Cape, 7 August 2009. Online. Available HTTP: http//:www.chet.org.za/news/manuel-castells-south-african-lecture-series (accessed 18 September 2012).

Chetty, N. and Webbstock, D. (2008) 'The taming of the intellectuals', *Weekly Mail & Guardian*, 19 February 2008. Online. Available HTTP: http://www.mg.co.za/article directaspx?articleid=332708&area=supahead0208_content (accessed 20 June 2008).

Clarke, J. and Newman, J. (1997) *The Managerial State*, London: Sage.

Cloete, N. (2006a) 'Policy expectations', in N. Cloete., P. Maassen, R. Fehnel, T. Moja, T. Gibbon and H. Perold (eds) *Transformation in Higher Education. Global Pressures and Local Realities*, Dordrecht: Springer.

—— (2006b) 'New South African realities', in N. Cloete., P. Maassen, R. Fehnel, T. Moja, T., Gibbon and H. Perold (eds) *Transformation in Higher Education. Global Pressures and Local Realities*, Dordrecht: Springer.

—— (2011) 'South Africa: radical new plan for higher education', *University World News*, 4 December 2011. Online. Available HTTP: http://www.universityworldnews.com/ article.ph (accessed 15 January 2012).

Cohen, G.A. (2000) *If You're an Egalitarian How Come You're So Rich?*, Cambridge, MA: Harvard University Press.

Cooper, D. (2001) 'Against the current: social pathways and the pursuit of enduring change', *Feminist Legal Studies*, (9): 119–48.

Cooper, D. and Subotzky, G. (2001) *The Skewed Revolution: Trends in South African Higher Education: 1988–1998*, Cape Town: Education Policy Unit, University of the Western Cape.

Council on Higher Education (2004) *Higher Education in the First Decade of Democracy*, Pretoria: Council on Higher Education. Online. Available HTTP: http://www.che. ac.za/documents/d000146/index.php (accessed 21 June 2008).

Crocker, D. (2008) *Ethics of Global Development: Agency, Capability, and Deliberative Democracy*, Cambridge: Cambridge University Press.

Cullinan, K. (2009) 'Number of public health nurses, doctors in decline', *Cape Times*, 11 December 2009, 6.

Delanty, G. (2001) *Challenging Knowledge. The University in the Knowledge Society*, Buckingham: SRHE/Open University Press.

Deneulin, S. (2006) *The Capability Approach and the Praxis of Development*, New York: Palgrave Macmillan.

—— (2010) 'Book review', *Oxford Development Studies*, 38(3): 383–8.

Deneulin, S. and Shahani, L. (2009) *An Introduction to the Human Development and Capability Approach: Freedom and Agency*, London: Earthscan.

Deneulin, S. and Townsend, N. (2007) 'Public goods, global public goods and the common good', *International Journal of Social Economics*, 34: 19–36.

Derber, C. (1983) 'Managing professionals: ideological proletarianization and post-industrial labour', *Theory and Society*, 12 (3): 309–41.

De Swaan, A., Manor, J., Øyen, E. and Reis, E.P. (2000) 'Elite perceptions of the poor: reflections for a comparative research project', *Current Sociology*, 48(1): 43–54.

DHET (2012) *Green Paper for Post-School Education and Training*, Pretoria: Department of Higher Education and Training.

DOE (Department of Education) (1997) *Education White Paper 3: A Programme for Higher Education Transformation*, Pretoria: Government Gazette, 386 (18207).

DOH (1997) *White Paper for the Transformation of the Health System in South Africa*, Pretoria: Department of Health.

—— (2008) *Policy and Guidelines for the Implementation of the PMTCT Programme*, Pretoria: Department of Health.

Downie, R.S. (1990) 'Professions and professionalism', *Journal of Philosophy of Education*, 24(2): 147–59.

Drèze, J. and Sen, A. (2002) *India: Development and Participation*, Oxford: Oxford University Press.

Drydal Solbrekke, T. and Karseth, B. (2006) 'Professional responsibility – an issue for higher education', *Higher Education*, 52: 95–119.

DSD (2005) *Recruitment and Retention Strategy for Social Workers in South Africa*, Pretoria: Department of Social Development.

Dugard, J. (1978) *Human Rights and the South African Legal Order*, Princeton, NJ: University Press.

Durand, J. (1985) 'Afrikaner piety and dissent', in C. Villa-Vicencio and J.W. de Gruchy (eds) *Resistance and Hope. South African Essays in Honour of Beyers Naudé*, Cape Town: David Phillip.

Du Toit, R. and Roodt, J. (2009) *Engineers in a Developing Country*, Cape Town: HSRC Press.

Earle, N. (2007) *Social Work in Social Change*, Cape Town: HSRC Press.

East, L., Stokes, R. and Walker, M. (2013) 'Universities, the public good and professional education in the UK', *Studies in Higher Education*, DOI: 10.1080/03075079.2013.801421

Economist, The (2010) 'Special Report on South Africa', 3 June 2010. Online. Available HTTP: http://www.economist.com/node/16248609 (accessed 15 February 2013).

Escrigas, C. (2008) 'Foreword', in GUNI (eds) *Higher Education in the World 3. Higher Education: New Challenges and Emerging Roles for Human and Social Development, GUNI Series on the Social Commitment of Universities 3*, London: Palgrave.

Field, J. (2006) *Lifelong Learning and the New Educational Order*, Coventry: Trentham Books.

Flyvbjerg, B. (2001) *Making Social Science Matter*, Cambridge: Cambridge University Press.

Fournier, V. (1999) 'The appeal of "professionalism" as a disciplinary mechanism', *The Sociological Review*, 47(2): 280–307.

—— (2002) 'Utopianism and the cultivation of possibilities: Grassroots movements of hope', in Martin Parker (ed.), *Utopia and Organisation*, Oxford: Blackwell.

Freidson, E. (2001) *Professionalism: The Third Logic*, Cambridge: Polity Press.

Gabara, N. (2012) 'National body to tackle gender violence', *SA News*. Online. Available HTTP: http:// www.southafrica.info/services/rights/gender-111212.htm (accessed 4 February 2013)

Gelb, S. (2004) *Inequality in South Africa: Nature, Causes and Responses*. DfID Policy Initiative on Addressing Inequality in Middle Income Countries, UCT Development Policy Research Unit, Cape Town. Online. Available HTTP: http://www.commerce. uct.ac.za/Research_Units/DPRU/DPRU-Conference2004/Papers/Gelb_Inequality_ in_SouthAfrica.pdf (accessed 20 May 2008).

Gernetzky, K. (2012) 'Zuma joins UN as a "champion" of education', *Business Day*, 27 September 2012, 3.

Giddens, A. (2001) 'Dimensions of globalization', in S. Seidman and J.C. Alexander (eds) *The New Social Theory Reader*, London: Routledge.

Greene, M. (1998) *The Dialectic of Freedom*. New York: Teachers College Press.

Grove, J. (2011) 'Sector must reject neo-liberal business-speak, event hears', *Times Higher Education*, 1 December 2011. Online. Available HTTP: http://www.timeshigher education.co.uk/story.asp?storycode-418295 (accessed 4 January 2013).

Guest, G., Bunce, A. and Johnson, L. (2006) 'How many interviews are enough? An experiment with data saturation and variability', *Field Methods*, 18(1): 59–82.

GUNI (eds) (2008) *Higher Education in the World 3. Higher Education: New Challenges Emerging for Human and Social Development*, New York: Palgrave.

Habermas, J. (1989) 'The idea of the university: learning processes', in J. Habermas, trans. S. Weber Nicholson, *The New Conservatism: Cultural Criticism and the Historians' Debate*, Cambridge: Polity Press.

—— (1990) *Moral Consciousness and Communicative Action*, trans. C. Lenhardt and S. Nicholsen, Cambridge: Polity Press in association with Basil Blackwell.

Habib, A. (2011) 'A league apart', *Times Higher Education*, 13 October: 28.

Hall, M. (2007) 'Poverty, inequality and the university', paper presented for The Poorest of the Poor: Institute for the Humanities, University of Michigan, February 2007.

—— (2012a) 'Public good and private benefits of higher education', in B. Leibowitz (ed.) *Higher Education for the Public Good*, Stellenbosch: SUN Media.

—— (2012b) *Higher Education and Inequality: marketplace or social justice?* London: Leadership Foundation.

Haq, K. (2008) 'Amartya Sen and Mahbub ul Haq: a friendship that continues beyond life', *Journal of Human Development*, 9(3): 329–30.

Haq, Ul M. (1999) *Reflections on Human Development*, 2d edn, Delhi: Oxford University Press.

Harvey, D. (2005) *A Brief History of Neoliberalism*, Oxford: Oxford University Press.

Hausmann, R. (2008) *Final Recommendations of the International Panel on Growth in South Africa*, Pretoria: Treasury. Online. Available HTTP: http://www.treasury.gov.za/ comm_media/press/2008/Final%20Recommendations%20of%20the%20International %20Panel.pdf (accessed 14 May 2008).

Higgins, J. (2007) 'Institutional culture as keyword', *Review of Higher Education*, Pretoria: Council on Higher Education. Online. Available HTTP: http://www.che.ac.za/ documents/d000081/index.php (accessed 21 June 2008).

Hochschild, A.R. (2012) *The Managed Heart: Commercialization of Human Feeling*, Twentieth Anniversary Edition, Berkeley: University of California Press.

Holmwood, J. (ed.) (2011) *A Manifesto for the Public University*, London: Bloomsbury Academic.

Hoogeveen, J.G. and Özler, B. (2006) 'Poverty and inequality in post-apartheid South Africa: 1995–2000', in H. Bhorat and R. Kanbur (eds) *Poverty and Policy in Post-Apartheid South Africa*, Cape Town: HSRC. (2007) *Pathways through Higher Education to the Labour Market: Factors affecting Student Retention*,

Graduation, and Destination. Case Study Report, Cape Town: Human Sciences Research Council.

Isa, M. (2012) 'World Bank warns of inequality threat to SA', *Business Day*, 25 July 2012, 1.

Jansen, J. (2009) *Knowledge in the Blood*, Cape Town: UCT Press.

Jansen, J. with Herman, C., Matentjie, T., Morake, R., Pillay, V., Sehoole, C. and Weber, E. (2007) 'Tracing and explaining change in higher education: the South African case', in Council on Higher Education, *Review of Higher Education*, Pretoria: Council on Higher Education. Online. Available HTTP: http://www.che.ac.za/documents/d000081/index.php (accessed 21 June 2008).

Jonathan, R. (2001) 'Higher education transformation and the public good', *Kagisano Higher Education Discussion Series*, 1: 28–63.

—— (2006) *Academic Freedom, Institutional Autonomy and Public Accountability in Higher Education: A Framework for Analysis of the 'State-Sector' Relationship in a Democratic South Africa*, Pretoria: Council on Higher Education. Online. Available HTTP: http://www.che.ac.za/documents/d000138/index.php (accessed 21 June 2008).

Joseph, N. (2008) 'As in UDF heyday, we must believe in ourselves – Manuel', *Cape Times*, 21 August 2008, 3.

Judt, T. (2010) *Ill Fares the Land*, New York: Penguin Press.

Kalati, N. and Manor, J.M. (2005) 'Elite Perceptions of Poverty and Poor People in South Africa', in E.P. Reis and N. Moore (eds) *Elite Perceptions of Poverty and Inequality*. London: Zed Press.

Karis, T. (1997) *From Protest to Challenge: A Documentary History of African Politics in South Africa, 1882–1990. Volume 5: Nadir and Resurgence, 1964–1979*, Pretoria: Unisa Press.

Kautzky, K. and Tollman, S. (2008) 'A perspective on primary health care in South Africa', in P. Barron and J. Roma-Reardon (eds) *South African Health Review 2008*, Durban: Health Systems Trust.

Keeley, B. (2007) *Human Capital*, Paris: OECD.

Keeton, G. (2012) 'No simple solution to SA's inequality problem', *Business Day*, 3 September 2012, 9.

Kraak, A. (2001) 'Policy ambiguity and slippage: higher education under the new state, 1994–2001', in A. Kraak and M. Young (eds) *Education in Retrospect: Policy and Implementation since 1990*, Cape Town: HSRC.

Larson, Sarfatti M. (2013) *The Rise of Professionalism: Monopolies of Competence and Sheltered Markets*, 2nd edn, New Brunswick and London: Transaction Publishers.

Lebeau, Y. (2008) 'Universities and social transformation in sub-Saharan Africa: global rhetoric and local contradictions', *Compare*, 38(2): 139–53.

Leibowitz, B. (ed.) (2012) *Higher Education and the Public Good*, Stellenbosch: SUNMedia.

Letseka, M. and Maile, S. (2008) *High University Drop-Out Rates: A Threat to South Africa's Future, HSRC Policy Brief March 2008*. Online. Available HTTP: http://www.hsrc.ac.za/Document-2717.phtml (accessed 21 June 2008).

Lobera, J. and Escrigas, C. (2009) 'Introduction: New dynamics for social responsibility', in GUNI (ed.) *Higher Education in the World 3: New Dynamics for Social Responsibility*. London: Palgrave.

Lombard, A. (2008) 'The implementation of the White Paper for social welfare: a ten year review', *The Social Work Practitioner-Researcher*, 20(2): 154–73.

MacDonald, K. (1995) *The Sociology of the Professions*, London: Sage.

McKinley, D.T. (1997) *The ANC and the Liberation Struggle: A Critical Political Biography*, London: Pluto Press.

McLean, M. (2006) *Pedagogy and the University*, London: Continuum.

McLean, M., Abbas, A. and Ashwin, A. (2012) 'The use and value of Bernstein's work in studying (in)equalities in undergraduate social science education', *British Journal of Sociology of Education*, 1–19, 34(2): 262–80.

McMahon, W. (2009) *Higher Learning, Greater Good: The Private and Social Benefits of Higher Education*, Baltimore, MD: Johns Hopkins University Press.

Magasela, W. (2006) 'Towards a constitution-based definition of poverty in post-apartheid South Africa', in S. Buhlungu, J. Daniel, R. Southall and J. Lutchman (eds) *State of the Nation: South Africa 2005–2006*, Cape Town: HSRC.

Mail & Guardian (2008) 'Actuaries estimates 5,6m have HIV/Aids in SA', *Mail and Guardian* , 6 May 2008. Online. Available HTTP: http://mg.co.za/article/2008-05-06-actuaries-estimates-56m-have-hivaids (accessed 20 June 2008).

—— (2013a) 'Section 27 threatens more court action over Limpopo schools', *Mail & Guardian* 14 February 2013. Online. Available HTTP: http://mg.co.za/article/2013-02-14-Section 27 (accessed 21 February 2013).

—— Mail and Guardian (2013b) 'Education Department in breach of court over textbooks', 18 April, 2013. Online. Available HTTP: http://http://mg.co.za/article/2013-02-14-Section 27 (accessed 25 April 2013).

Malan, M. and Ndlovu, N. (2009) 'Doctors "insulted". Strike talk goes on as medical professionals are offered a maximum raise of 2%', *Mail and Guardian*, May 15–21 2009, 12.

Mamdani, M. (1998) *Is African Studies to be Turned into a New Home for Bantu Education at UCT?*, Cape Town: Centre for African Studies.

Manuel, T. (2012) 'Do something that will make a difference', *Mail & Guardian*, 6–12 July 2012, 31.

Marginson, S. (2006) 'Putting "public" back into the public university', *Thesis Eleven*, 84: 44–59.

—— (ed.) (2007) *Prospects of Higher Education. Globalization, Market Competition, Public Goods and the Future of the University*, Rotterdam: Sense Publishers.

—— (2010) 'Creating global public goods', opening keynote for seminar on the Global University at the University of Virginia, USA, 14 November 2010. Online. Available HTTP: http://www.cshe.unimelb.edu.au/people/marginson (accessed 12 December 2011).

Maxwell, J. (2010) 'Using numbers in qualitative research', *Qualitative Inquiry*, 16(6): 475–82.

Moellendorf, D. (2009) *Global Inequality Matters*, Basingstoke: Palgrave Macmillan.

Molesworth, M., Nixon, E. and Scullion, R. (2009) 'Having, being and higher education: the marketisation of the university and the transformation of the student into consumer', *Teaching in Higher Education*, 14(3): 277–87.

Morris, M. (2004) *Every Step of the Way: The Journey to Freedom in South Africa*, Cape Town: HSRC Press.

Muller, J., Maassen, P. and Cloete, N. (2006) 'Modes of governance and the limits of policy', in N. Cloete et al. (eds) *Transformation in Higher Education. Global Pressures and Local Realities*, Dordrecht: Springer.

Nagel, T. (2009) *The Problem of Global Justice*. Online. Available HTTP: http://philosophy. fas.nyu.edu/docs/IO/1172/globaljustice.pdf (accessed 1 October 2012).

Naidoo, R. (2010) 'Global learning in a neoliberal age: implications for development', in E. Unterhalter and V. Carpentier (eds) *Whose Interests are we Serving? Global Inequalities and Higher Education*, New York: Palgrave.

Naryan, D. and Petesch, P. (2002) *Voices of the Poor from Many Lands*. Washington, DC: The World Bank.

Narayan, D., Chambers, R., Shah, M.K. and Petesch, P. (2000) *Voices of the Poor: Crying out for Change*, Washington, DC: The World Bank.

National Planning Commission (2011) *National Development Plan – Vision for 2030*. Online. Available HTTP: http://www.polity.org.za/article-national-development-plan (accessed 25 August 2012).

Naude, P. (2003) 'The theological coherence between the Belhar confession and some antecedent church witnesses in the period 1948–1982', *Verbem et Ecclesia*, 24(1): 156–79.

nef (2008) *University Challenge: Towards a Well-Being Approach to Top Quality in Higher Education*, London: new economics foundation.

Newman, J.H. (1852) *The Idea of a University, Discourse 9*, reprinted as J.H. Newman, (1960) *The Idea of a University*, San Francisco, CA: Rinehart Press.

Nixon, J. (2011) *Higher Education and the Public Good: Imagining the University*, London and New York: Bloomsbury.

Norberg, J. (2001) *In Defense of Global Capitalism*, Sweden: Timbro.

Nunan, T., George, R. and McCausland, H. (2000) 'Inclusive education in universities: why it is important and how it might be achieved', *International Journal of Inclusive Education*, 4 (1): 63–88.

Nussbaum, M. (1990) *Love's Knowledge*, Oxford: Oxford University Press.

—— (1997) *Cultivating Humanity. A Classical Defence of Reform in Liberal Education*, Cambridge, MA: Harvard University Press.

—— (1998) 'The Good as Discipline, the Good as Freedom', in D. Crocker and T Linden (eds) *Ethics of Consumption*. Lanham, MD: Rowman & Littlefield Publishers.

—— (2000) *Women and Human Development*, Cambridge: Cambridge University Press.

—— (2001) *Upheavals of Thought*, Cambridge: Cambridge University Press.

—— (2003) 'Capabilities as fundamental entitlements: Sen and social justice', *Feminist Economics*, 9(2/3): 33–59.

—— (2010) *Not For Profit*, Princeton, NJ: Princeton University Press.

—— (2011) *Creating Capabilities. The Human Development Approach*, Cambridge, MA: The Belknap Press.

Nussbaum, M. and Sen, A. (eds) (1993) *The Quality of Life*, Oxford: Clarendon Press.

OECD (2012) *Divided we Stand: Why Inequality Keeps Growing*, Paris: OECD.

Olssen, M. and Peters, M. (2005) 'Neoliberalism, higher education and the knowledge economy: from the free market to knowledge capitalism', *Journal of Education Policy*, 20(3): 313–47.

O'Neill, O. (1996) *Towards Justice and Virtue: A Constructive Account of Practical Reasoning*, Cambridge: Cambridge University Press.

—— (2002) *A Question of Trust. The BBC Reith Lectures 2002*, Cambridge: Cambridge University Press.

Open Society Foundation for South Africa (2005) *South Africa: Justice Sector and the Rule of Law*, Newlands: Open Society Foundation for South Africa.

Pakenham, T. (1979) *The Boer War*, New York: Random House.

Potgieter, C. (2013) 'Varsities have a local-global balancing act', *Getting Ahead, Supplement to the Mail and Guardian* 1–7 February 2013: 1–2.

Rantete, J. (1998) *The African National Congress and the Negotiated Settlement in South Africa*, Pretoria: J.L. van Schaik.

Rawls, J. (2001) *Justice as Fairness: A Restatement*, Cambridge, MA: Harvard University Press.

Rizvi, F. (2007) 'Global economy and the construction of lifelong learning', in D. Aspin (ed.) *Philosophical Perspectives on Lifelong Learning*, Melbourne: Springer.

Rizvi, F. and Lingard, B. (2006) 'Globalization and the changing nature of the OECD's educational work', in H. Lauder, P. Brown, J.A. Dillabough and A.H. Halsey (eds) *Education, Globalization, and Social Change*, Oxford: Oxford University Press.

Rizvi, F. and Lingard, R. (2010) *Globalizing Education Policy*, Abingdon: Routledge.

Robeyns, I. (2003) 'Sen's capability approach and gender inequality: selecting relevant capabilities', *Feminist Economics*, 9(2–3): 61–91.

—— (2005) 'The capability approach: a theoretical survey', *Journal of Human Development*, 6(1): 93–114.

—— (2011) 'The capability approach', in *Stanford Encyclopedia of Philosophy*. Online. Available HTTP: http://plato.stanford.edu/entries/capability-approach/ (accessed 18 September 2011).

—— (2012) 'Are *transcendental theories of justice* redundant? (Book review essay of The Idea of Justice, by A. Sen)', *Journal of Economic Methodology*, 19(2): 159–63.

Robins, S. (ed.) (2006) *Limits to Liberation after Apartheid. Citizenship, Governance and Culture*, Oxford: James Currey, Ohio University Press and David Phillips.

Roodt, J. and Du Toit, R. (2009) *Engineers in a Developing Country: The Profession and Education of Engineering Professionals in South Africa*, Pretoria: HSRC Press.

Saba, A. and Van der Merwe, J. (2013) 'South Africa has a protest every two days', Media 24 Investigations, *News 24*. Online. Available HTTP: http://www.news24.com/South Africa/News/SA (accessed 4 February 2013).

Salais, R. (2010) *What Reform for Social European Policies? Towards Full Employment based on the Politics of Work-and-Life Capability Development. CAPRIGHT Policy Report*. Online. Available HTTP: http://www.capright.eu/News/?contentId=9048 (accessed 20 May 2011)

Sall, E., Lebeau, Y. and Kassimir, R. (2003) 'The public dimensions of the university in Africa', *Journal of Higher Education Africa (RESA)*, 1(1): 126–48.

Samuelson, P.A. (1954) 'The pure theory of public expenditure', *The Review of Economics and Statistics*, 36(4): 387–89.

Sandel, M. (2009) *Justice. What's The Right Thing To Do?*, London: Penguin Books.

Sanders, D. and Alexander, L. (2008) 'The challenges for public health education in implementing primary health care in decentralised health systems', *New Directions for Public Health Education in Low and Middle Income Countries*, Hyderabad: Public Health Foundation of India, 22–33.

Sapa (2012) 'Income inequality divides SA; survey', *IOL*. Online. Available HTTP: http://www.iol.co.za/dailynews/news/income-inequality-divides-sa-survey-1.1303589 (accessed 25 September 2012).

Sawyerr, A. (2002) *Challenges facing African Universities*. Acra, Ghana: Association of African Universities.

Scheuerman, W. (2010) 'Globalization', in *Stanford Encyclopedia of Philosophy*. Online. Available HTTP: http://plato.stanford.edu/entires/globalization/ (accessed 12 January 2013).

Schofer, E. and Meyer, J.W. (2005) 'The worldwide expansion of higher education in the twentieth century', *American Sociological Review*, 70: 898–920.

Schön, D. (1983) *The Reflective Practitioner: How Professionals Think in Action*, New York: Basic Books.

Schouten, G. (2012) 'Fair Educational Opportunity and the Distribution of Natural Ability: Towards a Prioritarian Principle of Educational Justice', *Journal of Philosophy of Education*, 46 (3): 472–91.

Scott, I. and Yeld, N. (2008) 'The interface between further and higher education in South Africa: factors affecting the higher education sector's capacity to meet national needs', paper presented at the Association for the Development of Education in Africa Biennale Conference on Education in Africa, 5–9 May 2008, Maputo. Online. Available HTTP: http://www.adeanet.org/. . ./Session%204C%20presentation%201.%20SCOTT%20 Ian%20and%20YELD%20Nan%20ENG.ppt (accessed 21 June 2008).

Scott, I., Yeld, N. and Hendry, J. (2007) *Higher Education Monitor: A Case for Improving Teaching and Learning in South African Higher Education*, Pretoria: Council for Higher Education.

Sen, A. (1985) *Commodities and Capabilities*, Amsterdam: North Holland.

—— (1987) 'The standard of living', in Sen, A., Muellbauer, J., Kanbur,R., Hart, K. and Williams, B. (eds) *The Standard of Living: The Tanner Lectures on Human Values*, Cambridge: Cambridge University Press.

—— (1999) *Development as Freedom*, Oxford: Oxford University Press.

—— (2002) 'Globalism', *The American Prospect*, 1 January 2002. Online. Available HTTP: http://www.sas.upenn.edu/~dludden/SenGlobalism.htm (accessed 5 January 2013).

—— (2003) 'Human capital and human capabilities', in S. Fukuda-Parr and A.K. Shiva Kumar (eds) *Readings in Human Development*, Oxford: Oxford University Press.

—— (2004)'Capabilities, lists and public reasons: continuing the conversation', *Feminist Economics*, 10(3): 77–80.

—— (2008) 'The idea of justice', *Journal of Human Development*, 9(3): 331–42.

—— (2009) *The Idea of Justice*, London: Allen Lane.

Sheppard, S., Macatangay, K., Anne Colby, C. and Sullivan, W. (2008) *Educating Engineers: Designing for the Future of the Field*, Palo Alto: Carnegie Foundation

Singh, M. (2001) 'Re-inserting the "public good" into higher education transformation', *Kagisano*, 1, 7–22.

—— (2010) 'Re-orienting internationalisation in African higher education', *Globalization, Societies and Education*, 8(2): 269–82.

—— (2011) 'The place of social justice in higher education and social change discourses', *Compare*, 41(4): 481–94.

Soudien Report (2008) *Report of the Ministerial Committee on Transformation and Social Cohesion and the Elimination of Discrimination in Public Higher Education Institutions, Final Report*, Pretoria: DHET.

South African Government (1996) *Constitution of the Republic of South Africa, 1996*. Online Available HTTP: http://www.info.gov.za/documents/constitution (accessed 29 April 2009).

Spreafico, A. (2010) Applying the capability approach to higher education policy and quality assessment: the case of Barnard College, unpublished master's thesis, University of Pavia, Italy.

Stake, R. (1995) *The Art of Case Study Research*, Thousand Oaks, CA: Sage.

Statistics South Africa (1999) *Provincial Profile 1999, Gauteng. Report 00-91-91-07*. Online. Available at HTTP: http://www.statssa.gov.za/PublicationsHTML/Report-00-71999/html_20.html

Statistics South Africa (2007) *Mid-year population estimates 2007*, Pretoria: Statistics South Africa.

Stenhouse, L. (1978) 'Case study and case records: towards a contemporary history of education', *British Educational Research Journal*, 14(2): 21–39.

Stiglitz, J.E. (2003) 'Knowledge as a global public good', in I. Kaul, I. Grunberg and M. Stern (eds) *Global Public Goods : International Cooperation in the 21st Century*, Oxford: Oxford University Press.

Strain, J., Barnett, R. and Jarvis, P. (2009) *Universities, Ethics and Professions*, London: Routledge.

Stromquist, N.P. (2002) *Education in a Globalized World: The Connectivity of Economic Power, Technology, and Knowledge*, Oxford: Rowman & Littlefield.

Sullivan, W. and Roisin, M. (2008) *A New Agenda for Higher Education: Shaping a Life of the Mind for Practice*, San Francisco, CA: Jossey-Bass.

Sullivan, W., Colby, A., Wegner, J.W., Bond, L. and Shulman, L.S. (2007) *Educating Lawyers: Preparing for the Profession of Law*, San Francisco, CA: Jossey-Bass/Carnegie Foundation

Sullivan, W.M. (2005) *Work and Integrity: The Crisis and Promise of Professionalism in America*, 3rd edn, San Francisco, CA: Jossey-Bass.

Tawney, R.H. (1948) *The Acquisitive Society*, London: G. Bell and Sons.

Taylor, V. (2000) *South Africa Human Development Report*. Pretoria: UNDP.

Treasury (2008) *Budget Review 2008*, Pretoria: National Treasury. Online. Available HTTP: http://www.treasury.gov.za/documents/national%20budget/2008/review/Default.aspx (accessed 20 May 2008).

Umar, R.S. (2012) 'Bill places cap on legal fees', *Daily News*, 21 May 2012. Online. Available HTTP: http://www.iol.co.za/dailynews/bill/places-cap-on-legal-fees (accessed 21 January 2013).

UNDP (1990) *Human Development Report 1990*, New York: UNDP.

UNESCO (1998) *World Declaration on Higher Education for the Twenty-first Century: Vision and Action and Framework for Priority Action for Change and Development in Higher Education*. Online. Available HTTP: http://www.unesco.org/education/educprog/wche/declaration_eng.htm (accessed 15 December 2011)

—— (2003) *General Report by Mr Jacques Proulx, The Meeting of Higher Education Partners*, UNESCO, Paris 23–25 June 2003. Online. Available HTTP: http://portal.unesco.org/education/en/file_download.php/ (accessed 15 September 2012).

—— (2009) *Trends in Global Higher Education: Tracking an Academic Revolution*, Paris: UNESCO.

—— (2012) 'Trade-off, comparative evaluation and global obligation: reflections on the poverty, gender and education Millennium Development Goals', *Journal of Human Development and Capabilities*, 13(3): 335–51.

Unterhalter, E. and Carpentier, V. (eds) (2010) *Whose Interests are we Serving? Global Inequalities and Higher Education*, New York: Palgrave.

Van Vuuren, H. (2006) *Apartheid Grand Corruption. Addressing the Scale of Crimes of Profit in South Africa from 1976 to 1994*. Report prepared by civil society at the request of the Second National Anti-Corruption Summit, Pretoria: Institute for Security Studies.

Vernon, J. (2011) 'Canary in the coalmine', *Times Higher Education*, 1 December 2011, 42–7.

Walker, M. (2006) *Higher Education Pedagogies*, Maidenhead, UK: Open University Press and the Society for Research into Higher Education.

—— (2009) 'Making a world that is worth living in: humanities teaching and the formation of practical reasoning', *Arts and Humanities in Higher Education*, 8(3): 231–46.

—— (2012) 'A capital or capabilities education policy narrative in a world of staggering inequalities?', *International Journal of Educational Development*, 32(3): 384–93.

Walker, M. and Unterhalter, E. (eds) (2007) *Amartya Sen's Capability Approach and Social Justice in Education*, New York: Palgrave Macmillan.

Walker, M., McLean, M., Dison, A. and Vaughan, R. (2009) 'South African universities and human development: Towards a theorisation and operationalisation of professional capabilities for poverty reduction', *International Journal of Educational Development*, 29(6): 565–72.

Walker, M., McLean, M., Dison, A. and Vaughan, R. (2010) *Higher Education and Poverty Reduction: The Formation of Public Good Professionals in Universities*, Nottingham: School of Education: University of Nottingham.

WEF (2012) *Global Competitiveness Report*, Geneva: World Economic Forum.

Watermeyer, R. (2006) 'Poverty reduction responses to the Millennium Development Goals', *The Structural Engineer*, 84(9): 27–34.

WHO (1978) *Declaration of Alma-Ata*. Online. Available HTTP: http://www.euro.who. int/AboutWHO/Policy/20010827_1 (accessed 20 August 2009).

Williams, R. (1977) *Marxism and Literature*, Oxford: Oxford University Press.

Witz, A. (1992) *Professions and Patriarchy*, New York: Routledge.

Wolff, J. and De-Shalit, A. (2007) *Disadvantage*, Oxford: Oxford University Press.

World Bank (2002) *Constructing Knowledge Societies. New Challenges for Tertiary Education*, Washington, DC: World Bank.

—— World Bank (2003a) *Constructing Knowledge Societies. New Challenges for Tertiary Education*, Washington, DC: World Bank.

—— (2003b) *Lifelong Learning in the Global Knowledge Economy: Challenges for Developing Countries*, Washington, DC: World Bank.

—— (2009) *Implementing the Bank's Mainstreaming Strategy: FY08 Annual Monitoring Report*. Washington, DC: World Bank.

Wright Mills, C. (1959) *The Sociological Imagination*, London: Oxford University Press.

Young, I. M. (2011) *Responsibility For Justice*, Oxford: Oxford University Press.

Zipin, L. and Brennan, M. (2004) 'Managerial governmentality and the suppression of ethics', in M. Walker and J. Nixon (eds) *Reclaiming Universities from a Runaway World*, Maidenhead: SRHE/Open University Press.

Zymbalys, M. (2008) 'Adult learners' emotions in online learning', *Distance Education*, 29(1): 71–87.

Index

Bold page references denote a table.